All Girls

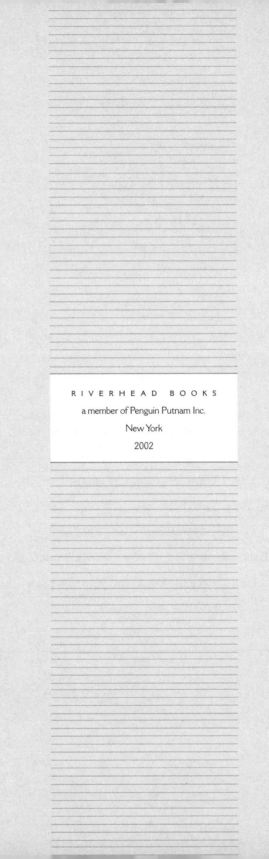

RIVERHEAD   BOOKS

a member of Penguin Putnam Inc.

New York

2002

All Girls

Single-Sex Education
and Why It Matters

Karen Stabiner

Riverhead Books
a member of
Penguin Putnam Inc.
375 Hudson Street
New York, NY 10014

Library of Congress Cataloging-in-Publication Data

Stabiner, Karen, date.
All girls : single-sex education and why it matters / Karen
Stabiner.
p.   cm.
Includes bibliographical references.
ISBN 1-57322-207-0
1. Marlborough School (Los Angeles, Calif.)   2. Young
Women's Leadership School of East Harlem.   3. Single-sex
schools–United States–Case Studies.   4. Women–Education–United States–Case Studies.   5. Educational equaliza-
tion–United States–Case studies.   I. Title.

LB3067.4 .S82   2002   2001048797 CIP
            371.822'0973–dc21

Printed in the United States of America
1   3   5   7   9   10   8   6   4   2

This book is printed on acid-free paper. ∞

BOOK DESIGN BY AMANDA DEWEY

To my sister, Lori, and to Dorene

All Girls

Introduction

A FRIEND WITH a daughter older than my own was trying to make an impossible decision. Should she send the girl to a coed school for seventh grade, or to an all-girls school? She had no idea what a girls' school was like; she and everyone she knew had gone to coed schools. The only information she had was theoretical: Some people believed that single-sex education was the best solution to pervasive gender discrimination in the classroom, while others dismissed it as a short-term fix for wealthy families who could afford private-school tuition.

What was best for my friend's daughter? There was no real way to tell. It was like making a choice between chocolate and vanilla without ever having tasted chocolate.

My daughter, Sarah, was in third grade at the time, brimming with the confidence and energy that researchers see in girls that age. But I had read about what was supposed to be in store come adolescence. By the time Sarah and her friends graduated from high school, too many of them would be unsure of themselves. They would judge themselves on how they looked or whether the boys liked them; they would look at images in the media and find themselves wanting. Girls who had the talent to pursue advanced work in math or science might not, because they doubted their own abilities in these fields. Their test scores would slip. For girls, the central lesson of coed middle and high school seemed to be about limitations.

So I did what any parent might like to do, given the chance: I went back to school to see firsthand what the alternative, a girls' school education, was like. In 1998, I approached the head of school at Marlborough School, a 112-year-old private school in Los Angeles, California, and the principal of The Young Women's Leadership School of East Harlem, a then-two-year-old public school for economically disadvantaged girls in New York City, and got permission to observe at both schools for the 1998–1999 school year.

I attended classes, tagged along with a handful of students, and talked to their parents and teachers, to find out for myself how theory translated into practice. The result is a look at two very different schools, where teachers and administrators are trying to define how best to teach girls. It is the story of some girls who feel happy and successful—no small thing, amidst all the stories of teenage girls' eating disorders, depression, and self-doubt.

The process changed my mind. I had carried around a rather musty, fussy, and completely uninformed image of what a girls' school must be: the sort of place where a child of privilege learned how to crook her little finger while she drank tea. I had thought that girls' school was for girls who could not handle the real world—until I spent time at two of them. The girls I met seemed almost arrogant at first, but I soon realized my mistake. They were not arrogant; they were self-confident, comfortable with themselves in a way I was not used to seeing. They had learned to speak, as one Marlborough teacher put it, in "a person's voice, not a woman's voice." They said what they meant, absolved of the social concerns that often made girls tone themselves down. They felt no need to defer or compromise their opinions in the name of getting along.

Had anyone told me when Sarah was born that we would someday enroll her at a girls' school where she had to wear a uniform, I would have laughed; I might have been insulted at the implication that she could not handle the rigors of a big coed school like the one I attended. By the time my family had to make a choice, though, we agreed that a girls' school would provide her with more opportunities than she would find anywhere else. A quality education is about much more than test scores and transcripts: It ought to open doors and keep them open for as long as possible. Our daughter enrolled at Marlborough last fall.

Most families do not have the luxury of that kind of choice; they have to work with their neighborhood public school or find a way around it. One of the reasons I observed at The Young Women's Leadership School was because it raises a difficult question: If girls' schools benefit their students, then what responsibility do we have to girls who cannot afford private school? Our public school system is based on the notion of equal access—but research shows that equal access is not the same as an equal education. Some of the most provocative research says that girls from poor ethnic communities benefit the most from a single-sex environment, and yet they are the ones who have the most trouble gaining access.

Their parents can lobby for change, though, whether for a school like The Young Women's Leadership School or for a revamped math class at an existing school. What I hope to do, with this book, is to give parents and educators a glimpse of a new model, one built on notions of what girls need. One they can borrow from, or seek to imitate, if they find concepts that will serve their daughters well. The best way to know what to do is to have firsthand experience; only then can we make a truly informed decision for our girls.

IT WOULD BE NAÏVE to assume that school is all that matters. One of the strongest students at The Young Women's Leadership School almost became a casualty of events outside of school—and although she and her family had agreed at the outset to let me use their real names, I have decided to change them. Diana Perez (her new name, for the sake of this book) had a rough time and got through it; she ought to be able to start college without being trailed by the past. I have also changed the name of one person who appears only briefly in the book.

I sat in on classes at Marlborough throughout the school year, and at The Young Women's Leadership School on several extended visits. I interviewed students and teachers during the school day, and visited regularly with the students' families; I also sat in on as many special events as possible—assemblies, performances, class meetings, conferences, and sporting events. With the families' permission, both schools furnished me with student records.

Along the way, the girls, their parents, administrators, and faculty often described how they felt about what was going on in their lives at that moment. If I refer to someone's feelings or private thoughts, it is because they told me about them.

Their frankness surprised me at first, until I began to understand that single-sex education is very much a work in progress: People like to talk about the process—not just what goes on in the classroom but how everyone feels about it—so that they can refine and improve a changing environment. I wanted to convey this desire to examine, to reconsider, because it is central to what goes on at both schools, and because it is just the kind of subtle attribute that defies quantifiable measure.

1

Marlborough School

Los Angeles, California, September, 1998

THERE WAS SO MUCH BRAVADO: SENIORS RULE chalked on the driveway, red and white crepe paper draped in the trees, a sprinkler shaped like an octopus spraying water at unsuspecting seventh graders. Some members of the Marlborough School class of 1999 painted "99" on their cheeks with the lipstick they never wore to class. Others pulled their hair into pigtails that they rolled and anchored high on their heads with bobby pins. Several girls wore shiny fuchsia tiaras, while others carried plastic tridents. They should have discarded their outgrown uniform skirts years ago, but instead they unbuttoned the tight waistbands and rolled them over, the hems hiked to mid-thigh; no point investing in a new skirt ten months from graduation. Underneath they wore boys' striped boxer shorts.

The parents had set out a breakfast buffet on long tables at either side of the school entrance, but the girls were too excited to eat. They hung on each other like drunks, laughing and shrieking, halfheartedly pledging to stop making so much noise. It was not yet eight o'clock in the morning.

One cluster of seniors stood under a sign that read FINALLY, OUR LAST FIRST DAY OF SCHOOL, fussing over the new "girl" in class—a tall, thin boy wearing a school uniform, his blond pageboy wig held in place by a headband, imitating the way Marlborough head of school Barbara Wagner wore her hair. The boy had bright-red lips and wore falsies, but the stubble on his jawline and the hair on his legs gave him away.

The seniors always sneaked a boy onto campus for the first day of school. It was a tradition, along with decorating the grounds and Ms. Wagner's home, which was on the next block, right behind the campus. After five grueling years, the seniors had earned the right to a raucous return—and for once, the faculty did nothing to stop them.

Leslie Klein, the senior class team leader and yearbook sponsor, darted through the crowd with her big Nikon 90, snapping away. Several teachers shepherded bewildered new students past the entrance, while others stood at the central hallway, ready to help a seventh grader stymied by her schedule. Many of the teachers wore brand-new white T-shirts over their street clothes, with the inscription COMPETENCE, CONFIDENCE, CONNECTEDNESS. T-shirts were a violation of the faculty dress code, which required collared blouses or sweaters for the women and dress shirts and ties for the men. But Wagner had made an exception today—in fact, she had handed out the shirts at a faculty meeting and encouraged her staff to wear them on the first day of school. The three C's were her theme for the year, borrowed from *How Girls Thrive,* an overview of single-sex literature that she had read over the summer. These were the qualities she wanted to instill in each Marlborough girl.

Monica Ward, one of the two college counselors, watched the antics of the class of 1999 silently and wondered how well they would survive the college-application process in the coming months. This year held the promise of success, and the threat of public disappointment and defeat. The three C's were one thing inside these walls; they might be harder to sustain as the outside world intruded and passed judgment. Let the seniors disrupt a single morning. Ms. Ward knew just how little time they had to make fools of themselves.

The seniors got rid of their silliness the way a dog shakes off water, in one great controlled shimmy, and then it was time to get to work.

Once the seventh graders had memorized their locker combinations and met all their teachers, they took a four-day trip to Catalina Island. A luxury bus full of jumpy girls and faculty chaperones pulled away down Rossmore Avenue early in the morning, leaving a handful of parents who were not quite sure what to do next. One mother sniffled, wiped at her eyes, and wandered down the street toward home. Another stood in the school's curved driveway and stared north, though the bus quickly disappeared from view. A relieved father who had screeched up in his mini-van just in time to deliver a forgotten pair of glasses sat in the driver's seat, laughing.

Girls were supposed to learn better if they worked and studied together, so the first assignment of seventh grade was to start making friends. The message was reinforced in each subsequent year: The eighth, ninth, and tenth graders were on their way to retreats in Big Bear, Sequoia National Forest, and the Marin Headlands, and this morning all seventy-seven members of the eleventh grade had met at Los Angeles International Airport for a class trip to Olympia, Washington.

The seniors stayed behind. Having learned to work together, it was time for them to separate, to begin to work solely for themselves. A year from now, the class of 1999 would be scattered at colleges and universities all over the country. To help them with the application process, Marlborough started the year with a three-day workshop on how to create a great college application—followed by a four-day weekend to give them time to visit campuses.

They shuffled into Caswell Hall, affecting nonchalance. The seniors were allowed to wear street clothes this week, but they all looked pretty much the same: The outfit of choice was a tiny cotton knit tank top, preferably in a pastel shade, worn over a bra of a different color, straps visible, and a pair of emphatically tired jeans. Choosing a more imaginative outfit would have been a drain on their energies. Today required absolute focus.

Marlborough students had been taught to expect that they would go to a great school. Many of them felt doubly entitled—money had bought them anything they wanted, and Marlborough had taught them that they were special, better prepared than girls who came from coeducational schools. They might complain about the rigorous schedule, the mountains of homework, and the absence of boys, but most of the girls assumed they would be rewarded for their sacrifice. Their parents, who had paid about $14,000 annually for tuition—and more for books, uniforms, and annual giving—also expected results.

This week was an attempt on the school's part to impose order on the chaotic process of choosing a college. It was far more competitive than it had been when the girls' parents were high school seniors. Mothers and fathers who had applied to two or three schools listened to their daughters discuss a dozen prospects, up from half that just five years earlier. They heard their daughters' friends talk about the same schools and silently worked the odds in their heads.

At the beginning of the year, any dream was up for grabs: a scholarship to Harvard College, recruitment by Stanford University, the dizzy possibility of having to choose between Brown University and the University of Chicago. Marlborough seniors aimed high. Although there were more than 3,000 colleges and universities in the United States, the girls in this room would limit themselves to about 130 schools. The least competitive of those 130 schools might take half their applicants, but the top schools took less than ten percent. Everyone in the room knew the numbers, but no one, on this first day of the future, believed that she would be one of those turned away.

Or rather, no one admitted it. Anxiety was the first item on the day's agenda, and a trio of staff members was ready to address it. Dr. Susan Lewandowski, in her second year as director of college counseling, was the first to speak. A short, neat woman whose frank manner was sometimes mistaken for pessimism, Dr. Lewandowski tried to be reassuring without ever losing sight of reality. As an associate director of admissions at Smith

College for nine years before coming to Marlborough, she knew firsthand just how difficult that could be.

"I want you to know you have a *team* here," she said, to a sea of blank faces. "We've heard your anxiety about the college essay, about how to put yourself on paper; a lot of anxiety in general. It's a stressful year. There will be major periods of deadline distress." She reviewed a list of important dates—the deadline to register for the October Scholastic Achievement Tests, the deadline to get teacher recommendations, the schedule for parent-and-student conferences with the two college counselors. Girls who were set on a single college were already at work on their early decision applications, and would hear back in mid-December. The rest of the girls had to turn in their applications between November and January and would receive word in the spring.

Dr. Lewandowski and Barbara Wagner were concerned about the growing number of seniors who had decided to apply early, and the accompanying pressure on the other girls to make a choice before they were ready. There were two kinds of early applications—early decision, which was binding, and early action, which allowed a student to consider other schools—but the distinction was lost on most of the girls, who only cared about not having to wait until the spring. Wagner preached patience to all but the most determined students; early applications deprived the rest of what she called "important maturational time." They made up their minds too fast in the name of security, when sometimes the best decision came with time.

An early rejection could be particularly devastating. One application, one rejection; there was nothing to buffer the disappointment. In April it was easier. A girl who had followed the college counselors' advice and applied to a range of schools was likely to get accepted somewhere, and good news had a way of eclipsing the bad. Wagner encouraged the counselors to keep early applications to a minimum. She advised families that it was easier for a girl to "keep her head" when she did not feel that her future rode on a single envelope.

Talk of process did little to dissuade the seniors or their parents, though. The percentage of girls who applied early had risen steadily over the past seven years; over one-third of the girls in the auditorium that day hoped to get the application process over with as quickly as possible. Early decision, once the province of the exceptional student, was now the frantic playground of girls who were wary of being left out.

Katie Tower slumped in her seat clutching the first draft of her college essay, wearing a skimpy black T-shirt over baggy khaki pants, which she jokingly called her "fashion statement for the year," as though she cared about such things. A slender, pale young woman with hazel eyes and chin-length dark-brown hair, Katie was a clever, high-pitched girl who loved science, books, and not quite fitting in. She had attended the United Nations School in Manhattan until she was ten, when her parents, a freelance lighting director and a freelance sound technician, decided to move to Pacific Palisades, a comfortable residential neighborhood on the cliffs overlooking the Pacific Ocean, just west of Los Angeles.

Katie had spent two years at the Lycée Français before she came to Marlborough for seventh grade. She still carried herself with an East Coast immigrant's pride: Her clothes might look like the other girls', but with a slight edge, and if she liked the same movies they did it was always with a knowing air, as though she understood something that the other girls had missed about the literary antecedents of *Scream*.

She was hardly a snob, but she did consider herself an individual. Katie had no use for what she saw as the enforced camaraderie of team sports, even though female athletes were now recruited by colleges with a fervor once reserved for boys. Sixty percent of Marlborough students participated in school sports. Katie chose instead to pursue a black belt in karate, because she liked the self-discipline and was more comfortable working on her own.

Her nearly straight-A record was marred only by an occasional B, usually in math, but she refused to take classes just because they might look good to an admissions officer somewhere. Some girls took college-level Advanced Placement (AP) classes in every possible subject, even if it meant staying up until two in the morning doing homework for a class they didn't care about. Katie took AP classes in subjects that interested her, like biology and dramatic literature, and settled comfortably into regular or honors sections of calculus and physics. She intended to suffer through the math

SAT a second time to see if she could raise her math score of 610, but she assumed that some admissions committee, somewhere, would see beyond it.

Katie planned to apply to several Ivy League schools, because this might be the year they wanted a black belt with an interest in science and international relations; to the University of Chicago, because it sounded right for her; to Johns Hopkins for its science program; to the University of California at Berkeley because it was the most academically challenging of the California campuses; and to the University of California, San Diego because she was fairly sure she would get in.

Like Katie, most of the seniors had sorted their schools into the three categories the college counselors had defined for them: the "reaches," where acceptance might require a little luck; the "likelies," where they had a good chance; and a couple of safe schools, where they could pretty much depend on getting in. The counselors wanted the girls to be comfortable with all the schools on their lists, so that they would not feel like failures if they ended up at a safe school. But the good students, like Katie, were not ready to settle. They wanted to submit essays that would impress the Ivy League schools. The less satisfying work of identifying schools that might be happy to have them could come later on.

The seniors were supposed to hand in drafts of their essays this morning, so that a team of faculty advisors could read them; on Wednesday, the girls would meet in small groups with the advisors to begin rewriting. Katie balked. Marlborough had made it easy for her to develop her own point of view, but this time she was writing for strangers, and she felt uncertain. She needed to talk to someone before she relinquished her pages.

Dr. John Wands had run the Marlborough English department for thirteen years, and in that time he had developed a refined sense of just what kind of essay an admissions committee wanted to see. He warned the girls that a good essay could take two or three months to develop, and that what they were about to hand in likely would not be what they finally submitted. They should expect revisions and frustrations—in fact, they might end up starting over more than once. This was not the kind of essay that they had been writing for five years, in which they expressed their thoughts and feelings about what they had read. These essays required more awareness of the potential audience.

"You have to become an informed consumer," he said. "Realize what a particular school is looking for—and, in an honest way, slant your essay to respond to that."

What every admissions officer wanted, he told them, was an essay that made the applicant "come alive as a human being." The girls in this room would have to try harder than their counterparts on the east coast. "There is probably a prejudice against the west coast," Dr. Wands warned the girls, "that we're laid-back and spacy. Now, Marlborough girls, as a rule, don't fit that profile, but you may have to convince an admissions officer that you're dedicated and determined to do things well."

He wanted the girls to understand who was going to be reading their work. An admissions officer was usually more liberal than the general population, "so if you enjoy dirt-biking or polluting the environment, you might not want to mention it. That probably won't go over very well. And they're idealistic. If you're a scientist and you chose fifty thousand dollars to teach at Berkeley instead of a hundred thousand to work at Hopper Chemical, that means you think there's something more important than money. Many of them aren't rich, so when you come from Marlborough you have to prove you're not a spoiled rich kid; that you care about more than wealth and social status. They frown on people who see an education as a ticket to a bigger car and lots of money. They're dedicated to what the University of Chicago calls 'the life of the mind,' and they need to know you care as well."

He gazed at the girls. The senior class included daughters of screenwriters, producers, a judge, corporate lawyers, doctors. About fourteen percent of Marlborough students received financial aid, but for the most part this was a privileged group. Dr. Wands wanted to help them strike a balance in their essays—to sound confident but not arrogant.

"The spoiled, selfish life," he said, "does not sell."

He had several other bits of advice:

"Admissions officers are older than the norm, so a split infinitive might bother them."

"They appreciate risk-taking."

"They appreciate brevity."

"They want to see dedication—that you have a sense of where you want to end up in four years—and yet they want to see resilience: that you won't be crushed if it turns out you do not want to be pre-med after all."

"They don't want daily grinds, people who care about schoolwork and nothing else. But they're not impressed by laundry lists of what you have done."

"The point here is not to scare you," he said, "but to make you realistically aware."

With that, he dismissed them for lunch and a senior-class meeting. Katie Tower ran up to him, clutching her pages in her hand. She had written a first draft about the question of free will versus fate in her favorite play, Tom Stoppard's *Rosencrantz and Guildenstern Are Dead*. She wanted Dr. Wands to tell her right that minute whether she ought to turn it in or start over.

He skimmed it quickly. "Many people try to use fate or predestination as an excuse for their own mistakes or misfortunes," Katie had written. "In *Rosencrantz and Guildenstern* Stoppard shows the absurdity of allowing this belief to rule your life. Instead of trying to pin down the exact moment when everything 'happened' to you and changed your life, like Rosencrantz and Guildenstern, you should act. This is what I finally took from Stoppard. Predestined or not my future depends on my actions and my life will only change if I act. According to Stoppard's philosophy, life is a box, and the only meaning it has is what you put in it. Rosencrantz and Guildenstern spend the entire play allowing themselves to be carried along by other peoples' actions and morals. I realize that only actions that follow *your own* moral code add to the meaning of your life. The only way I can fill my life with meaning is to act according to what I feel is right."

But Katie and her parents were masters of the wicked aside, and they liked to play sincerity with a sly grace note. Katie recognized the absurdity of what she was being asked to do: to summarize, in 500 words, who she was and why they should care about her. The final line of her essay quoted a line from the play, "'Shouldn't we be doing something more constructive?'" Did Dr. Wands think she was being too flip?

He suggested that she hand it in the way it was and let her advisor read it. There would be plenty of opportunities, over the next two days, to reconsider—and months after that for extended second-guessing.

On the following night, the girls' parents came to school for a presentation on college strategies and the accompanying emotional stress. Jon Tower, Katie's father, arrived late and stood at the back of the library rather than take one of the folding chairs that had been set out. Having spent his entire working life as a freelancer—one boss this week, another boss the next, never identifying with any of them—Jon was always slightly uncomfortable at this sort of institutionalized event. He and his wife, Cabel, lived with uncertainty all the time: One week they both had jobs, the next week they didn't. The kids were used to the ups and downs. If there was a lot of work, they might take a trip to Europe. If there wasn't, they ate at home more often.

Acceptance and rejection were part of daily life, and they were always based on ability, not image. At fifty, Jon Tower refused to look the part of the middle-aged private-school dad. He preferred baggy khaki shorts for almost any occasion, wore his gray hair in spikes, and assumed a working-man air that held up only with people who had never seen his house full of books. He was not interested in finding out how best to package his daughter. She was a bright, interesting kid. That might not be enough for some schools, but he was sure she would end up in a good college, on her own terms.

This kind of event ate away at his self-confidence, though. He could barely imagine what it was doing to people who led more ordered lives, the ones who assumed a causal link between effort and results. They must really be squirming. Five years of believing they had provided their daughters with an academic edge, and still there were no guarantees.

As head of college counseling, Dr. Lewandowski felt that it was her obligation to remind parents of the odds. She might not end up the most beloved of faculty members, but she would not pretend that every story had a happy ending. "The competition is very, very stiff," she told them, "and we want your daughter to be willing to go to her 'likelies,' as well as to the other schools on her list. The problems come when all the energy is focused on getting into one school. If she's comfortable with all the schools on her list, she'll have an easier time with rejection. Because remember: With some of the top schools, ninety percent of the applicants don't get in. A student who shoots too high may get seven rejections out of ten, which is not going to make a happy camper."

And happiness—or, rather, self-satisfaction—was an essential part of the Marlborough curriculum. The whole point of segregating girls was to focus their attention on academic achievement, and have them define themselves in terms of accomplishment, not by the more fleeting measures of appearance and popularity. Marlborough cleared their path: Having a boyfriend meant nothing here, because it happened offstage if it happened at all. Having a beautiful wardrobe was beside the point in a place where status seemed to be tied to how long you could wear the same old uniform skirt. The period from seventh through twelfth grade was supposed to be a time not of turmoil and self-doubt but of dedication to task.

It was impossible to eliminate competition completely, whether for grades or for the sleekest figure, but nothing these girls had experienced could prepare them for what was to come. Dr. Lewandowski had invited a handful of Marlborough parents whose children had graduated the previous year to offer advice to the assembled senior parents, and one college freshman's mother implored her audience to watch for signs of trouble.

"These are all very competent girls," she said, "but sometimes they don't feel that way, especially when it always seems there is someone who's more competent. Especially in a place like this. So this year is a real chance for you to make your daughter feel competent. Stress her strengths."

Jon shifted from one foot to the other, and sighed, and left as soon as the last speaker was finished. At this point in the process, most of the parents in the room were floating on the same mix of love and adrenaline that made Jon and Cabel sure that their daughter would face a happy choice come spring. He kept telling everyone he wasn't worried.

But someone would be disappointed; hadn't the counselors just said as much? If Jon hung around here too long, he would start making the inevitable comparisons—that guy's daughter was a volleyball star, that woman's kid was a science whiz. He would try to handicap the odds of Katie's bright future, which was the last thing he wanted to do.

2

The Young Women's Leadership School of East Harlem

New York, New York, September 1998

THE SUN WAS not yet up at five-thirty in the morning, when Maryam Zohny got on the city bus at 94th Street and Third Avenue, two blocks north of her family's apartment. On a normal school day she would have walked to The Young Women's Leadership School of East Harlem, on 106th Street just east of Park Avenue, but it was too early, and she and her friend were carrying too much stuff. They rode the twelve blocks to 106th Street in drowsy silence, Maryam glad that she had told her mother not to come. Afaf Zohny worked all week; Maryam had said there was no use coming along just to turn around and go back home alone once the girls had left on their trip.

What she needed from her mother was food, not companionship. Maryam was a city girl, used to good food available at any hour. The prospect of a thirty-six-hour camping trip in the middle of nowhere did not excite her, so yesterday she had implored her mom to make a bunch of sandwiches and pack frozen fruit drinks. Maryam got on the city bus carrying three backpacks, one exclusively devoted to food, rather than risk a day and a half in the wilds of Brooklyn without provisions.

The fifty members of the ninth-grade class at The Young Women's Leadership School of East Harlem were going to Gateway National Park in Brooklyn, the site of an abandoned airfield, for an overnight camping trip arranged by the Outward Bound organization. TYWLS, pronounced "twills" by everyone involved with the school, was a two-year-old public school for girls; the ninth graders had been dubbed "the pioneers" by the principal, Celenia Chevere, because in the fall of 1996 they had been the first to enter the school in seventh grade. There had been a new class of seventh graders every year since, and this year, TYWLS had added a tenth grade as well. Starting on Monday, two hundred girls would attend classes in the top three floors of an eleven-story office building in East Harlem, just a few doors east of the elevated train tracks that carried wealthy commuters to and from Westchester County and Connecticut.

Philanthropist Ann Tisch had come up with the original idea for the school, which had been endorsed by then–Department of Education Chancellor Dr. Rudy Crew and was overseen by Chevere, a twenty-six-year Board of Education veteran. TYWLS was a showcase school, a laboratory experiment in gender equity for girls who could never afford an independent girls' school. If it worked, grades and test scores would improve, and girls who previously had hoped only to graduate from high school would instead aspire to college scholarships.

The school's detractors hoped that TYWLS would never reach that first graduation day. Several groups, including the New York Civil Liberties Union and the National Organization for Women, had already lodged complaints with the federal government's Department of Education, accusing TYWLS of using public funds for a school that discriminated against boys. The suggestion that the entire public school system discriminated against girls—and that TYWLS was merely an attempt to achieve parity—did not interest them, since it involved interpretation, not absolutes.

The federal investigation moved slowly, though, and TYWLS was still open two years later, its program enhanced by a series of profitable alliances. The girls were going to Brooklyn because Outward Bound had provided food, supplies, and an agenda designed to make the girls feel even more confident about their abilities. Eight tenth graders had been dispatched to the park on Friday night to set up. Just after 6:30 on Saturday morning, the bus rolled away carrying the ninth graders and three teachers: Shirley Gasich and Suzanne Kerho, who both taught science, and Peter De-Wan, who taught history.

Maryam was not pleased about the location: It was too hot, the airstrip was barren and dusty, and there were tents for sleeping and portable toilets. These were unpleasant revelations for a girl who was fastidious about both her privacy and her appearance. Maryam was tall and full-figured, with long, black hair that fell in a symmetrical pageboy from an impeccable center part. Her big, brown eyes were encircled by fine, black eyeliner and a bit of pale shadow, her eyebrows were carefully groomed, and she wore a natural shade of lipstick. Her school uniform was always perfectly pressed. Even her clothes for this outing were neat. It was not a look that would survive a night in the park.

Still, the first assignment was fun. Shirley Gasich gave each of the girls a piece of paper and an envelope and instructed each of them to write a letter to herself about her goals for ninth grade. Gasich planned to give the letters back to the girls in January, so that they could see how close they were to reaching their goals and figure out what they needed to do during the second semester.

Maryam loved to write. "To myself," she began,

> My short term goal for this year is to remain with a straight A average as well as have a social life at the same time. This year I promise myself to do all my work to the best of my ability. In addition, I promise to have fun at the same time. I do not want my life to be spent with books and school supplies. Besides having a social life I need to begin to KNOW God. I have to become more of a spiritual person.
>
> My long term goal in life is to graduate high school with high honors, after passing all my regents and scoring an average or above score on my SAT's. Go to a college of my choice with a

scholarship, become an architectural or computer engineer, or a physical therapist/psychologist. Then I want to get married and have seven kids (four boys and three girls). However my main focus is education. What strives me so much is my parents, but mainly my father. Although he has passed away, I know if he was alive he would have wanted me to do really well in school. Therefore I'm trying to live out his dream since he can't live it for himself. I also want to strive in school for my mother because she works soooooooooooo hard raising us kids, therefore it would be nice if she is able to see the job she's done, because we reflect her. And if we succeed then she succeeds, and that's what I want most.

Therefore Maryam, you have to do well for yourself and for mama and baba. Hopefully I will succeed in my goals.

She signed it, "Love, Myself."

The rest of the day's activities included a talent show, dinner, a night hike, and a campfire that made it impossible to go to sleep until the rest of the girls had stopped talking. On Sunday morning they faced the big physical challenge of the trip, a climb up the outside wall of the sixty-foot airport control tower. Outward Bound stressed physical challenge as a way for city kids to get a sense of their own abilities and build a community spirit, and the ninth graders cheered each other on as, one by one, they headed up the tower. Almost all the girls completed the climb.

Sitting in a circle while they waited for the bus, they talked about the trip and how much fun they had had. But as soon as Maryam heard the sound of the bus engine she was on her feet, ready to go home. School, for her, was about quantifiable progress. It was time to go back to class.

The next morning, a cluster of neighborhood kids stood by the coffee cart on 106th Street between Park and Madison, chatting in Spanish with the proprietor, buying spongy bagels and big cups of steaming sweetened coffee. They were on their way to the local high school—or maybe not—and they cast furtive glances at the students who entered the office building at

105 East 106th Street, all decked out in their uniforms and their superior attitude. One girl on the street caught her boyfriend staring, and muttered with a mix of envy and disdain about the girls who went to "*that* school"; who clearly were not going to bother to look back at him.

It was part of Celenia Chevere's plan to separate her girls from the people they passed on the way to school. The girl at the coffee cart and her boyfriend represented to her a pervasive threat; they seemed to have only a tangential relationship to education, and acted as though school were merely something to be endured until they were old enough to strike out on their own. TYWLS students did not come from a background of opportunity or privilege. Most of them belonged to ethnic minorities, and were survivors of public schools where metal detectors were part of the daily ritual, where gangs were a more common social configuration than sports teams and the only uniforms were gang colors.

The luckier girls had come to Chevere from specialized public elementary schools, by virtue of their test scores or their parents' determination or both. She made it clear from the start that escape demanded something more than the obvious attributes of dedication and academic excellence. A successful young woman made TYWLS her community, and left the temptations of her neighborhood behind.

Some of the girls resisted the cosmetic aspects of the transition and proudly wore vestiges of the life outside: big gold earrings, necklaces that spelled their names in ornate gold script, long fingernails painted in deep colors with raised detail. Maryam had nothing to do with them. Her faith in TYWLS was absolute. She believed that if she played by its rules, in four years she would be strolling across a college campus. Not a school in New York City, but perhaps UCLA or Berkeley. The world just outside TYWLS threatened her with poverty, pregnancy, drugs; worse, it encouraged resignation. Maryam rejected it all. She refused to think of her neighborhood as anything but a way station.

She picked as her best friends girls who shared her dedication: Diana Perez, a quiet girl with a quick mind, and Amy Lopez, who with Maryam had attended The New York City Laboratory School for Gifted Education, another of the public schools Chevere had started. They were among the girls who had attended a special summer program in science and the humanities at Smith College. They were the ones who spoke up in class and got their homework done on time.

Maryam Zohny's father, Sami, the eldest of five brothers and two sisters, came to the United States from Cairo, Egypt, in 1969, and got a job at the Chase Manhattan Bank. His wife, Afaf, joined him in 1976, by which time he had gone to work for the Metropolitan Transit Authority. He retired in 1984, the year his fourth child, Maryam, was born, and opened Zohny Travel with two of his brothers.

But when Maryam was only two, Sami Zohny died suddenly of a heart attack, leaving Afaf to raise a boy and three girls alone. His relatives joined together to help, supporting the family financially so that Afaf could stay at home until Maryam was six and at school for a full day. In 1990, Afaf went to work part-time at the travel agency, but it was with the understanding that the children came first.

By the time Maryam entered TYWLS, Afaf had made sure that her youngest child had everything she needed to succeed, including her own desk in her bedroom and a desktop computer. All Maryam had to do, in return, was make her mother's efforts worthwhile. Homework came before television; grades were more important than a social life.

Maryam was happy to comply, because she had always had big plans. When she was a little girl, she had gone for a walk with her mother down Fifth Avenue in the shadow of increasingly elegant buildings. There were doormen in fine uniforms, and the people who came in and out moved with sure purpose. Maryam imagined that the apartments inside must be like castles.

She turned to her mother, a small, pale woman, a devout Muslim who always wore a head scarf and walked with deferential, downcast eyes. Maryam solemnly announced that when she grew up, she would be rich and live in one of these buildings.

Nine years later, she had gotten her first glimpse of the inside of one of those grand buildings. In eighth grade Maryam, full of school spirit, decided that the girls needed a school store where they could buy pencils, notebooks, and other supplies emblazoned with the school crest. Ann Tisch, eager to reward enterprise, invited Maryam to come by after school to discuss the idea. Tisch's husband, Andrew, was a scion of the family that controlled the $20 billion Loew's Corporation, and they lived with their two young daughters in an airy Park Avenue duplex. Maryam spent a giddy hour in Tisch's home office, discussing how large a loan Maryam needed to stock the store and how she intended to pay it back.

She was inside, and all it had taken was initiative. Some of the girls at TYWLS treated school like a cruel joke, a tantalizing glimpse of a future they would never attain. Maryam told everyone her goal, as though repeating it often enough would make it come true: She was going to be the best student in her class, the kind of girl a top college would want to recruit.

She expected that it would be hard to leave her mother. Maryam had been terribly homesick during the month she spent at Smith, even with Diana and Amy to keep her company, but she was determined to go away to college. She informed her teachers that she intended to get straight A+'s from the ninth through the twelfth grade. She was going to make it impossible for anyone to ignore her.

3

Marlborough School

A S A TEENAGER in the late 1960s, Barbara Wagner was as oblivious to the compromises she made as any good midwestern girl. When she looked back now on her high school days in rural Michigan, the Marlborough head of school marveled at some of the things she had done in the name of acceptable social behavior. One emblematic incident stuck in her mind: the time she fell down on purpose during a big water-skiing show, just to avoid being noticed for her ability or accused of showing off.

She got her bachelor's degree in music education at Michigan State University. In 1977, she was lured to the University of Colorado in Boulder, which had an intriguing program in group piano instruction—a notion that appealed to her after too many lonely hours in practice rooms. After she received her master's degree, she stayed on for two years, teaching other students how to teach music, and then, in 1979, she began her career in independent schools. Wagner started at Denver's coeducational Graland

Country Day School as chair of the fine arts department, continued to teach music, and in 1982 became the head of the Middle School.

Despite having had what she considered a traditional upbringing, Wagner prided herself on her awareness of gender issues. She had seen the early research about how boys tended to dominate in the classroom, and she had attended several workshops on how to make sure that girls and boys had equal opportunities in hers.

A straightforward, confident woman, she welcomed an observer who wanted to videotape one of her sixth-grade music classes. "I would have bet my house," she said, that girls got as much attention as boys. The researcher came to a startlingly different conclusion. They watched the videotape together and tallied the number of times Wagner called on the boys and the girls. The boys responded five to seven times more often than the girls, often not even bothering to wait until Wagner acknowledged them.

She was taken completely by surprise, and, in the weeks that followed, that surprise soured into an uncharacteristic pessimism. Wagner considered herself well-intentioned and aware. If she could not adjust the balance in her classroom to an equitable level—if she had failed even to recognize the problem—then what hope was there for all the children whose teachers had not attended workshops and read the literature on gender equity? If Wagner herself was any example, it was going to take some time, and more effort, to insure that a girl got a fair shot at a good education.

Soon after the videotape incident, she got a call from her former boss at Graland, who had moved to California and heard about a job Wagner might want. He had been in touch with Robert Chumbook, the head of school at Marlborough, a girls' school for the seventh through twelfth grades in Los Angeles. Chumbook had run Marlborough for twenty years, and he needed a new director for the Upper School.

Wagner had been thinking of leaving Graland and had gone out on several job interviews, but she was quite clear about what she did not want: Los Angeles, a high school, a girls' school. As aware as she was of the problems at her own school, she knew nothing about single-sex education. But she called Chumbook and, after several conversations, agreed to visit Marlborough.

The girls were a revelation. "They impressed me immediately," she recalled. "They had the ability to articulate what they thought, to ask tough questions; they had a great sense of themselves." She went back to Colorado and joked with her colleagues that there must be something in the water in Los Angeles. She had never before met a group of girls like that.

Wagner allowed herself what she previously would have considered a traitorous thought, given her attempts to achieve a fair classroom environment: Maybe girls were better off on their own. The ideal of equal coeducation seemed to her to be just that—an unattainable ideal. The hundred-year-old Marlborough School promised a committed group of girls in an unequivocal environment. Wagner accepted the position of director of the upper school in July 1989.

What she could not know was the magnitude of the opportunity. One month after she arrived, Chumbook announced his intention to retire. At first, the board of trustees said it would not consider internal candidates and mounted a search for a new head of school. Four months later, the board approached Wagner about the job. The alumnae had spoken up with what Wagner called a "vehemence of sentiment": They wanted to see a woman in a leadership role. She became Marlborough head of school on July 1, 1990, one year after she had arrived.

At first glance, Barbara Wagner seemed a central-casting choice for the role. Her fine blond hair, tucked neatly into a headband or barrette, looked as perfect at four in the afternoon as it had at seven in the morning; nary a strand had the will to defy her. She exerted the same control over her clothing, which obediently refused to wrinkle. Her uniform of choice was any of a number of good wool suits worn with a silk blouse or plain sweater, sheer stockings, plain pumps, and tasteful gold jewelry—or, on a more casual day, a twin sweater set and slacks. Her handshake was firm, but not the aggressive grasp of a woman who needed to prove something.

A more considered appraisal betrayed small, subversive details: One of the suits the forty-six-year-old Wagner wore to an open house for prospective parents was fire-engine red, with matching pointy-toed, high-heeled red pumps. The set jaw beneath the pageboy was decisive. And if Wagner gave the impression of being a very good listener, it was not because she was reluctant to speak up, but because letting other people talk was the best way to find things out.

She was, in fact, a woman with an agenda. She had on her desk a gift from Cabel Tower, Katie's mother; a framed cover of *Newsweek* magazine from February 2, 1959. Over a picture of two sweet, smiling girls in school uniforms, the headline read, GIRLS AT WORK: FINISHING SCHOOLS ARE FINISHED. As far as Wagner was concerned, they were. She rejected the "old notion" of a girls' school as a cloistered place where privileged girls could escape the real world for a more ladylike learning experience. She wanted a school that prepared them for the world better than even the most enlightened coed school could.

Marlborough was a luxurious place for an educator to effect change. When Wagner noticed that girls tended to get up from their individual science-lab stations to work together in small groups, she ripped the labs out and replaced them with new stations designed for groups of four. When her faculty wanted more special sections of classes in response to perceived differences in ability, they got them. A half-dozen bright girls were a mandate, whether for a science research group or a foreign language tutorial.

Wagner's definition of growth meant more than improving the curriculum, though. She wanted those who followed her at Marlborough to speak of her as the woman who expanded the school's horizons. On a practical level, that meant an ambitious $17 million plan to nearly double the size of the campus and consolidate its athletic program. For years, the school had been buying up the row of houses on the block behind the campus. This year, once all the hearings were completed and the permits acquired, they intended to raze the houses and replace them with an athletic field, a new and larger swimming pool, two new tennis courts (in addition to the existing one), a garden, and more parking spaces.

That would be the visible monument to her administration. Her other goal was to make Marlborough "an urban school, not a suburban one"; a school that better reflected the demographics of Los Angeles, which meant a level of diversity previously unknown at the school. Marlborough was in Hancock Park, a moneyed neighborhood of handsome old homes, influential families, and an exclusionary past. There had been a time, less than twenty years earlier, when black and Jewish students knew better than to apply, because they had no chance of being accepted.

The school's conservative reputation, in terms both of ideology and demographics, had persisted well into the 1970s. "Marlborough was not welcoming to entertainment money, which often meant Jewish money," said Wagner. "Marlborough was a school where a certain kind of family sent their daughters."

The school had grudgingly begun to yield to "entertainment money" before Wagner arrived, since as a practical matter it depended on wealth for its financial stability—whether old Hancock Park money or newer fortunes. Wagner took her job with the stated intention of opening the doors even wider. Success, as she defined it, meant pulling in students who previously might not have considered Marlborough. She felt a particular affection for one group of seniors, dubbed "The Internationals" by one girl's mother—eight friends who had been together since seventh grade, four of them black, one Asian, one East Indian, and two Caucasian.

She wanted an expanded curriculum that served a heterogeneous group of girls, and she wanted to figure out how best to teach the girls what they needed to know. It all came down to teaching style; to what went on in the classroom of even the most well-intentioned teacher. That was where Wagner sometimes felt she was trying to jump onto a moving train. Her best teachers had in common an intense commitment to what they did, but beyond that they were a fractious group. John Langdon, known to all as "Doc," the beloved head of the history department, ran his classes like an old-style college professor. He talked, the girls took copious notes, and then he drilled them and gave exams. Right next door, Myranda Marsh taught seventh-grade history in direct repudiation of Langdon's technique, using the newest approach from the latest paper on how to teach teenage girls. She had one game for memorizing facts, another to encourage classroom participation, and an origami-like paper-folding technique to help the girls study for quizzes.

Some of Wagner's teachers believed that projects—drawing maps, making posters—appealed to a girl's visual imagination. Others dismissed projects as distracting busywork. Some believed in what Wagner called "teaching to the test," preparing the girls for the inevitable raft of tests that stood between them and college acceptance, while others bemoaned the demise of learning for its own sake. Education had its trends and fashions, and the best Wagner could hope for was to hire faculty who were passionate about their approach, whatever it was, but willing to entertain new ideas. She told parents that the benefit of all this variety was that any girl could likely find a teacher to inspire her.

If anything, the older girls griped about having too much choice—such an embarrassment of advanced-placement and elective courses that it was hard to choose. But Wagner wanted the same diversity in her curriculum that she wanted among the students, and she pressed the teachers, particularly in science and math, to come up with new ways to engage the girls.

Wagner had no interest in running a school that girls attended by default. She wanted to be at the vanguard of a new era in education, a model both for other all-girls schools and for coeducational schools eager to improve a girl's chances. Marlborough was where a girl should be if she really intended to learn. It ought to be her first choice.

Her timing was perfect. Wagner believed that between 1970 and 1990, girls' schools had been mired in confusion as they sorted out the "residuals of the finishing school thing" and faced a women's movement that defined liberation as access to a man's world, not retreat from it. Parents who valued the proper social environment continued to enroll their daughters, while the families who wanted something more too often stayed away.

Some parents still saw it that way. It was usually the father of a prospective seventh grader who approached Wagner or one of the admissions staff during an open house to insist that his daughter did not need a special environment in order to excel. He considered Marlborough a remedial setting, and wondered if his daughter might not get exactly the opposite of the school's intended message. Wouldn't she feel that there was, in fact, something wrong with her? Something that required special attention? And how would she cope with the real world after having been shut away from it for six formative years?

Wagner saw it differently, as did many of the girls' mothers, who had come of age with distinct memories of what it was like not to have an equal chance. She defined equality in terms of outcome, not process. What mattered was giving girls as good an education as boys got, not how they got there. After almost ten years as head of school at Marlborough, Wagner believed that critics of single-sex education were asking the wrong question first.

"The bottom line," she said, "is less about 'Do we separate?' and more about 'How do we effectively educate?,' and the answer to that question may lead to separate classes. It is a travesty in this country that there are so many girls who, if you believe the research, are not being well educated."

Let the theorists discuss ways to improve the coeducational classroom for all students; Wagner was determined to offer a quality alternative to families who preferred not to wait until someone figured it out. As for coping skills, a girl who knew who she was would be better equipped to deal with boys. The girls who really wanted boyfriends usually managed to find them, but for seven hours a day, five days a week, all they had to think about was themselves.

She was equally impatient with prevailing ideas about how to build self-esteem in adolescent girls. If girls' schools were to be faulted for anything over the last ten years, it was their preoccupation with making girls feel good about themselves—an understandable initial response to research about the precipitous drop in self-confidence among teenage girls, but, as far as Wagner was concerned, a misguided effort. A nurturing environment was meaningless, even deceptive, since the real world was often short on empathy. Lasting self-esteem required a foundation of competence, and this year Wagner had instructed her staff to emphasize academics even more than they had in the past.

Not every girl could hope to be a straight-A student, and the teachers had to make sure that a girl who did her best and got a B+ felt proud of the achievement, rather than hating herself for not getting the A. But every student had to work to the limits of her ability. An A student who let herself slide was not to be patted on the back. Self-confidence did not exist in a vacuum. It had to be tied to effort.

The yearly increase in admission applications, which had begun in the early 1990s, was proof that more and more families saw Marlborough as an opportunity, not an escape. With an average income of $150,000 annually, Marlborough families were far wealthier than most, but it was not just the established wealth of the past. In the previous year, Wagner had noticed that several mothers jumped up to return to work after a parents' lunch at school. She estimated that about one-third of Marlborough families required two incomes to meet the costs of private school.

Wagner worked hard to extend the school's reach even farther into the community. Students on financial aid now comprised fourteen percent of the student body, including the likely valedictorian for the class of 1999, Christina Kim, the daughter of Korean immigrants. One of the Internationals was Sommer Louie, an African-American girl whose father was a retired electrician and whose mother worked for the director of the Los Angeles office of the Southern Christian Leadership Conference. This was what inspired Wagner: a diverse community of girls who, with luck, would never understand why she had chosen to fall off her water skis.

4

The Young Women's Leadership
School of East Harlem

CELENIA CHEVERE, Barbara Wagner's counterpart at The Young Women's Leadership School of East Harlem, was "the godforsaken middle child" who had always found happiness at school. Her Puerto Rican immigrant parents had settled in East Harlem, where her father ran a little grocery store and sold cigars he made by hand. They ran a strict home: Celenia and her sister and brother went to school every day, on time, properly dressed. Her parents would not tolerate excuses.

"They believed," she said, "that education was something no one can take away from you."

Chevere was eager to cooperate. She liked making friends with the teachers, and even now, at fifty-four, she remembered her favorites—the one who wrote to nine-year-old Celenia over summer vacation, and the fifth-grade teacher who had always had time to listen. When Celenia playacted, she cast herself as a teacher.

An early marriage and the birth of her first daughter did not deter her.

She enrolled in the City College of New York and got her first job, as a teacher's assistant for pre-kindergarten through third grade, in 1972, while she was still a student. She had worked for the New York City Board of Education ever since.

She made her way through the 1970s without giving any particular thought to women's rights. Chevere had no time for political theory: As a working mother, she was too busy trying to provide the kinds of opportunities that girls from more comfortable backgrounds took for granted. She sent her older daughter to a private Catholic junior high and high school and sent her younger girl, born in 1977, to independent schools from the time she entered kindergarten. She had seen enough of the city's public schools to convince her that her daughters would be lost there, so she got them safely installed at private schools and then went back to the business of improving what she considered an almost hopeless public school system.

Over the years, Chevere gained a reputation for chipping away at mediocrity and for working with the neglected poor, who stood to profit most from a decent education. She established one outpost after another, including an elementary school for gifted children in District 4, where she grew up. She kept the names of families she met along the way, people whose commitment equaled her own, in the hope that one day she might be able to help them again.

She took no time for herself. After a 1985 divorce she worked even harder, paying for her older girl's college education, cadging the time she needed to attend her younger daughter's school meetings and conferences. It was a different kind of gender politics, not the upheaval engineered by privileged women who could decide to change, and do it, but a slower process of improvement, generation by generation, plotted by women who counted progress by the methodical half-step.

By 1995, she could look back on her life with a weary satisfaction. Celene, her older daughter, was working for a law firm and planned to return to college for her degree. Serena, her younger girl, intended to major in psychology at Wesleyan University in Connecticut. Chevere was a fierce advocate for the city's disadvantaged students. She grew new schools, in an often hostile environment.

Ann Rubenstein, the daughter of a well-to-do couple in Kansas City, Missouri, had flirted with the idea of becoming a teacher until she was sidetracked by journalism. Her parents, who were active in Jewish charitable organizations, had instilled in her the importance of giving back to the community, so she gravitated toward stories about people trying to improve their situation—first at a local television station in Topeka, Kansas, and later at *The NBC Nightly News*.

In 1986, Rubenstein visited a Milwaukee high school that had built a day-care center next door to enable teenage mothers to finish high-school. The idea was that a high-school diploma would buy a better future, so she asked one of the girls where she imagined she would be in ten years.

Rubenstein was a tall, fresh-faced woman with a quick smile and an empathic air, the kind of reporter who inspired confidences, but she was not prepared when the girl burst into tears. A diploma would not erase the fact that she was a child responsible for another child's life; good intentions had come too late to make a difference for her. Rubenstein returned to her hotel room shaken, and sat there, alone, wondering about what she had seen. That girl did not need a day-care center; she needed not to have gotten pregnant in the first place. She needed a school that made her feel worthy of a more ambitious future.

Three years later, Ann Rubenstein went on a blind date with Andrew Tisch, and three years after that, in 1992, she married him. She was now an extremely wealthy woman. Though she hardly needed to continue working, Ann Tisch proudly dismissed the society couture-and-charity circuit. She worked at NBC while she looked around for something new to do.

One afternoon she came across a quote from Mother Teresa that said, "If I look at the masses I will never act. If I look at one, I will." Suddenly, she knew what she wanted to do. Tisch, who now had a toddler daughter of her own, had been reading some of the new literature on single-sex education. She remembered the teenage mother she had interviewed in Milwaukee. She asked herself, "What if you offered inner-city kids some of the same opportunities that wealthy girls have, and that Catholic girls have? Put them on an entirely different path?" Girls' schools had always been the exclusive province of the wealthy. Catholic schools were less expensive than independent schools, but they still cost thousands of dollars each year. If subtracting boys from the equation was a solution, it ought to be available to all girls, regardless of how much money their parents made.

Separating students for any reason—gender, religion, language, ethnicity—threatened the principle of equal access, but Tisch felt that the reality, for girls, was quite different from the ideal. The research to date showed that equal access did not mean an equal education for girls; they sat in the classroom with boys, but they got less attention, less acknowledgment when they did well, and less encouragement in fields like math and science. As far as Tisch could tell, the coed classroom denied more than half the population its vaunted right to an equal education; she was determined to even things out.

She could close her eyes and imagine the school, which in her mind looked just like the private school her young daughter would likely attend someday, minus the costs: "A college-prep environment, high expectations. 'If you're coming here, you're going to college. You're coming here, you're not getting pregnant.' Uniforms, small classes, everything. I could see it all."

She and her husband hired a lawyer to make sure that such a project would survive the inevitable legal challenges, and he assured them that it did not fall under Title IX, which prohibited discrimination at schools that received public funding. In the lawyer's opinion, the 1972 federal legislation targeted colleges and universities, not kindergarten through twelfth grade.

Next, Ann Tisch polled the experts. She visited New York University adjunct professor of education Diane Ravitch, a prolific and controversial writer on educational reform. Ravitch regularly confounded her adversaries by refusing to align herself with a particular educational doctrine; although she publicly questioned whether girls continued to suffer in the coed classroom, the Wellesley College graduate endorsed their right to choose a single-sex public school. She encouraged Tisch to pursue the idea, and invited her to a publication party at the home of the then-chancellor of the New York City Board of Education, Ramon Cortines. By the end of the evening, Tisch had his blessing. The logistics were up to her.

Manhattan has thirty-two school districts, each one with its own superintendent and a community school board made up of local residents. Tisch decided to focus her effort in Manhattan School District 4, in East Harlem, which she felt would be a "friendly" district because of its history of innovation. In 1973, District 4 had been the worst district in the city, but by 1987 it had risen to fifteenth place, higher than some schools in more affluent neighborhoods, thanks to a network of twenty-six alternative public schools.

Convincing District 4 that an all-girls public school was legal took so long, though, that Tisch ran into two school-board elections and had to start over each time. Finally, she got their approval. The district agreed to help her find a home for the school and to appoint a principal who would hire the teachers.

It was time to start looking at buildings. Tisch spent two years and much of her second pregnancy taking calls from realtors who had heard about her project and were sure they had the perfect space. She looked at a bargain building that required "fifty million dollars of repairs," a beautiful space that didn't work out on the campus of Bronx Community College, a Girl Scout facility on 116th Street.

Then she found what she was looking for. The Board of Education had a fifteen-year lease on the top three floors of a small office building on 106th Street between Park Avenue and Lexington Avenue. It had been completely renovated just a year and a half earlier to house a public performing-arts school that needed a temporary home while its own building was being repaired. Now the performing-arts school was ready to move back home—and the Board had an empty space already outfitted to be a school.

Tisch had an ally in Seymour Fliegel, the director of the Center for Educational Innovation and one of the architects of District 4's rebirth. Fliegel knew how to navigate the city bureaucracy, and his word carried weight; together they lobbied the people at the Board of Education who made decisions about high schools and buildings. They cajoled disgruntled board members who resented Tisch's progress when their own projects had not worked out. She quoted her lawyer, time and again, to bureaucrats who feared paralyzing lawsuits. She told all of them: "You have to spend your ninety-two-hundred-dollar-per-pupil-per-year allocation somewhere. You might as well give us a try and see if you get more for your money."

She told anyone who would listen that this was the best possible way to improve the public schools. Conservative politicians had terrorized the public school system by endorsing a system of vouchers, in which disadvantaged families would be given financial aid to send their children to private or parochial schools. The idea at the heart of the voucher program was to improve the public schools by forcing them into competition with private schools, but critics of the plan feared that it would result, instead, in a hemorrhaging of talent. Public schools would become little more than holding tanks for the children who had failed to impress an admissions officer somewhere else—the ones who most needed attention.

Tisch wanted, instead, to rebuild the system from within. Wholesale reform was probably impossible; the New York school system was too big, and too dysfunctional, to respond to a blanket plan. But she could continue Sy Fliegel's legacy, save a few hundred girls, and provide a model for others who could do the same. She was not asking the public schools to spend more money per student—only to spend it in what she believed was a more productive way.

"We don't dismantle, we don't brain-drain, we don't do vouchers," she said. "We don't do anything to destroy our public school system. We strengthen a weakened system. That's why it's so important."

The Tisch family could have built a private school from the ground up and stocked it with disadvantaged girls, but that was not what Ann Tisch wanted to do. She wanted to help get a girls' public school off the ground, to show other school districts that they could do the same without a big infusion of private money. The family's financial outlay, most of which went for lawyers' fees, was "less than a hundred thousand dollars," according to Tisch—low by philanthropic standards—and she was slightly embarrassed to tell people what she had spent.

By December of 1995 she had a potential site, a reassuring lawyer, the support of the chancellor and the Board of Education and District 4, and still no deal. Then she lost Ramon Cortines, who resigned as chancellor and was replaced by Dr. Rudy Crew. Exasperated, Tisch decided to throw a cocktail party to welcome the new chancellor—and to ambush him before the other guests arrived.

When Dr. Crew arrived, she shook his hand, told him how nice it was to meet him, and started in. "Look," she said. "Let me tell you about a little thing I've been working on." She ushered the unsuspecting Dr. Crew into her living room, figuring that this was her only chance to make him an ally, and that he wouldn't yell at her in her own home.

"So okay," she began, trying not to talk too fast. "We've got this idea, and we've been working on it for a couple of years, and what would you think of a public girls' school, totally college-prep, public school with a private mission, uniforms, first-class education? Just fabulous."

She realized that she was moving closer and closer to the chancellor, who had begun to edge away from her.

"Oh, God," he said. "You're going to open up a whole can of worms."

"Oh, I know," she replied, "but not to worry about that. Public opinion will be on our side. This is a good idea."

She waited, knowing that if Dr. Crew turned her down she would have no recourse.

Finally, he said, "All right, look. Just do one thing if you go forward with this."

Tisch could hardly believe that it was going to be this easy.

"Oh, anything, sure, tell me, what?" she replied.

"Just do one thing for me. Make it replicable."

Which was exactly what Ann Tisch had in mind.

The call from District 4 came just as Celenia Chevere was beginning to think about retirement. For the first time in her life, she was about to be free of the responsibilities of raising a family and the pressure of doing it on her own. Now District Superintendent Evelyn Castro wanted Chevere to start up yet another school, The Young Women's Leadership School of East Harlem, scheduled to open in the fall of 1996. The offer obliterated all her incipient retirement fantasies. This school could be her lasting legacy, the embodiment of all her ideas about education. She accepted the job in the spring of 1996 and immediately began to look for faculty and recruit her first seventh-grade class.

Finding the right teachers turned out to be slightly easier than it should have been, in part because the Manhattan High School District, along with District 4, was committed to making the school work. Chevere should have had to stand in line for available teachers like any other school principal, interviewing teachers who had seniority on the eligibility list whether she wanted them or not. But Granger Ward, the high school superintendent, instructed the district personnel office to screen the list of applicants for Chevere; to look for teachers who would appreciate what the school was trying to do. She got a better sampling than she should have, and the district let her interview the candidates herself. No one got a job without passing Chevere's inspection, and she was very clear about her expectations: Her teachers would have to take a bunch of girls who might not otherwise make it through high school and transform them into college-scholarship material. Coming to work at TYWLS was more like taking religious vows—or enlisting in the military—than applying for a teaching job.

Chevere did not anticipate being a beloved principal, because she believed in hard work and more of it, but she did think she could get results. The important thing was to find families like the ones she had worked with at the Laboratory School for Gifted Students. She went through her files and began to call parents who had not heard from her in years, like Afaf Zohny, whose daughter, Maryam, had been in the first grade when Chevere left the Lab School.

As word of the new school got out, families started to call to schedule admissions interviews. A teacher who had heard about the school contacted Maryam's good friend Diana Perez, whose mother, Maria, quickly requested an appointment. Amy Lopez, who had gone to school with Maryam since first grade, came in despite her skepticism about life without boys.

One by one, the families came to school for their interviews, and when they got off the elevator at the ninth floor, Chevere was waiting for them. She was a short, slender woman with a take-no-prisoners air and a reason for everything she did: Shoulder pads in her suit jackets made her seem a more authoritative presence, tasteful stud earrings and pale fingernails suggested an alternative to the flashier styles on the street, and her soft, sensible pumps were a practical concession to a chronic bad back. Chevere had straight black hair that she usually pulled tight off her forehead into a bun, dark eyes behind oversized glasses, and a thin, determined mouth that only occasionally relaxed into a surprising, little-girl grin. She was excited at the thought of what these girls might become, but she did not give herself away. What the families saw was a determined woman with a tough proposition.

She had a list of "non-negotiables" that she explained to every prospective student and her parents. Chevere was not just looking for the best students. She wanted the best families, because she had met too many parents over the years who "promised me the moon," she said, only to lose interest the moment their children left home for school. However talented these girls might be, it meant nothing without their parents' watchful support.

Each prospective family had to promise to come to school in the fall for a "goal-setting conference" with an advisor, in which they filled out a form that listed a girl's individual goals and described how she intended to attain them. There would be mandatory conferences during the year. And there had to be a sympathetic environment at home—a time and a place for a girl to do her homework, when she would be free from the kinds of responsibilities a girl with younger sisters and brothers might have, like babysitting and helping with meals. The girls themselves? They had to be religious in their devotion to school. If a girl faltered, Chevere would ask her to leave and give her spot to a more deserving candidate.

A Marlborough girl enjoyed a surfeit of choice; most students came from private elementary schools and were well ahead of the national norm in test scores and grades. They picked Marlborough from among a half-dozen competing college-prep schools and spent six years on a happy plateau, far from the strapped reality of many public school systems. Marlborough was part of a grand landscape of opportunities.

Getting in at TYWLS meant something quite different. The rest of the world was not friendly to Chevere's target families. Nationally, Hispanic girls were frequent casualties of the public schools: In 1995, 30 percent of them between the ages of sixteen and twenty-four had dropped out and had failed to earn a high school equivalency degree. Overall, only 50 percent of New York City high-school students graduated on time, 30 percent never graduated at all, and 75 percent did not test well enough to earn a Regents diploma, the prerequisite for admission to a good college or university. Chevere's applicants had nowhere to go but TYWLS, and plenty of remedial work ahead if they were to do well enough to stay there.

5

CELENIA CHEVERE WORKED FAST. By June of 1996, three months before TYWLS was supposed to open, she had hired three teachers and admitted about half of the fifty girls for her first seventh-grade class. On July 15, the *New York Daily News* ran a feature about the school. The next day, *The New York Times* ran a front-page story, "Plan for Harlem Girls School Faces Concern Over Sex Bias," which reported that New York Civil Liberties Union Executive Director Norman Siegel had written to Chancellor Crew asking him to prevent the school's planned opening.

What unnerved Chevere was the response of the chancellor's spokesman, Frank Sobrino, who admitted to reporter Jacques Steinberg that "neither the chancellor nor the central Board of Education had officially approved the proposed school—as is required." The implication was clear: Approval from District 4 was not enough to guarantee the school's survival.

Steinberg cited a discouraging list of decisions that seemed to establish a precedent against the school, including the recent Supreme Court ruling that the all-male Virginia Military Institute was required to admit women because it received state financial aid, a decision that in turn referred to a 1982 Mississippi case in which a single-sex women's nursing school was ordered to admit men. The last all-girls public school in New York City, Washington Irving High School, "was ordered to admit boys in 1986 by Chancellor Nathan Quinones, for fear its existence violated civil rights law," according to the *Times*. Plans to create all-boys schools for minority students in New York City and Milwaukee had failed because of legal challenges like the ones that now threatened TYWLS, and in Detroit, the Malcolm X Academy and two other all-boys schools had been forced to admit girls when a judge ruled that they violated Title IX.

Chevere called Tisch, frantic with worry.

"What are we going to do?" she asked.

"I don't know yet," replied Tisch. She called her lawyer and Sy Fliegel at the Center for Educational Innovation and asked them to start looking for what she called "wiggle room." She did not anticipate being able to resolve the conflict before school opened in September. All she wanted was a loophole large enough to keep the Board of Education from shutting the school down.

The next day, the *Times* ran another article, this one about whether TYWLS violated an obscure 1991 city law that forbade single-sex public schools. The article noted, "None of the lawyers now quarreling about the legality of the school on either side seems to have known about the law; no one has cited it in an argument against the school." But the NYCLU's Siegel said that he intended to add the law to his complaint, which meant that the city's Human Rights Commission would have to investigate.

In the meantime, Tisch's lawyers had discovered what they considered a temporary loophole, a technicality that distinguished between a new school and a new "program," and allowed an educational program to exist by virtue of district approval, at least for the seventh and eighth grades. They would have to rename the school The Young Women's Leadership Program and officially make it an extension of Junior High School 13, a nearby coeducational school, but they would be able to open on time. This maneuver would delay a confrontation until the girls were ready for ninth grade, at which point the program, or school, would require the sanction of the city's board. If the girls did as well as everyone hoped they would, shutting down the school would be a public-relations disaster.

Tisch worried that this strategy only postponed the inevitable. If critics were willing to sacrifice the girls to principle, which was how she saw their position, then reason, in the form of better grades and test scores, was not going to derail them. Having come this far, she wanted the "full-blown support" of Dr. Crew and his board.

A week later, the chancellor's representatives were still discussing his reluctance to endorse a school that could end up a casualty of legal challenges. Tisch and her supporters were involved in daily conversations with the chancellor's office, trying to find a solution acceptable to both sides. The school could agree to take applications from boys, even though the class was almost full and no one quite believed that a boy could successfully complete the interview process, which was geared toward selecting girls interested in leadership roles. Or the chancellor could open an allboys' school in District 4.

By mid-August, Tisch feared that she would have to agree to something or the chancellor might in fact withhold his approval. All she cared about, she said, was "getting the girls in the door." If need be, TYWLS would form an alliance with an existing school or agree to take applications from boys, though there would be no recruitment effort and no plan to increase the size of the class.

Tisch continued to fight for a formal endorsement. She kept making calls in advance of an August 22 Board of Education meeting—and two hours before that meeting was scheduled to begin, the board added to its agenda a resolution to endorse the school. The TYWLS lawyers attended the meeting and presented their case, as did the city's lawyer, but Tisch stayed home, too emotional to sit and listen to the debate.

She waited, and paced, and muttered to herself, "There's no word, there's no word, there's no word." Then the phone rang. It was the chancellor's office, calling to say that the board had just voted unanimously in favor of TYWLS. The New York City Board of Education, in an alliance with District 4, endorsed the school and intended to make it an all-girls public high school, with no contrived relationship to any existing school.

Immediately the New York Civil Liberties Union and the New York Civil Rights Coalition filed complaints with the Federal Department of Education, charging that the school discriminated against boys. The National Organization for Women joined the complaint, fearful that public acknowledgment of a distinction between girls and boys would hinder the cause of women's rights; if girls were so different from boys that they required their own school, and the public school system endorsed that segregation, women would have a harder time arguing for equality.

Tisch ignored them. She called a school-uniform company, to make sure the girls had something to wear on the first day of school. The man she talked to apologized and said that this close to the beginning of the school year, all the company had left were some pieces in navy blue.

"Send it," she said. "Let's get this done."

To Diana's mother, Maria Perez, TYWLS was justice, not discrimination. The people who complained about it failed to see what she saw in her neighborhood every day. Real discrimination meant abandoning kids like hers to overcrowded classes, battle-weary teachers, and the vocabulary of the streets: drugs, gang fights, weapons, teenage pregnancy.

When she heard that someone wanted to shut down TYWLS before it even got started, she had to laugh. A short, stocky woman with freckles, tousled hair, and a pugnacious attitude, Maria had no patience for people who spouted theory at her family's expense. No one was going to sacrifice her daughter to some highflown notion of equal opportunity. Discrimination was a problem, all right, but the discrimination Maria Perez saw was economic. Because they were poor, her kids never got an even break.

There had always been people with more, and those with less, and Maria hardly expected someone suddenly to provide her family with a ˙ʳ apartment, a computer, new clothes for the kids. But education was Without a decent school, her daughters would stay poor; with .night break the cycle.

To Maria, the issue was quite simple. "Why," she liked to ask, as if daring a listener to attempt an answer, "shouldn't my girl have what the rich girls have?"

EDUCATING WOMEN in the United States has always been defined in deference to the needs of men. Colonial girls learned the domestic skills they would need as adults; there was no reason to send them to school, since school prepared men for careers. If girls learned to read at all, it was only to read the Bible. The few who learned more did so by eavesdropping on the boys' classes.

As American University professors of education Drs. David and Myra Sadker noted in their 1994 book, *Failing at Fairness: How America's Schools Cheat Girls,* girls in the late 1700s learned what they needed to know in "restraining chairs," into which they were strapped for hours on end, motionless, with nothing to do but work, passively, on proper posture. At the end of the eighteenth century, some girls got to attend elementary school—but only early in the morning and late in the afternoon, before and after the boys' classes. Unlike the boys' parents, the girls' parents had to pay for the privilege.

By the early 1800s, American girls who could afford it were allowed to develop their minds, but not too far: They were encouraged to seek an education so that they could oversee the intellectual growth of their children. A second tier of schools, like The Young Ladies Academy in Philadelphia, sprang up, "to transform girls into strong and intellectually able mothers," according to the Sadkers. The seminary school movement, begun by Emma Willard, who opened the private Troy Seminary in 1821, represented incremental progress—girls received a high-school education, while continuing to learn what they needed to know for their domestic futures.

The public school system tried to respond, without disrupting the boys' education. In the late 1820s, the city of Boston opened a high school for girls, and the response was dramatic—so many applicants that the city had to turn away three-quarters of them. Their incensed parents complained to the mayor, who devised what he considered the only fair solution, and simply closed the new school. It was not until his reelection defeat that the school reopened.

Poorer communities could not afford to maintain a separate facility for girls; faced with increased demand for girls' education, they opened coeducational high schools. At first, the schools segregated boys and girls, reflecting the persistent notion that they needed to learn different things. As the years passed, more and more of these schools allowed coeducational classes, and this polarized the community. Critics complained that putting boys and girls in the same classroom would dilute the boys' experience and unnecessarily expose the girls to information they did not need. Supporters said that the mix would breed more civilized boys—and more stimulating mothers.

Women at the college level faced even more resistance than did younger girls. During the first half of the nineteenth century, a girl who managed to complete high school found few opportunities beyond the insistent expectation of full-time domesticity. In 1858, the University of Michigan rejected the applications of three women. Twelve years later, the university reversed its decision—because the Civil War had reduced the number of male students, and tuition dollars had to come from somewhere.

The University of Rochester agreed in 1898 to admit women only if they were able to raise a donation of $100,000 to be used to expand the facilities and hire more teachers. The prospective students raised $40,000, at which point the university trustees, motivated more by the prospect of ready cash than by any sense of fairness, reduced their ransom demand to $50,000. Suffragette Susan B. Anthony cashed in her life-insurance policy to make up the difference. The male student body actively resisted the move, however, and in 1913 the school decided to open a separate women's college, to keep the peace.

The Ivy League women's colleges began, according to the Sadkers, as "~isible" schools, intended as a way to educate women without intruding ᵇlished routines of the male students. Harvard professors taught ᴧ in nearby rented homes. Even after Radcliffe College ₁893, its students had to send messengers to the Harvard library, after school hours, to check out books. Skeptics met every measure of progress, however small, with a call for a return to the past. In his 1873 book *Sex in Education,* physician Dr. Edward Clarke suggested that coeducation would actually compromise a young woman's reproductive system. He liked the idea of girls' schools because they could be designed to protect the weaker sex from the rigors of a real school.

It was in this charged atmosphere that Mary S. Caswell opened the Mrs. Mary S. Caswell's School for Girls in 1889, in Pasadena, California, a wealthy enclave northeast of Los Angeles. After twenty years as a teacher in New England, Mary Caswell had emigrated to southern California from Maine for the express purpose of opening her own quality boarding school for high-school-age girls. She told her young students, "The day when it was interesting to be helpless is far in the past," and encouraged them to follow her example: to take charge of their lives and venture into the world looking for opportunity. But there were limits, still: The "Caswell don'ts" defined the way a girl ought to behave in public. Tuition limited access to families who could afford the expense, and quiet tradition ensured that only girls of a certain background would attend.

In 1916, the school moved to its permanent home, built on what had been a barley field at the corner of Third Street and Rossmore Avenue; it was now known as Marlborough School, after the Pasadena hotel that had been its previous residence.

Its genteel reputation prevailed for most of the school's life. In the 1920s and 1930s, perhaps half of Marlborough's graduates went on to college; the rest had ambitions that were more social than academic. Even as late as the 1960s, Marlborough, like most girls' schools, tended to attract girls like the ones cited by the Sadkers, who said they most hoped to be a "teacher, secretary, nurse, or mommy" when they grew up. Girls' middle and high schools were most often a marginal intellectual enterprise, a way station for privileged girls who would become the wives of the next generation of wealthy, powerful men.

The dawn of modern feminism in the early 1960s put the educational system on notice. The politically correct position was gender equity, in quantifiable terms, and separate was definitely not considered equal. Private girls' schools were a backward vestige of a bygone era when sex defined destiny, and public schools were scrutinized for any evidence of taxpayer-subsidized discrimination. With the implementation of Title IX in 1972, the days when a state university spent big money on football at the expense of girls' athletic programs were over. The road to equality was paved, dollar for dollar, with program parity.

Private Ivy League men's colleges began a gradual metamorphosis: Radcliffe graduates began to receive Harvard diplomas in 1963; residences at both schools became coeducational in the 1970s, and at the end of that decade the two schools formed a joint admissions office. In 1969, Yale University and Vassar College began merger talks and, a year later, broke them off in favor of each school going coed. Brown University merged with Pembroke College in 1971, and over the next few years, Dartmouth College, Amherst College, and Princeton University all agreed to accept women. In 1982, Columbia College decided to admit women, which put it into direct competition with another division of Columbia University, the all-girls Barnard College.

The truly independent woman took her place alongside men in the classroom, abandoning all-girls schools to students who were not up to the challenge. Suddenly, remaining separate meant accepting a lesser status for women.

While the government attempted to impose order from the outside, researchers around the country, their curiosity piqued, began to wonder about other, less obvious obstacles to girls' academic achievement. Perhaps opening the doors to women was not enough. The next question was, how were they treated once they took their government-mandated place?

Myra and David Sadker, both doctoral candidates in education at Georgetown University, had run headlong into gender discrimination in their own department: professors who ignored the outspoken Myra in favor of a male colleague or referred to the couple's joint grant proposal as David's alone. The experience led Myra to write *Sexism in School and Society*, published in 1973 as a teachers' guide to classroom inequities. The Sadkers next embarked on an ambitious classroom research project, while others, like Harvard psychologist Carol Gilligan and Colby College education professor Lyn Mikel Brown, studied adolescent girls.

Teachers began to hear about the research in the late 1970s and 1980s, but it was not until the early 1990s that the information reached a broader audience. In 1992, The American Association of University Women published "How Schools Shortchange Girls," a report researched by The Wellesley College Center for Research on Women. A review of existing research on gender in the classroom, the AAUW report was enough to terrify the parents of any girl. If anything, girls entered kindergarten with a slight advantage over boys in fine motor and verbal abilities. By the time they graduated from high school, they had fallen behind in mathematics and science, their self-esteem had crumbled, and boys outperformed them on standardized tests.

Worse, much of the research about the American educational system failed to address gender issues at all. Girls were still invisible, just as they had been at the turn of the century. The AAUW report dismissed the 1991 National Education Goals, as defined during George H. W. Bush's administration, because they were not gender-specific. "Solutions designed to meet everyone's needs," wrote the authors, "risk meeting no one's."

Lyn Mikel Brown and Carol Gilligan's *Meeting at the Crossroads*, published the same year, described in painful detail, and in girls' own words, the wrenching passage from childhood to adolescence in a culture that did not easily tolerate authoritative, independent young women. Two years later, the Sadkers published the result of two decades of research, the comprehensive *Failing at Fairness*. Together, the books painted a picture of a generation of unhappy teenage girls whose problems seemed to be exacerbated by their school experience.

They were part of a vicious cycle: Schools did not give girls an equal opportunity; since those girls were at a particularly vulnerable point in their lives, they too willingly accepted the notion that boys were smarter. Girls censored themselves in the classroom, as though deference were the proper order of things, and this enabled the boys to hold center stage. Often without realizing it, coeducational schools perpetuated old discriminatory habits, educating boys first and girls only when it was convenient. A literal notion of equality—that of equal access—might in fact guarantee that girls continued to function at a disadvantage.

Parents and educators who had grown up during the first years of the women's movement looked for an escape for their daughters, and came back around to an unlikely place—the all-girls school, an institution originally founded on the notion that girls did not need to learn what boys did. Its future could be something quite different: It might become a progressive alternative to the documented prejudices of a coeducational classroom. If the enemy was society, with its seemingly indelible assumptions about girls, then why not secede from it, at least temporarily, in order to better prepare girls for the adult world?

In the early 1990s, schools like Marlborough experienced a rush of applicants whose parents doubted that reform of the coed classroom would come quickly enough to serve their daughters. At the same time, supporters of public schools began to demand what they saw as equal opportunity: the chance to find out if their girls' performance would improve in a different environment.

As the school year at TYWLS got underway, Celenia Chevere dismissed what she considered pious concerns about discrimination voiced by those who opposed TYWLS because it did not admit boys. "The school system in New York City is one of the most discriminatory public school systems in the country," she said, because it perpetuated privilege for those who already had it, and relegated poor and ethnic families to the worst schools. New York's hierarchy was based on money: White students in well-off neighborhoods went to better schools than did the minority kids in the projects; the end result was racial discrimination, but the real villain was property taxes.

Poor girls faced a double disadvantage. They suffered for living in the wrong neighborhood—which meant too little money spread too thin—and for being girls, which the AAUW said guaranteed them a raw deal in the classroom. To Chevere, shutting down TYWLS because it discriminated against boys was a ridiculous notion. It would penalize families who wanted more for their daughters and had no access to it.

She also had harsh words for those who made the overhaul of all the schools in the New York City system their priority. After more than two decades inside the Board of Education bureaucracy, Chevere did not see how such sweeping change could come about fast enough to help this generation of students. "And what," she asked, "am I supposed to do with these girls in the meantime?" In her view, there were too many things that needed fixing, and not enough time, money, or personnel to do the jobs. The New York City Board of Education had no hope of winning that war. The only answer was little pockets of resistance, guerrilla incursions, like TYWLS.

6

Marlborough School

September 1998

MYRANDA MARSH, the self-appointed scourge of the Marlborough history department, was lying in wait for her new seventh graders. After five years at Marlborough, she had come to expect one thing: They would act like they knew more than they really did. Perhaps only a quarter of them were truly capable of abstract thought, but they liked to sound sure of themselves. It was her job to make them more comfortable with not knowing; to dismantle them and build them up again, better.

Seventh graders were not supposed to know everything; some of her eighth-grade students were still more comfortable memorizing dates and names than they were with open-ended conceptual discussions. Ms. Marsh wanted the girls to understand that there was no shame in not having all the answers. Seventh grade was all about creating a new, more efficient system for learning. Marsh was here to build a foundation for college-level work. If she was successful, her students would leave her class, "Your World and You," both humble and more sophisticated.

The girls had heard only that she graded hard—it was almost impossible to get an A in the first semester—and that she loved surprises. They filed into her classroom and took their seats with apprehensive, downcast eyes, too overwhelmed by the newness of school to feel anything but wary.

She waited until they had settled into their chairs and tucked their backpacks next to their seats, and then strode to the blackboard and surveyed the room. There was little about Myranda Marsh to put people at ease. Even her physical appearance was something of a challenge: she favored colorful shirts on her heavyset frame, blood-red fingernail polish, and big earrings. Her hair was a constant battle between style and efficiency, a wavy, dark brown pageboy kept out of her way by a strategic assortment of clips and barrettes. She was a walking dare: Let *anyone* try to tell her that she ought to be thinner, more tailored, more discreet.

She consulted her class roster and groaned. There were three girls named Jamie.

"You have no idea," she said, in her clarion voice, "how hard it is for old people to remember names—and *three* Jamies."

"One girl switched to another class," offered one of the remaining Jamies.

"Oh, good," said Marsh. She flashed a wicked grin. "We'll miss her dearly." She glanced at her book one last time, closed it, and rattled off all the names from memory. Triumphant, she began to pace back and forth in front of the girls.

"Something very strange happened last night," she began in the tone of voice a camp counselor might use for a campfire ghost story. "While you were asleep, an alien sucked you up and placed you on an island like Gilligan's Island." She paced from one table of four to another, saying, "You guys are on one island, and you guys are on another island," and then she told them the rules:

- Don't try to escape.
- There's an international language, so you all can communicate.
- You're with people of all ages, some of whom have been injured when the aliens dropped them.

- You're from all over the world.
- All you have is the clothes you are wearing.
- There are 50,000 of you, all tired, hungry, and thirsty.

"Now," she said, "talk to your table and decide what you're going to do."

She walked over to a table at the back of the room, where four girls were huddled together, two already talking away and two listening, not sure what to say. Lisa, an antic brunette, said, "We could shave our heads to make blankets."

"With what?" asked Marsh. And then, abruptly, "Do you have gum in your mouth?"

Lisa swallowed, hard.

"No."

"Don't *swallow* it," said Marsh. "It stays in you for some disgusting amount of time. Now decide what to do—the day's getting warm." She moved on to the next group.

Nicole, who was sitting next to Lisa, wanted to cut down trees, and at that Alexandra Siegel had to speak up.

"There's nothing to cut them down with," she said, staring at her hands. A quiet, slender girl with long, black, wavy hair and big, darting eyes, Alex was uncomfortable in the spotlight—but even more uncomfortable at things getting out of hand. She could not let Nicole go on about cutting down trees. They were part of a team now, their performance intertwined, so Alex had to stop her from making them all look foolish.

Nicole insisted that they could break branches and rub them together for a fire, while Lisa wondered if they could shave their heads by rubbing them with smooth rocks.

Marsh appeared again. She wanted the girls to start to think more carefully, and to befriend one another. If she played the outside agitator, they would have to become allies.

"You know, two babies have died while you're talking about shaving your heads," she barked. "One man has bled to death."

"We'll build a hut," said Lisa.

"By then, ten people will have died," said Marsh, and before anyone could reply she had turned her back on them.

"Well, then," said Lisa, grimly, "we'll eat the dead babies."

Alex groaned.

By the time Marsh started her third circuit of the room, three of the four girls at Alex's table were wondering if they could find enough coconuts in the trees to feed all 50,000 of the aliens' hostages. The fourth girl at the table had remained silent throughout the class. Marsh listened for a moment and then addressed her directly.

"Is this okay with you, people dying on the beach while they go look for coconuts?"

The girl shook her head. "I'll stay behind," she said.

"I'll stay with her," said Alex, staunchly.

"Won't work," said Marsh. "Think bigger."

The alien island project might seem goofy to girls who were used to a more traditional lecture-and-discussion format, but Marsh had created the lesson plan because it promised her absolute control. By the time it was over, she would know more about each girl than she could have figured out any other way.

"It's a great assessment tool," she said. "It's the cornerstone of my approach." She made a mental inventory as she visited each table: There was a girl who blurted out answers without thinking and seemed to believe that the number of times she spoke up was more important than what she said; she would have to be taught to consider and analyze. There were girls who might require an extra moment to compose their answers, but were capable of a more subtle response. And there were dutiful girls like Alex, a classic example of the kind of student who was supposed to profit most markedly from the single-sex environment.

Marsh had seen plenty of seventh graders like Alex before. She referred to them as "the good girls, who would rather be silent than wrong." They were the "biddable" students, eager to do what the teacher asked them to do, reluctant to take the initiative—and they were the most difficult to evaluate, because they volunteered so little information about what they thought.

Alex had done everything to ensure that her first year at Marlborough would go well. She had a laminated copy of her schedule taped to the outside of her binder, each class color-coded, so that she could see at a glance where she was supposed to be at any given time of day. She had labels, subject dividers, and a calendar to help her keep track of homework and long-range assignments. But it was clear to Marsh, after only a few visits to the table, that Alex was going to have a problem with classroom participation. When Marsh asked her a question, Alex inevitably knew the answer, but she clearly did not like to speak up. When she offered halting comments within her alien-island group, it was because she saw the conversation getting out of hand.

As far as Marsh was concerned, there was a big gap between what Alex did and what she was capable of doing, and it was the teacher's job to close that gap. From the little that Alex did say, Marsh knew that she was one of the girls who could already grasp abstract concepts; what she needed to learn was how to take a chance. Marsh did not expect miracles. She doubted that Alex would ever be comfortable speaking up in front of the whole class. So she set a private goal: by the time Alex moved on to eighth grade, she would be at ease in front of half the class. Eight girls. That would be a big improvement.

The central memory of Myranda Marsh's childhood was coming home proudly with five A's and a B on her report card, only to have her father say, "What happened in science?" Her parents expected a straight-A student, and they delivered their judgment from on high: Both of them were college professors. Education was the currency of Marsh's youth, and anything less than the best felt to her like failure.

She struggled for many years to live up to her parents' standards, at a performing arts public high school in Los Angeles's San Fernando Valley, at the University of California at Berkeley, and in law school, where she lasted one year. The law school faculty seemed to her as demanding, and unyielding, as her father was, but since they were strangers, not family, she could afford to give vent to her irritation. She recalled being delighted at the invitation to join the prestigious Law Review, because "I could tell them where to *put* their Law Review."

She entered Mills College for Women, where she completed a year's course-work toward a master's degree in education and got a teaching credential. It was her ticket of admission to a very private revolution: Myranda Marsh, estranged daughter of a man who taught educational theory to aspiring teachers, chose to practice rather than preach. She was going to find the hardest cases around, teach them properly, and change their lives.

She landed at Pasadena High School, where 54 percent of the students were "Chapter 1," which meant that they were at least three years behind their grade level in standardized test scores for reading and math. For three years, Marsh told herself that her students surely would start to behave if only she were a better teacher. When she received a letter threatening rape from one of the school's star athletes, she wondered what she had done wrong. When a student grabbed another teacher by the hair, Marsh reminded herself that better teaching would change the world. But in her fourth year, the violent incidents increased, and she began to think that being a good history teacher was not going to fix things.

She joined a teachers' headhunter organization and was sent to Marlborough, which had advertised for "someone who had strong classroom-management skills."

To Marsh, strong classroom skills meant "you could prevent students from throwing chairs." At Marlborough, it meant being able to handle eighth graders who were "testing their limits" by being out of uniform. Marsh felt terribly guilty about abandoning the revolution, but she took the job.

It was not an easy transition. Marsh described her first year as "being trapped in a Disney movie." She kept waiting for the seventh graders to act up, to challenge her, but they never did. One afternoon, right before the winter break, she had to leave the classroom for a moment, and as she came back down the hall, she heard the girls making noise. She sped up, relishing the possibility that finally, someone was doing something she was not supposed to do. When Marsh opened the door the girls were lying on the floor on their backs, vigorously moving their arms against the carpet, trying to make the Southern California equivalent of snow angels. They were singing "Rudolph the Red-Nosed Reindeer."

That was as naughty as the youngest girls got.

By her fifth year, Marsh had embraced Marlborough as one of the "few places where it is safe for a young woman to exercise her power." In an odd way, she benefited from the single-sex environment as much as she imagined her students did. She was going to rewrite her personal history through the Middle-School girls, and everyone would end up better off for it.

Marsh proselytized about newfangled study techniques that would help the girls through the mandatory history-class maze of dates and names. If her study aids didn't work well enough—if a parent came to her saying, "I don't want you telling me, or telling my daughter, that it's okay to get a B"—Marsh told them the story of her own report card and how unhappy her parents' response had made her. She told them to read *Reviving Ophelia*, Mary Pipher's best-selling book about adolescent girls struggling to find themselves.

Some of the more traditional members of her department were skeptical about her approach, but she welcomed their questions. Marsh needed an establishment to rebel against. She found the world a hostile place, a "truly impossible situation" for a capable woman, and she wanted to make sure that her students were better prepared for it than she had been.

The most important lessons she had to teach had nothing to do with content; she wanted the girls to learn "that you have to be a fighter, that it is a struggle, and that you need to understand logical arguments, prioritizing, choosing your battles. . . . It's really important that they know that even if they're outraged by their life experiences, they're not alone. That is often enough to create psychic survival."

For the rest of the period, Marsh berated Alex's team. Each of the other tables had drawn up a list of rules for their new communities, but Alex's group remained mired in specifics and comic asides. They were not thinking about the consequences of their ideas, so Marsh shot them down no matter what they suggested. Even if they found a way to retrieve the coconuts, had they considered how to handle the frantic mob that was waiting for them? Those hungry people might be so excited that they would trample an old man to death in their haste to get to the food—or they might drop the coconuts and waste most of the milk, enraging those who had not yet had anything to eat or drink.

The girls got cranky. Nicole wondered if they ought to kill everyone else and go on themselves, since four people were far more manageable than tens of thousands. Lisa hoped she would never find herself stuck on an island, because she wasn't willing to haul coconuts or tend the wounded with bandages made from the clothing of the deceased. Even the quietest girl, Carol, gave up her rationality and suggested that they use a ship to collect what they needed.

Alex protested. "She didn't say anything about there being a ship."

"Make it up," came the tired reply.

Marsh pointed out that there were monkeys on the island, but the girls balked at the idea of killing monkeys and eating them.

"So you want your community to be vegetarian," said Marsh.

"Couldn't we swing them by the tails—that'd kill them—and then eat them?" asked Nicole.

"So you're hungry," said Marsh.

"Yeah," said Nicole.

"Well, I'm not killing monkeys," said Lisa.

"You guys aren't listening to each other," said Marsh, raising her voice to address the whole room. "Listen and work together."

After another exasperating round, Nicole finally blurted out, "We need to get our priorities straight." For that she got a smile and a thumbs-up from Marsh. The girls agreed that the first order of business was to get as many people as possible to a water source. They figured out how to help the wounded make the journey, accepted that there would be casualties along the way, and were feeling rather smug when Marsh returned to see how they were doing.

"Okay," she said, "so you lose a couple hundred along the way, but when you arrive at the stream you have a riot. Fights break out. People are starving, they're dying."

"That's okay," said Nicole.

"Good. By nightfall people are getting cranky, hungrier."

"Seafood," said Carol.

"From where?" asked Marsh.

"The river."

"Nope," said Marsh, with a gay smile. "Want to eat the dead people?"

"No," said Nicole.

"I don't think so," said Alex.

"Maybe," said Lisa, who was getting tired.

"Okay," said Marsh. "Then maybe a bunch of religious fanatics hang you." She glared at Lisa. *Think about your ideas.*

When she walked away, Lisa leaned over and whispered to the others, "Let's not tell her any of our ideas until we're sure they work. We're twelve years old. What are we supposed to do?"

That was the response Myranda Marsh wanted: Alex's table might have lagged behind the others when it came to making a list of ideas, but her group had come quickly to the epiphany their teacher had in mind for them. The first step toward knowledge was accepting just how much they did not know.

"That is *exactly* the symbol of the seventh-grade transition," said Marsh. "They come in thinking that they know how to solve all problems, and that if they were just put in charge of the world, everything would run beautifully. *But they're not really thinking about it.* They need to understand that there's no way to win at desert island. Nobody succeeds. Because human beings aren't capable of building a peaceful, wonderful, utopian civilization, and it sure as heck isn't going to happen with a bunch of seventh-grade girls.

"It's a setup," she said. "It's to make them realize that nothing is as simple and straightforward as you think. Learning—especially social science—is about questioning and bad choices and the lesser of two evils. And desert island sure beats the heck out of sitting there and listening to a lecture."

The only way to fail the alien-island unit was to stop talking, a foreign concept to girls who were used to a causal link between being right and getting a reward.

"They're programmed to work for the cookie," Marsh complained, "and sometimes there is no cookie."

Alex approached the next class session with a new vigor. When Lisa insisted that the death penalty was the best way to enforce order and protect the meager food supply, Alex resisted.

"It's really not a good idea," she said gently.

Lisa was offended. "You want fighting?"

"It's really not a good idea. It's *really* not a good idea," Alex insisted. When Lisa interrupted, Alex cut her off. "Will you please stop talking? We don't want the death penalty because there are so few people. Or maybe for something really serious—but not for stealing coconuts." She wanted to try to find more food instead, and Nicole and Carol quietly backed her up. Marsh approached as the girls talked, but this time she chose to listen rather than intrude on the argument.

Lisa replied that some form of imprisonment was necessary—and if people happened to die in prison, that would be all right.

"Less people to feed," she said.

Alex would not back down. "Less people to work," she replied.

Marsh bent down and whispered to Alex, "Keep an eye on her. She's out of control." The next time Lisa tried to interrupt Alex, Marsh replied sharply, "Listen to Alex. She has something to say, and you have to listen to her." Marsh already had high hopes for her quiet student. She had had a glimpse of what she called Alex's "intellectual power," and was determined to make Alex feel more comfortable about showing it off.

A T FIFTY, a graduate of a big public high school in suburban Chicago and the University of Iowa, Leslie Klein was old enough to look over her shoulder at the shirtwaisted past, where dads commuted home on the

Northwestern line and moms took the kids out for an after-school snack. She was carried into adulthood on the first wave of the women's movement, and she was a contradictory product of that cultural shift: a self-avowed "very left-of-center feminist" who called herself Les and yet looked, with her straight sunflower hair and conservative tailored clothes, like the women who a generation before had driven to the station to pick up their husbands.

Klein had taught English literature for twenty-five years, the last eight of them at Marlborough. It had turned out to be her favorite job. Over the years, Klein's politics had landed her in arguments with male students who, she felt, were propelled by a desire to win and so found it necessary to prevail in any debate. She had the opposite problem with the girls, who often were too quick to capitulate. The youngest girls were the hardest; they were what Klein called "outwardly identified," their happiness still measured by what other people, primarily their teachers, thought of them, and they were reluctant to disagree with an authority figure. Middle school was about preparing them to think for themselves, a discipline that Klein found frustrating.

A year ago she had stopped teaching middle-school classes to focus her energies on the older girls, but even the tenth graders sometimes misinterpreted her fervor. They assumed she was trying to show them that she was right, and were too quick to back down. She explained, over and over, that a good argument was an exercise, a way for both sides to refine their ideas, and not a power struggle.

She loved the seniors, particularly the girls who had signed up for the Advanced Placement Dramatic Literature elective. Klein could see right away that this was a strong group, "able to focus on the material at hand, and not be distracted by hormones. If they break up with somebody or get together with somebody, at least the somebody isn't right there." She had "the two Katies": Katie Tower, whose arch cynicism guaranteed bracing debate, and Katie Briggs, an earnest, good-natured girl whose dependability would set a standard for the others. To spice it up, there were an actress, a jock, a musician, and a couple of wiseacres.

Like Myranda Marsh, Les Klein was a chaperone on a yearlong transition. The seventh graders might be bewildered, but they were in a controlled environment for seven hours each day, spared some of the pressures that accompanied puberty. The seniors were the opposite: far more sure of themselves, but completely uncertain about their future. There were girls in this room who were competing against each other for admission to some of the most selective schools in the country. Klein had to enforce attention without forgetting the extreme distractions the girls faced. She was strict about her expectations in terms of participation, assignments, and tests, but inside that box she hoped mostly to have a wonderful time.

She and the girls sat in a circle, surrounded by a collection of bumper stickers, postcards, posters and prints that made Klein's uncompromising point of view very clear:

IF MEN BECAME PREGNANT, ABORTION WOULD BE A SACRAMENT.

WHEN YOU TEACH . . . YOU TOUCH A LIFE FOREVER.

IF YOU THINK EDUCATION IS EXPENSIVE, TRY IGNORANCE.

IF YOU CAN'T CHANGE YOUR MIND, ARE YOU SURE YOU STILL HAVE ONE?

One little postcard read,

I WAS EDUCATED ONCE, AND IT TOOK ME YEARS TO GET OVER IT.

Klein never indulged in romantic notions of her own importance in the girls' universe. The best students would likely do well wherever they went to school, whether there were boys in the classroom or not. But she did believe that Marlborough made a difference with the "middle" student by making it easier for her to concentrate on her work. There was just the work—and, if the teachers did their jobs right, an increased willingness to take chances with it.

She regarded plays as a great way for the girls to learn about literature and figure themselves out at the same time. Fiction could be considered at leisure, reflected upon from a safe distance. A play was immediate, and the emotional response could be powerful. Klein loved to have the girls read plays aloud, taking turns at various parts; let a girl try on King Lear's anguish one day and his daughter Cordelia's loyal affection the next, so that she could see that relationship from both sides. Seniors were at just the right age to appreciate this kind of class: adamant about their need for in-dependence and still terrified, in some private corner, that they would achieve it.

She began her introductory lecture. "Drama *lives*," she began. "It seems like all of you were really excited to be in this class, but why? What is it about drama that floats your boat?"

"It's dramatic," said one girl.

"It's fun to act," said another.

"For two hours, the play is your reality," said a third.

"That's good," said Klein. "When the curtain opens, you're sucked into that reality. I respond—if it's good—as it happens. It's the big difference be-tween drama and fiction. Drama exists in the present tense, and you react in the moment."

Without stopping, she nudged the small blond next to her. "You're not going to fall asleep on me, are you?"

She launched into an explanation of the conventions of drama: the use of masks, the introduction of the curtain—but she got sidetracked by her real interest. "How can imagined experience," she asked, "be a way of knowing and understanding?"

"You get knowledge by doing," said the first girl, "instead of being told by a narrator, like you are in fiction."

"An imagined experience is a trial run of real experience," said Klein. "You watch a play and think, 'What would it be like if I were in that situa-tion?' You can think about how you'd react without really being there. And you've probably met all these people in your real life."

The girls waited to see what she would say next. Many of them had juggled schedules and given up other classes to get into this room, because Klein had a knack for the unexpected insight and a real empathy for the seniors. No one knew exactly what they would end up talking about this term, which was the point of being here.

The first play on the syllabus was *Oedipus*, and today Klein wanted to know how the girls felt about what happened to the king. "Do you all be-lieve in destiny?" she asked. "Is there free will, or is there fate? That's the big question in *Oedipus*. Is what has befallen him his fault, or are the gods playing with him? Did he cause it or walk into it? Was there any moment when his life could have taken another course?"

She looked at them expectantly. When Klein's class worked at its best, it existed on two tracks simultaneously, and she knew it. They could talk about free will and destiny in *Oedipus,* and at the same time talk about free will and destiny for a bunch of girls who were waiting to hear where they were going to college next year. Most of the seniors tried to play it cool and act as though the future was out of their hands—but she had heard them talking about their essays, and she had seen the strain on their faces. Some girls had already asked her to read a draft, or maybe two, and she had agreed to write several letters of recommendation, including one for Katie Tower. Klein imagined a lot of inner turmoil as each girl reviewed her time at Marlborough and wondered what, if anything, she might have done to enhance her position.

She got a couple of halfhearted answers about life being a hybrid; there was destiny, but then there were all the things a person could do to change it. So she told them about a question she had asked her tenth graders the previous year. "If life is a box," she said, "when you open the box, is there something in there? Is there meaning to life, and if so, who put it there? Is it your job to discover it? Or do *you* put meaning in the box, which is the existential position: There is no meaning to the box except what you put into it?"

She waited a beat. "Then, to be negative, there's nihilism. You're born. You die. That's it. Adios."

Katie Tower was the first to respond. Like Klein, Katie was born into comfort, not privilege. She did not believe in fate or its upscale cousin, entitlement. Katie believed she was the master of her own future—a useful defense for someone surrounded by so many girls who already enjoyed the external trappings of success. "I think you're born a blank," she announced, "and then you make choices. It's the opposite of fate. The choices you make are what you want at the time, and then you end up with your choices, your regrets, your mistakes. And when you die you're a complete person, made up of the choices you made."

Klein wondered if anyone had read Sartre's *No Exit,* and only Katie

Tower raised a hand. Klein asked her what she thought of the final scene, where three characters with no eyelids face each other onstage, "the point of which," she said, "is that hell is other people."

"They have to face up to who they are," said Katie, "and how they led their lives. The decisions they made. It's the actions of the other people in the room that show them their lives in another way."

Klein liked Katie's perspective. In a school this small, upper-school teachers often knew about students before they met them in class, and Katie came to Dramatic Literature with a reputation that stretched back to Myranda Marsh's eighth-grade history class. Marsh had made her out early as a girl who knew how to think, and she had let it be known that she expected great things of Katie. A voracious reader who needed debate skills simply to hold her own at the family dinner table, Katie had impressed a string of subsequent teachers as a girl who liked to chew on ideas. This year she was a member of the Marlborough debate team. Klein assumed that she would be one of the students who kept the discussion from becoming predictable.

Still, Klein had to be careful not to lose the rest of her audience. She had no specific strategies for involving the quieter girls, just an instinctive rhythm born of years in the classroom.

At the start of the year, she wanted the girls to feel that they were all about to embark on an adventure together—and that this room was still a safe place for them, where for an hour they could forget an upcoming exam or college interview. AP Dramatic Literature was Klein's valedictory to some of her favorite seniors. She intended that they learn as much about themselves as they did about the plays she asked them to read.

"I love teaching this course," she told them, "because again and again it's a life-changing thing. It can be really political, if you let it, and also aesthetic. You can always look at a play like *Oedipus* and say, 'What can I learn about my life from this man? What lessons are there for me?' Okay?"

She got no reply, but it was only September, and Klein was a patient woman.

She picked up the discussion of fate versus free will the next time the class met. Klein suggested that what happens to Oedipus is not fate, not a willful destructive act, but simply a mistake. "He merely makes a great mistake," she said, "and a series of events are catalyzed by a single misstep."

As she spoke, she remembered "Death Speaks," a W. Somerset Maugham story that John O'Hara used as the epigraph of his novel *Appointment in Samarra*. She told the girls the tale of the manservant who encountered Death in the Baghdad marketplace and ran home to ask his employer for the loan of a horse, so he could flee to Samarra. When the merchant went down to the market, he saw Death, approached her, and asked why she had threatened his servant. She protested that her gesture had been one of surprise. She had not expected to see the servant in Baghdad, for she had an appointment with him that very night in Samarra.

Perhaps everything was preordained, suggested Klein—and Oedipus, the servant at Samarra, and the seniors were all part of a larger plan that they could not alter. Destiny was a tempting concept, after all, because it exonerated every girl in the room from any responsibility for her future, but Marlborough, as an institution, endorsed free will, which tossed them right back into a soup of test scores, grades, and endless college-essay revisions. Klein was not about to endorse a point of view; she preferred simply to present them for the girls' consideration.

"It's a mind game," said Klein. "It's a lot about control. Some people think they're in charge of their lives, some people have faith in a larger entity, and most of us are caught square in the middle, thinking, 'Oh, what if I choose Columbia over Harvard. . . .'"

"Oh, yeah, like that's a choice," muttered one girl. The others giggled nervously.

"Okay," said Klein, "Santa Monica City College." That got a bigger laugh. SMCC was a nearby junior college, hardly the kind of school a Marlborough girl aspired to attend.

7

The Young Women's Leadership
School of East Harlem
September 1998

M OST OF THE GIRLS at Marlborough considered a good education their birthright; their parents, and many of their grandparents, were college graduates. It was one of the perquisites of a comfortable existence, along with travel, access to cultural events, lessons, and sports. Life exposed them to the infinite possibilities of a world outside their own.

At TYWLS, many of the girls would be the first in their families to graduate from high school. Their lives were defined more commonly by their neighborhoods. The world outside their tiny slice of the city might as well be in another galaxy.

TYWLS was supposed to change all that, to confer on each student a new status as an enfranchised member of society. Schoolwork mattered now, because it was the means to an end. Whatever the lesson on the blackboard was, the teachers always had a second agenda: to convince the girls that all this work would pay off someday, and that it was worth being frustrated to tears.

The ambitious students, like Maryam, Diana, and Amy, knew what they did not want—to end up like some of the girls who lived in the projects, high-school dropouts, teenage mothers, stuck in dead-end jobs; the most marginal residents of Manhattan. They were specific about what they did want, their choices influenced by stories they had heard about other kids who made it out, or by the after-school mentoring programs that TYWLS set up. Maryam wanted to be a psychologist, an obstetrician, a computer engineer, or an architectural engineer. Diana wanted to be an actress or an archeologist. As for Amy, she aspired to be a pediatric surgeon—a desire so strong that her parents had already bought a stethoscope to encourage her.

Not everyone at TYWLS shared their sense of purpose. Some of the girls had trouble in class or broke concentration as soon as they left the building. They were here not because they yearned for an education but because their parents were desperate for an antidote to daily life. The trick, for the teachers, was to challenge them without defeating them.

Like most of the TYWLS teachers, Peter DeWan was new to the profession. After a year teaching mathematics at a Los Angeles private school, he had moved to New York to attend Columbia Teachers College and had spent the past year as a student teacher at Manhattan's John F. Kennedy High School. DeWan, who grew up in Washburn, a poor neighborhood of Boston, had been home-schooled until his family moved to Kansas when he was eight. He liked the idea of a public school that challenged accepted wisdom about what a school ought to be.

DeWan told the girls just enough to convince them that he, like they, had not had an easy time of it: divorced parents, the move away from the rest of his family when he was eight, shuttling between his folks. He had found order within himself. He exuded pride and discipline, from his ramrod posture to his no-maintenance brush cut. Although it was not required, DeWan almost always wore a tie. His manner conveyed a clear message: Excuses would not be tolerated in room 908. There would be no negotiations, no flirtatious appeals for clemency. He had never asked the world for special favors, so he would not grant them.

He taught a ninth-grade history class called Global Studies, which with these girls required extra effort on his part. Most of his students came from immigrant families, and when they thought of home, they thought of somewhere else. They had no history here; the country they now lived in belonged to people who had been here longer. Before DeWan could expect them to learn, he had to make the girls feel that they belonged.

Early in the school year, he asked each girl to draw a map of her neighborhood, and as they walked into his classroom on a Wednesday morning, all the buzz was about Maryam's, a huge map divided into neat little rulered boxes, each one identified: the dry cleaner, the copy shop, the neighborhood market, the apartment building. It was drawn on a large board cut out in the shape of a girl, complete with a head, hands, and feet. A few girls had hastily sketched crude maps on notebook paper, and when they saw Maryam's map they quietly shoved their more meager offerings under their binders.

DeWan announced that the bulletin board outside room 908 was empty. "If you think you did a nice job on your map, you should put it outside, right now," he said. No one moved, not even Maryam. He persisted. "I trust you," he said. "If you think you did nice work that other people should see, put it up."

Three girls got up, but still Maryam kept her seat. Diana could not stand it. Her own map was hand-drawn with fluorescent markers, and the accompanying report handwritten, since the Perez family did not own a computer. But Maryam's was beautiful, and she ought to pin it up. Diana loudly nominated her best friend's map, and DeWan came over to take a look. It was by far the most ambitious effort, but Maryam was a perfectionist who, like many girls her age, judged herself on what other people said about her. No matter how good she thought her map was, she assumed it could have been better. DeWan knew that she would not put it on the board unless he confirmed its worth.

As usual, she had done far more than the assignment called for. Maryam was in DeWan's advisory group, which meant that she and a dozen other girls checked in with him every day before school. DeWan felt he knew her better than he did the other girls, and he worried that she drove herself too hard.

"C'mon," he said, as though she ought to know better than to hold back.

Silently Maryam got up and took her map outside, while DeWan collected the other girls' maps and written descriptions and marked a check, a check-plus, or a check-minus in his grade book. The four girls at the back table, already notorious for not paying attention, loudly proclaimed how bad their maps were, as though noise would distract DeWan from their slapdash efforts. They tried to catch a glimpse of their grades, but he held the grade-book close to his chest so they could not see. The last girl, feigning indifference, handed him a nearly blank page.

"You didn't put any stores or anything in here," said DeWan.

"There's nothing there," she protested. She had also failed to write the accompanying description, and when she saw the disapproving look on DeWan's face, she realized she had gone too far.

"If I write my description in study hall," she said, "will you accept it?"

"I'm sorry," he said. "I can't. I have to stick with the rules."

She looked down, petulant. At that moment, DeWan became the enemy; one of those distant, disapproving adults who, she expected, would get in her way forever. This business about taking the word of the outside world worked for everyone: If Maryam believed in herself in part because her teachers told her it was appropriate to do so, the girls who were having a hard time took every criticism as proof that they were failures.

TYWLS students came from what was delicately called a disadvantaged environment—they knew it, the staff knew it, the whole point of this single-sex school was to see if it could compensate for life outside of school. The question was whether to hold them to a standard of behavior or cut them some slack; whether to treat them like any other kids or acknowledge that they might need some special handling. DeWan believed that treating them like remedial students was an insult, and refused to negotiate, but he ran the risk that a girl would balk at his authority, become belligerent, and shut down.

Today's lesson was about culture. DeWan had written on the board, AIM: WHAT IS CULTURE? and began the day's lesson with a question.

"Who in the room considers herself an American?"

No hands.

"What, then?"

The girls shouted out answers: "Dominican," "Puerto Rican," "African-American," "Egyptian," "Ecuadoran," "Mixed."

"What about me?" DeWan asked.

In chorus they answered, "American."

"What else?"

They asked where he was born, and he answered Roxbury, Massachusetts. Where were his parents born? New Jersey and upstate New York. Two generations born here. It made all the difference.

"You're American," one girl insisted.

DeWan protested that his ancestors were Irish, so the girls grudgingly allowed that he was Irish, too. But they insisted on the distinction: He was an American, and they were not, even though all but two of them had been born in the United States.

So he asked each table of girls to come up with a list of at least ten things that made them part of a particular culture. "If you say you're different from somebody else," he said, "you should be able to think of specific differences, as specific as possible." They ought to be proud of what it was that distinguished them from others, but they also needed to understand that they were part of a long tradition of immigration. Maryam's mother was more Egyptian than American; Anna, who sat at her table, had started kindergarten unable to speak English, and to this day her Dominican parents could not. But the same had been true of earlier waves of immigrants. It was no reason for the girls to feel shut out.

He walked between the tables, peering over the girls' shoulders, offering encouragement and advice. Diana, Maryam, and their tablemates did not require help as they scribbled and muttered comments to each other. When he got to the back table, the lists were shorter. "You can come up with more," he said. "I *know* you can." No one picked up a pen.

"Why don't you consider yourself American?" he asked them.

"Because it's not our own culture," said one girl.

He pushed her for specific examples. If his folks had been visiting Puerto Rico when he was born, would he be Puerto Rican? All four girls burst out laughing at his inability to comprehend the difference.

"Spanish people are *loud,*" said one.

DeWan said that he had noticed one difference: White people on the Upper West Side did not tend to sit outside on the stoop listening to the radio turned up loud. At that, one girl took offense; the line between observation and insult was a fine one to girls who were sensitive to being outsiders. DeWan quickly explained that he had not meant it as an insult.

"It's just a difference in how people entertain themselves," he said.

Toward the end of the period, DeWan wrote the lists on the board. Most of the girls were the children of Puerto Rican immigrants, and considered themselves Puerto Rican. Diana was the first to volunteer her list. A tall, slender girl with a high forehead and full features, Diana wafted through life without complaint about its difficulties. She recited a full-page list of happy associations: Puerto Ricans had a native dance, the salsa; instead of Christmas they celebrated the Catholic holiday, Three Kings' Day, giving gifts as the Magi gave gifts to the baby Jesus; and, she said, "The food is good." Other girls were more embarrassed by what they saw as their cultural heritage, which included overeating, being loud and aggressive, and speaking a hybrid language they called Spanglish.

Anna, the girl from the Dominican Republic, liked her family's strong discipline, and loved to dance the merengue and the bachata, but she had no patience for the way her parents and their friends looked or sounded. "They don't know what to wear, and they don't wear socks," she recited, to a chorus of giggles. "They've got this loud, rough accent."

The one reason she could think of to be proud of her ancestry, at the moment, was the performance of her countryman, the Chicago Cubs right fielder Sammy Sosa, who was in a race with St. Louis first baseman Mark McGwire to break the major-league home-run record.

The African-American girls talked about Kwanzaa and rap music, and the few girls from Ecuador, suddenly concerned that they would be the only ones not to have contributed, blurted out two things that set them apart from the Puerto Ricans: their Protestant religion and a marinated raw fish salad called ceviche. As they all began to pack up, DeWan tried to explain that culture was something to be proud of in a country founded by people who had come from somewhere else.

"This is the important thing for today," he said. "Culture is a group of people's unique way of life, including religion, food, clothing, music, language, superstition, manners, art, ideas." It was not, as some of the girls assumed, their destiny.

The level of energy in the room encouraged Peter DeWan. He did not care what the girls had said. What mattered was that they spoke up—that they thought about their lives, thought about how they felt different, and were willing to share their observations. Last year, at the coeducational Kennedy School, he had gotten used to being challenged in class, particularly by the boys. His one frustration at TYWLS was a pervasive cautiousness: Neither the best nor the worst students liked to take risks. The girls were so polite that sometimes he missed the energy level that came with having boys in class.

DeWan urged the good students to speak up in class, even if it meant disagreeing with their teacher, so that they would develop what he called "independent and creative minds." He encountered more resistance than he had anticipated, because the best girls already worried about how they would look to a college admissions committee three years down the line. What good was original thinking without A's on a transcript and respectable test scores? If TYWLS was about gaining access to a larger world, all that a girl like Maryam cared about was having her exit visa in order.

DeWan had already informed her that she would not be allowed to do as much extra-credit work as she had in the past. Maryam liked to compensate for her weaknesses—the occasional B on a test, a real reluctance to talk in front of the whole class—by doing the kind of elaborate homework assignment she had just completed. DeWan wanted Maryam to work on thinking, not doing; to improve her ability to respond spontaneously, whether in his classroom or on an exam. He believed that she had a shot at getting into an Ivy League college in four years, but not if she held back.

"At some point, in college," he told her, "it's not so much how hard you work, but how well you think."

He was not sure if he had had much of an impact; Maryam had not said a thing today about her cultural background. It was going to be a complicated year. DeWan wanted Maryam to speak up, but he worried, always, about falling into an informal tracking system, where the most promising girls got his attention, "and the people at the bottom did worse and worse and worse." Every class session was a balancing act.

The class needed lessons that made it easy for them to speak up, like today's. All they had to do was answer questions about themselves; no endless memorization to evade, no difficult readings about a distant and long-dead civilization. DeWan had to prepare them for the global-history Regents exam at the end of tenth grade, but first he had to make them willing, and that often required a more imaginative lesson plan than what he found in the Regents review literature.

He would not write off any student, no matter how obstinate she was. After all, DeWan thought that Amy Lopez was one of the brightest girls in her class, and right now she was an unfocused mess of competitive energy, unwilling to do A-level work even though she was capable of it. He had to be patient. DeWan looked forward to teaching these girls straight through twelfth grade and then sending them off ready for college. In that context, a full hour of attentive girls was a victory.

The subject of the next day's history class was the difference between power and authority, which seemed to DeWan a particularly important lesson for these girls. He wanted someone to disagree with him—to understand that while he might be an authority figure, he was not interested in exerting power over what they thought.

As soon as the girls sat down, he started to fire questions at them.

"If I say 'Quiet in the halls,' do you listen to me more than to your friends?"

A chorus of voices answered, "Yes."

DeWan smiled. "And if I said, 'I think you should study harder?'"

"Sure, I'd listen," came the quick answer from a girl in the front of the room. "You have power over my grades."

What about a minister? The perfect example, DeWan said, of authority, but not of power. A guy with a gun who takes your money and says "Never wear blue again"? Power, but no authority.

He asked the girls to draw up their own lists of who in their lives had authority and power. In return he got a lot of blank stares, the silence broken only by a whispered exchange between two of the back-table girls.

"You pregnant?"

"No."

Everyone in the room began to laugh, so DeWan quickly altered his tactics. He would allow the girls to discuss the question with the other girls at their table—a calculated risk, since the conversation immediately turned to gossip, even at Maryam's table. But the serious students in the room finally prevailed. Maryam and Diana simply refused to respond to any question that did not pertain to the lesson.

Maryam requested a dictionary so she could look up the definitions of "authority" and "power," but DeWan wanted her to think about the words on her own. As usual, she was the first to speak up. "I think power is somebody who can really have an effect on your life," she said. "Authority, they have an effect but it's not that important."

Diana chimed in. "Yeah, we've had so many teachers, it's hard to think of them as having power. Just authority. Now, parents—*they* have power."

DeWan asked if the girls knew anyone who respected the police.

"My dad," said Diana. "He respects the police, the army, all those guys."

But there was a difference, DeWan said, between fearing that the police might arrest or beat you, which means that they have power, or just knowing that the police are around and acknowledging their authority.

"Respect," he said, "is an important part of authority."

"Okay," said Maryam, "power is me, myself, my mom, and any member of my family. Power is where maybe I do something because I'm afraid of what's going to happen if I don't. I'm not going to fear a teacher, though. They're an authority."

Diana's list of the people who had power included her parents, herself, and her grandmother. And God. Authority meant the police, her parents, her priest, her teachers, her uncle David, and the government.

Anna and Inez, the fourth girl at the table, were reluctant to share their lists, preferring instead to listen as Maryam and Diana debated about who should be included. Maryam and Diana were in demand as table partners in every class they shared. Classroom distractions were often hard to ignore, and the best thing for a girl to do if she wanted to do well was to sit with the serious students. As Diana explained some of her choices, Inez quietly revised what she had written down.

When class was over, Inez approached DeWan about the C he had given her on a recent paper. An eager but erratic student, Inez lacked focus; she paid attention as long as she understood what the teacher was saying, but as soon as she got confused she gave in to loud, often angry frustration. She knew enough to be unhappy about the C. What she did not know was how to improve her performance, except to appeal to a teacher's sympathy.

But DeWan never budged on grades. If he started listening to excuses, the girls would think that every grade was open to challenge. "It won't prevent you getting an A in this class," he said, "if the rest of your work is A quality."

"Okay," Inez replied. Just in case her work turned out to be on the borderline between an A and a B, she wanted DeWan to know how much school mattered to her. Trying ought to count for something.

"Because I cried when I got that C," she said, plaintively. "I *did.*"

8

ARAH KIRKPATRICK'S APPROACH was entirely different from Peter's. Even the layout of the room suggested that she was a potential friend and confidante, the desks shoved close together to leave a large, less-formal area where the girls could sit and talk or work. Sometimes she taught a lesson there, a handful of girls seated on a weathered couch and easy chairs, the rest scattered at her feet. Today she announced that she would be happy to share her summer wedding photographs with any girl who dropped by after school.

Kirkpatrick had started at TYWLS a year ago, in the fall of 1997, after two years of teaching at a rural school in her hometown of Baton Rouge, Louisiana. A graceful woman who wondered if she would ever get used to the frenetic pace of her new home, Kirkpatrick exuded an almost naïve optimism. But for all her lightheartedness, she had a master's degree in education and definite ideas on how to make up for lost time.

TYWLS students may have had to compete for admission, but they still lagged behind grade level in their reading and writing skills. English was the class that determined success in all others, and Kirkpatrick intended to send the girls on to tenth grade able to read more complicated works, analyze what they had read, and communicate their thoughts.

She threw everything she could think of at her students: vocabulary lists, book reports, reading and discussion sessions in class. She began each class by checking everyone's homework and journal entries, and she followed that with a look at the day's new vocabulary words, which were written on a board at the front of the room. Today's words were "erratic," "futility," and "resolute."

"Anyone have a sentence for 'erratic'?" she inquired.

"I am a very erratic person," one girl called out.

"Anybody else?"

No reply. The girls had to learn to compose sentences that proved they understood a word's meaning. Kirkpatrick said, "My dog's behavior was very erratic, so we had to put him to sleep," and got a chorus of "Aww"s in response.

"It isn't true," she confessed. "But I bet you'll remember it now."

When no one could define "futility," she supplied a sentence. When she got to "resolute," one eager girl turned it into a verb.

"I resolute to do better," she said.

Kirkpatrick was not going to embarrass her by pointing out the error in front of the whole class, not when she was the only one to make an attempt. She corrected by example: "I *know* I will pass my test," she said. "I have studied very hard—and I am resolute."

She looked at the girls. "Let me hear an 'Amen' to that."

"Amen," they said, in chorus.

Next, she handed out format instructions for the book reports. The girls had to get her approval on any book for outside reading, but Kirkpatrick intended to be fairly lenient. She tried to make the challenge sound flattering. "We are reading things that interest us," she explained, "and are at our level." But "our level" encompassed a broad range of titles. Kirkpatrick had put a quote from William Faulkner up on her wall that read,

"Read, read, read. Read everything—trash, classics, good and bad, and see how they do it. Just like a carpenter who works as an apprentice and studies the master."

The first assigned reading for class was *Gilgamesh,* a story in verse about an ancient king. Kirkpatrick was nervous about starting off with a story that might seem irrelevant to the girls as well as difficult to read, but TYWLS wanted to connect what was taught in English and history whenever possible, and ninth-grade history included the study of ancient civilizations. So *Gilgamesh* it was.

Kirkpatrick could feel an almost palpable resistance from some of the girls. The assumption at TYWLS was that a good school would make the difference in a girl's life. But what if it did not? What if the girls carried limits around inside them that all the special handling in the world could not change? Any student who had trouble with *Gilgamesh* might wonder if this was as far as she was going to get—if, as she secretly feared, she had reached the outer edge of her ability. Every teacher came up against the kind of fatalism that DeWan had encountered on the map assignment: girls who took a demanding assignment as proof of their limitations.

And failure, in this place, was harder to bear than it was in an overcrowded classroom with fights breaking out. A girl who performed poorly there could spread the blame around: not enough money for special programs, harried teachers and too few of them, the weight of the bad kids pulling everyone down. The exceptions in those public schools were the ones who managed not to drown. TYWLS, by comparison, had eager teachers, small classes, even special classes on study skills run by Holly Simon, the guidance counselor. There was no crippled bureaucracy to blame for poor performance. Failure here reflected back on the girl, and it carried a very real threat. Each year, the eighth graders had to take a test to qualify for the high-school portion of the program. If they did not pass, they were banished to the schools they had tried to escape.

DeWan's solution was to try to maintain momentum. Kirkpatrick was more of a strategist. She told the girls that they might have trouble with *Gilgamesh,* so that they would not feel quite so bad when they encountered it.

She frequently reminded them that it was all right—even a good thing—to admit that they needed help.

"If you're having trouble and you don't want to talk about it in class, I'm off while you're in study hall," she said. "Make an appointment and come and see me. And say, 'Here's the part of *Gilgamesh* I'm having trouble with, and here's what I don't understand.' What's not helpful to me is if you just say, 'I don't understand *Gilgamesh.*'"

For today, the girls were to have read a section where Gilgamesh went on a quest for eternal life. Kirkpatrick asked them what they thought, but all she got in reply was halfhearted shrugs, which was just what she had feared. Straightforward prose was challenge enough for the ninth graders. Verse was trickier, and their defensive response was to back off; being silent was always preferable to sounding stupid.

Kirkpatrick anticipated a prolonged standoff unless she figured out some way to make the story more relevant to the girls. She decided to take a chance.

"Tell me," she said. "How many of you have lost a loved one?"

Nearly every girl in the room raised a hand. Kirkpatrick called on Inez, a combustible girl who already today had invoked tears with DeWan and yelled at her math teacher for not explaining an equation to Inez's satisfaction.

She spoke in an uncharacteristically quiet voice. Inez's father had been in prison all her life; she barely knew him, since her parents had split up before she was born and her mom had since remarried. "I thought life was good," she said, "so I didn't write to my dad." He had died a year ago, still in prison, never having heard from his daughter.

She stopped to wipe a careful index finger under each eye, trying not to disturb her makeup. "When he died, I felt so guilty," she said. "I couldn't eat. I was depressed."

No one said a word, including Kirkpatrick, whose training had hardly prepared her for this kind of confession. She knew so little beyond generalities about the girls' lives outside school. Suddenly she had a room full of attentive girls, which had been her intention—but for a long moment, she could not think of a reply.

"Can't eat," she said, with a faltering smile. "I do just the opposite. I eat too much. But thank you, Inez, for sharing that with us. Now, has anyone felt anger at a loss?"

Anna's hand shot up. Her favorite aunt had died recently. "She was an angel," said Anna, "and all I could think was I was so angry. *I* should have died, because my aunt was so good, she helped my mother. . . ." Anna began to cry.

Kirkpatrick asked if anyone else wanted to speak, and glanced over at Maryam, who silently shook her head and looked away. Maryam resisted all of her teachers' efforts to get her to talk about anything personal. Twelve years after her father's death, Maryam still did not discuss it in public.

Kirkpatrick tried to shift the discussion back to the text, but it was no use; the girls continued to talk among themselves. When the bell rang, she asked them to add one thing to their homework assignment. They were to reread the passages about Gilgamesh and grief, and write a short paragraph about the section that best expressed grief to them.

After the girls were gone, Kirkpatrick sat at one of the empty tables and wondered about what had just happened. Many of the TYWLS teachers had more ideals than experience, while the girls often had more experience than they could handle. The best lesson plan was no match for real life. Kirkpatrick was pleased that Inez and Anna had spoken up, but not at all sure that she had enhanced the girls' understanding of the assigned reading.

Celenia Chevere was in the hallway watching the girls change classes. Amy Lopez ran by, clutching a new souvenir T-shirt from the summer program at Smith College, and when Diana heard that the box of shirts had arrived, she bolted for the office to pick up her own. Chevere proudly watched her go. Maryam, Diana, and Amy had come back from Smith talking about what they had to do to be able to apply to colleges of that caliber. It gave her chills just to think about it.

When Chevere had first taken the job as principal, she promised herself that she would stick with it for three years. Looking at the ninth graders, she knew she would be here for at least six, until they graduated, in June of 2002. She had a particular affection for the pioneer class. In seventh grade they had adored her. "I was this busy woman building a school for them," she said. "In eighth grade I graduated to the wicked witch, very clear on the standards I expected, trying to keep the school the way it should be. The ninth graders now, it's getting better, maybe they're starting to realize what I'm working for. I see them in the hall, I say hello, I can talk to them."

She let them call her Celenia, just as they called the other faculty members by their first names. Chevere had always done it this way, to teach students that respect was something to be earned, not part of an empty ritual. "These girls come from such varied backgrounds, where respect is often measured in archaic ways," she said. Sometimes the parents complained that first names seemed too familiar, but Chevere insisted, "It's not a matter of calling someone by their last name. It's how you behave, how you act when you're with them."

The girls had to win the teachers' respect as well, and that was going to be more difficult than Chevere had anticipated. She remembered how shocked she had been back in the fall of 1996, when the pioneers got their first TYWLS report cards. "There were some girls here that were so-called straight-A students—and then they got their first report cards, and surprise, surprise, they were no longer straight-A," she said. "They lacked so many skills, it's really amazing."

Chevere had a theory on how these girls had earned such good grades only to falter when they got to TYWLS. She figured they were gratitude grades, awarded by battle-weary teachers to anyone who showed up in class and did not make trouble. A girl who posed no overt problem and made the slightest effort was a stellar pupil.

To compensate for the gaps in the girls' abilities, Chevere had developed a curriculum plan that she called a "spiral," using the seventh and eighth grades to prepare the girls for more intensive work in high school. Peter De-Wan's history course, Global Studies, was a two-year course that began in ninth grade and culminated in a Regents exam at the end of tenth grade, and Chevere considered it "very difficult" because of its scope. The seventh- and eighth-grade teachers had to ease into the work, emphasizing study skills as much as the material. Once a girl got to ninth grade, there was little time for compensating. The high school classes were a forced hybrid of supportive teaching techniques—games, team projects; long on participation and short on lectures—and the regimentation required for success on standardized tests.

In January, the ninth graders would have to retake the state-mandated Regents exam in earth science because they had failed it in eighth grade. In June they would take Regents exams in biology and mathematics, and if they failed either of those, they would have to take it again in tenth grade, in addition to Global Studies. That would be too much of a burden. The science and math teachers were on notice: The girls had to be ready for the tests.

Chevere had promised they would be. At the beginning of the school year she had told Granger Ward, the district high-school superintendent, that 90 percent of TYWLS students would pass their Regents exams this year, almost as many as had failed the earth-science test the year before. She had to make up a lot of ground.

Chevere had dangled big dreams in front of the girls, talked to them about how colleges would love to recruit a minority girl with an exemplary record. The truth was more complicated, and she knew it. Success required strategy, determination, perhaps a little begging to find a volunteer college counselor—but it was possible, which was all that mattered.

Chevere believed that prestigious schools would solicit the pioneers three years from now, if only she could keep them on course. It would be all too easy to settle for less, because every girl who scurried past on her way to class faced the handicap of poverty, and sometimes more: Maryam, growing up without a father; Diana, who endured exhausting bouts of asthma; Amy, who had yet to develop the self-discipline that high school would require of her. Chevere could have patted them on the backs simply for trying, but she had loftier goals. Let them think she was too strict, too rule-bound, too demanding. No one got an A at her school simply for showing up.

9

Marlborough School

October 1998

M ARLBOROUGH WAS a young school in old clothes. Its traditions were more than a century old, but the questions that preoccupied Barbara Wagner's administration were new ones. The goal at graduation was clear: to send a group of competent, self-confident young women to some of the finest schools in the country. The question of how to do it was more complicated.

On a practical level, Wagner and her staff tried to build an Upper-School curriculum that satisfied the needs of the most accomplished students and encouraged every girl to excel. Preparing students for those advanced classes was a more subtle challenge, though, and the role of the Middle School at Marlborough was the subject of some disagreement. The program could emphasize either a girl's emotional and developmental growth or the academics required to get the girls into shape for high school. One of those two things had to come first.

A former Middle School head had begged his colleagues to build what he called a "safe haven" for middle school girls. He had conducted his own media workshop, buying magazines aimed at twelve- to fifteen-year-olds, surfing the web, and talking to the girls, and had arrived at a sobering conclusion. "However bad you think it is," he told his colleagues, "however bad it was when you were a kid, it's worse."

Magazines that a generation ago had told seventeen-year-olds how to look, how to act, and what to wear now targeted a younger, more vulnerable audience. Computers offered the same advice, but with a damaging twist: they isolated a girl just at the time when she ought to be wondering who she was and where she fit in the larger universe. The Middle School director had campaigned for a supportive atmosphere not because girls were somehow weaker than boys, but because the culture outside school was more than any girl should have to deal with.

Other staff members believed that the best way to build a strong girl—and satisfy her ambitious parents—was to prepare her for the academic demands of high school. If they worked too hard to make the youngest girls feel comfortable, they came dangerously close to the kind of remedial environment that skeptical parents worried about. Wagner often reminded her staff that this was a "college preparatory school." They could not ease the girls along for three years only to hit them with a tougher schedule when they entered the Upper School in tenth grade.

It was hard to strike the proper balance. After the 1996–1997 school year, forty Marlborough students transferred to other schools amidst complaints that the Marlborough program was too much of a grind. As one girl put it, "I do everything I can and I feel like I'll always be a B student."

The following year, Wagner instituted five changes designed specifically to make the Middle School girls feel better. On the list: Improve staff accessibility, revise the daily schedule to emphasize relationships, coordinate the curriculum to "reduce the overwhelm factor," clarify expectations, and inject a little happiness with special assemblies and events. She refused to back down on academic expectations, but she did shift to the ninth grade some of the increased workload that had previously begun in the eighth grade, to give the girls one more year to acclimate themselves.

The new program seemed to work. At the end of the 1997–1998 school year, only twenty-one girls transferred, the lowest number in the school's history. The only complaints came from some of the parents, who were concerned that any lightening of the load might adversely affect their daughters' chances of getting into good colleges.

Wagner assured them that it was possible to make Marlborough a more pleasant place for the younger girls without compromising the academic program. Middle school was the time to build a solid educational base for the challenges that lay ahead, in an environment tailored to encourage achievement and reward best effort. It was not an extended group-therapy session. No one forgot the exodus of 1996–1997, but no one was going to ease off just to make a girl more comfortable.

Some of the Middle School teachers took it upon themselves to monitor the girls' comfort level. Myranda Marsh, whose brain always seemed to be operating on several channels simultaneously, kept a private record of behavioral changes in her students. As the weeks went by, Marsh was happy to see Alex Siegel becoming slightly less exacting about her appearance. She had started to wear boxer shorts like the other girls. She even chatted with her tablemates during history class—and while Marsh would not tolerate it, she was glad, on another level, to hear it.

"Alex needs to experiment," she thought, "with yapping."

Another Middle School history teacher rounded up a dozen Upper School volunteers and encouraged them to befriend the Middle School girls, but the effort backfired. Being a mature senior involved some amount of denial about the distant, silly past. The older girls were incredulous about the seventh graders, who, as far as they could tell, lived a simple life—as one senior described it, "Eat. Sleep. AOL." The seniors had far more important things to do than bond with such youngsters.

THERE WERE GIRLS at Marlborough whose parents could send three children to private colleges, at over $30,000 per child per year, without difficulty. There were others, like the Tower family, who had long ago devised a financial strategy that would enable them to send Katie and

her younger brother wherever they wanted to go. And there were the ben-
eficiaries of Wagner's commitment to economic, as well as ethnic, diversity: families who had no chance of college without financial aid. Like the
girls in East Harlem, they had to hope that they could cobble together
some combination of scholarship money, grants, loans, and a part-time job
to pay for the next four years.

On the evening of October 6, an exceptional line of cars pulled into
the school's curved driveway. Not the usual assortment of perfectly de-
tailed foreign luxury sedans and hulking sport-utility vehicles, but citizens
of Los Angeles' automotive underclass: a Nissan Sentra, a vintage Volvo, a
faded brown Oldsmobile Cutlass, a 1960s Toyota Corona wagon.

Phyllis Louie came straight from work, her head swimming with numbers. She defiantly told anyone who asked that she had started thinking
about colleges for her only child, Sommer, "on August fourteenth, 1981,"
which was the day Sommer was born. Last year, when Sommer was a junior, Phyllis had begun to educate herself about finances in earnest, compiling information about any scholarship, however small, that benefited
black students. She had never allowed circumstances to get in her way before, and would not be done in by them now.

Phyllis was a secretary who had taken classes at the University of Wis-
consin, taken a year off to earn some money, and never returned. Her husband, Robert, a retired journeyman electrician, had attended Los Angeles
Trade Technical College, and now spent his free time restoring old cars, including a pristine white 1972 Cadillac Eldorado that bore the vanity license
plate LOUIE. They lived in a small, immaculate stucco house in a neighborhood with more self-esteem than square footage. If Robert doted on his
daughter, Phyllis strove on her behalf. It was Phyllis who had dubbed Sommer and her friends "the Internationals," elevating racial diversity into an
exclusive club; Phyllis who, last year, had converted the dining room into
the "college room," full of catalogues and file boxes.

She was one of the first to arrive for the meeting, pad and pen in hand.
If determination could take physical form, it would be Phyllis Louie: She
was one of those short women who seem larger than they really are, everything about her magnified by a sense of purpose. She strode into the li-

brary, her close-cropped hair and chiseled features making it seem that her face had been sculpted out of stone.

Phyllis needed to talk to Sommer's college counselor. Monica Ward was a stylish, self-confident young black woman who had worked in admissions at Vanderbilt University before coming to Marlborough, and Phyllis adored her. Ward was the crucial link in the Louies' college plan, the one who would turn Phyllis's yearning into a successful strategy.

It had been an exasperating day: Sommer had returned, sick, exhausted, and unimpressed, from a free minority-recruitment weekend at Amherst College in Massachusetts, and had expressed no interest in the Martin Luther King scholarship her mother had discovered at Brandeis University, despite the fact that it meant a free ride. Sommer wanted to go to Rice University in Houston, or maybe to Stanford University, and then to become a gynecologist. She did not want to listen to her mother's oft-repeated warning that price, in the end, would determine their preference.

Phyllis walked a fine line. She wanted Sommer to believe in herself. At the same time, she needed her daughter to face reality, which might not look quite as glorious as Sommer's imagined future. Money made a difference. So did competitive test scores, no matter how much a school talked about minority recruitment. Sommer was known at Marlborough as a dogged, hardworking student who welcomed a challenge, but her test scores needed to come up. She had a combined SAT score of 1260 out of a possible 1600 from the spring of her junior year, and the top schools liked to see a minimum of 1300 to 1400. Some schools used scores as a way to make an initial cut, refusing even to consider a candidate who did not meet their minimum requirements.

With her daughter collapsed in bed and the next SATs six days away on Saturday morning, Phyllis wanted to talk to Monica about a rumor she had heard: that Stanford required a minimum combined score of 1340 on the SATs. Ms. Ward said she was right. "That's what you need to be competitive."

There had been no money in the Louie budget for the expensive SAT-preparation courses that most of the Marlborough girls took. The best Phyllis could do was to get her daughter over this miserable cold and shoe-horn some good nights' sleep between now and the October 10 test. They were too close to their goal to let eighty points get in their way. "I know my daughter. I know what she's going to do," she told Ward, as though saying it aloud would make it so. "She's going to raise that test score, I just know it."

At seven o'clock, twenty-one anxious parents took their seats, with Phyllis in the first row. Monica Ward introduced the speaker, David Levy, a financial-aid officer from the California Institute of Technology. Phyllis took notes on everything he said, even though Levy had handouts for the parents. The only time she rested was when Levy discussed early-decision applicants. Sommer could not afford to consider early decision. They had to look at everyone's financial package and make a choice based on that.

Levy's list of estimated costs, including room and board, was a daunting one, although at $13,500 the UC campuses were cheaper per year than Marlborough. An out-of-state public school would run between $15,000 and $20,000—and the independent schools Sommer had her heart set on could cost as much as $35,000 a year.

Looking at the parents' long faces, Levy quickly moved to the next slide: "Two words of comfort when going to college. Anyone know what they are?"

Rodney Forneret's older daughter, Erica, was a friend of Sommer's and an early-decision applicant to Brown University, and his younger daughter, Martine, had just begun seventh grade at Marlborough. Without hesitation, he called out "'Mom' and 'Dad.'"

Levy laughed. "At one of these, one man said they were 'Good' and 'bye.' But they're 'financial aid.'"

He went on to describe the various kinds of aid and ways to find them, and after a while, Phyllis stopped taking notes and sat with her palm against her cheek, listening to the avalanche of information. She needed nine more months' energy to complete the central project of her life: to launch a young woman of color from a poor neighborhood into a prestigious school that would guarantee a promising future.

Her husband, Robert, was happy to let the two women in his life define it. A skinny man with a heart-shaped face and a quick smile, he stood in awe of his wife and daughter. Sommer seemed to him to have been in charge since the day she was born, and while her mother wove fantasies of ambition and achievement, Robert supervised her musical education. He loved all kinds of music, especially jazz, so he had often put on a record and danced around the house with his infant daughter in his arms. Sommer listened, danced with her father, and developed an eclectic set of musical preferences. She liked vintage Sinatra as much as she liked the bands her friends listened to.

When she got to Marlborough, she eagerly took her place alongside trained dancers in the introductory dance class, and by the time she was a junior she was one of only a dozen girls accepted into the elite Dance Dimensions group. Many of them were classically trained; long, slender girls on pale-pink toe shoes. Sommer, who also ran track, had the broad shoulders and bunched muscles of a sprinter, and she had never been *en pointe*, but she felt entitled to her place. Her mother's grit and her father's dancing were as good a set of credentials as years spent at a dance academy.

She approached the college-application process in much the same way. Monica Ward wrote a cover letter to accompany Sommer's applications, asking that the schools waive their application fees because the Louies could not afford to pay each of a dozen schools. No one in the family, or at school, suggested cutting back on the number of applications. For her part, Sommer proceeded on the assumption that the world would accommodate her, because it had so far; because being a hard worker had to matter more than being rich.

It was hard to eliminate any of the schools. She tried to throw out the catalog from the University of Michigan, but as she reached to put it in the wastebasket, she wondered, "Is this my ticket to—*everything*?," and put it back in the stack.

Erica Forneret, who enjoyed hyperbole, told people that she would die if she did not get into Brown University. She joked that she loved the school because there were no math requirements, but in fact she loved it because it promised a forgiving atmosphere. Erica was a lopsided student who personified textbook generalities about girls: that they excelled at writing and were intimidated, and finally defeated, by math.

She did not care. The child of two professionals—Rodney was a municipal court judge and Phyllis was a speech therapist who worked part-time to accommodate her daughters' schedules—Erica had been raised to think highly of herself. Her parents had always made the world work for them. Phyllis Forneret was a statuesque, soft-spoken woman whose two daughters jokingly introduced her as "the black Martha Stewart," and their rambling, pink-stucco two-story home was testimony to her will, from the seasonal floral arrangements to her collection of old china and vintage table linens. She knew all the shops that sold designer clothing at discount prices, so that the girls would always have a remarkable dress for any social occasion. She tinkered with reality until it looked the way she wanted it to.

Erica's father might gripe about the cost of sending two girls to private high school and private colleges, but he was prepared to refinance the house if he had to. Phyllis Forneret built an elegant universe, and Rodney somehow figured out how to subsidize it. Erica expected that such privilege would continue without any major adjustments on her part.

She was proud of who she was, and more concerned with finding a place where she would fit than with changing herself to meet someone else's expectations. Erica had already scored a perfect 800 on her verbal SAT at the end of her junior year. She was not about to tempt fate by taking the test again this year just to raise a disappointing math score.

She was a budding actor and writer, a dreamy girl with feline eyes and her father's rascal smile. Despite all the warnings from the college counselors, Erica had fallen in love with a single school, and that infatuation informed everything she did. Many colleges requested first-semester mid-term grades before making a final decision on an early applicant, so Erica had designed a first-semester schedule that would highlight her strengths, centered on an AP elective called Literature of the Supernatural. All she cared about was maintaining her A in that class.

To her dismay, it quickly became clear that showing off was not going to be easy. There were a couple of girls in the class who were aggressive about participating, including the likely valedictorian, Christina Kim, and Erica had trouble getting a word in edgewise. As the days went by, she began to worry about the participation part of her grade, and to wonder why Dr. Morgan, one of her favorite teachers, did not come to her aid. She complained plaintively to her mother and sat silent in class, doodling long, curly vines on the edge of a sheet of notebook paper.

Erica's predicament was supposed to be a function of the coeducational classroom, in which boys shot their hands up first, and more frequently, and girls' participation dwindled because they were tired of fighting for attention or worried about upstaging a potential boyfriend. But there was a range of response among girls as well, and Marlborough teachers disagreed on how to give everyone a fair shot. Myranda Marsh played a game with the seventh graders in which students got cardboard "coins" that they spent each time they spoke in class. Once a girl had used up her money, she had to remain silent, and this kept the talkative girls under control. Marsh wanted everyone to be broke by the end of the session, so girls like Alex Siegel, who were too quiet, had to figure out a way to jump into the conversation.

By the time the girls were seniors, though, most of the teachers expected them to solve such problems themselves. Erica refused, and complained to her mother that Dr. Morgan had let the class get out of hand. Phyllis encouraged her to make an appointment to see Dr. Morgan before it was too late. Phyllis worried that both Erica and Martine tended to back off when they felt unhappy. "If you hide your light under a bushel," she counseled Erica, "no one will know what you're thinking. You have to tell the teacher what you think." With an acceptance at Brown at stake, Erica scheduled a meeting with Dr. Morgan for Monday, October 12—not so much to talk about how to improve her participation grade as to explain why she had not contributed, and to make sure her A was safe.

Erica's meeting with her teacher did not go well. Genevieve Morgan had been surprised by Erica's reticence this term, but she did not believe in intervention. The girls had to learn how to take charge in the classroom. Erica would be in college in a year, and her professors were not going to bother with a girl who said she was smart but who never showed it. Dr. Morgan warned Erica that at this point she could expect a C-plus in participation, which would bring her mid-term grade down to a B-plus.

Erica was horrified, and not a little indignant. "I've never had anything lower than an A in English," she said.

Dr. Morgan did not care how many A's Erica had had, particularly since she felt she was one of the more lenient teachers when it came to classroom participation. Les Klein told her Dramatic Literature students that participation counted for 30 percent of the grade, and if a girl failed to speak up, Klein called on her anyway, to see if her reluctance was a matter of not knowing the material, or of not knowing when to jump in. Dr. Morgan reminded Erica that in her class, participation counted for only ten percent of the grade. A girl could speak up, or she could hope that her tests and written work would carry her. Erica had to decide if she wanted to take that chance. Her teacher's only responsibility was to apprise her of the potential consequences.

Erica continued to resist. It wasn't her fault that she failed to speak up. The two or three girls who dominated the discussions made it impossible for everyone else—except the parrots, who merely repeated what the other girls had said, a role Erica considered beneath contempt.

"By the time I have something to say, they've already said it," she said.

Dr. Morgan admitted that Christina and one or two of the other girls were fast with their comments. "I do try to curb them a bit," she said, "but they're so excited about learning. I'm not going to say, 'No, don't do that.'" She advised Erica to find a way to resolve the problem.

"It's something you have to overcome," she said.

After school, Erica reported the conversation, and her dissatisfaction with it, to her mother. Phyllis immediately wrote a conciliatory note to Dr. Morgan, saying that Erica understood she needed to participate and would be a more active member of the class from now on. She and Rodney had successfully raised Erica to think of herself as a special child; the discarded first draft of her college essay had been about being an African-American girl who for a long time had felt estranged from that community; who preferred Beethoven to rap music and proper grammar to street parlance, and felt left out because of it.

But Phyllis was aware that "special" could easily tip over into smug. Erica had a reputation for being smarter than her grades; for refusing to work up to her potential unless the work really interested her. Phyllis had to make sure that Erica played by the rules.

CHRISTINA KIM KNEW there was a problem in Dr. Morgan's class, but she was not about to undercut herself to fix it. The older daughter of a Korean house painter and his wife, a nurse, Christina drove herself so hard that her parents and teachers could only stand by, shaking their heads. They might as well try to get her to stop breathing as persuade her to slow down.

The Korean community in Los Angeles had a reputation for demanding excellence from its children, but Christina's parents would have accepted a more reasonable pace, had their daughter asked. They were not consulted. Her father, Yong Cheol, retreated into his work and left the primary responsibility for his daughter to his wife, Youngsook. She in turn made gentle suggestions about her daughter's welfare, until it became clear that Christina was not listening. Junior year had been a nightmare of AP classes, a schedule so demanding that the head of the Upper School had offered Christina the chance to back out of some of them. She politely refused, at which point her mother gave up and decided simply to ride out the year as well as she could.

Over the summer before her senior year, Christina and her mother had agreed that Christina would try for Harvard College, early decision. Given her academic record and a combined score of 1580 out of 1600 on her junior-year SATs, they had every reason to believe she would be accepted. Just in case, they composed a short list of alternatives, including Brown University, Princeton, Columbia, and MIT, all of which had one thing in common: They were on the east coast. Christina had no interest in the UC system. Never having gone anywhere alone, Christina wanted to go as far away as she could.

She was the object of universal admiration at Marlborough, and was the marker by which the other seniors mapped their place in the world. Assuming that Christina went to Harvard, they could work their way down the scale and estimate the odds that they would land at Yale or Brown, or one of the UC campuses. She glided happily from one class to another, a tall, slender, quiet girl whose composed features were shielded by glasses and a curtain of long black hair. She had an unexpected giggle, but few of the girls had heard it. She had a mind for science, but few of the girls understood it. Christina lived a solitary existence. The time that other girls devoted to sports, or plays, or doing nothing, Christina invested in her schoolwork.

She was used to leading whatever class she was in. Her parents had enrolled her in a highly competitive SAT preparation class, from which any student who failed to score 1500 on periodic sample tests was eliminated. She remembered with disdain the "submissive" girls in the class, who sat like stone and wasted their time and their parents' money. The atmosphere at Marlborough was more to her liking.

Christina had taken an honors English class with Erica Forneret in their junior year, and had enjoyed the dynamic conversation. She did not understand why Erica refused to speak up in Dr. Morgan's class, and she did not know what to do. Backing down made no sense; then there would be two capable students who were not taking part. Besides, Christina genuinely enjoyed classroom discussion. And if Brown wanted to know how Erica did this semester, Harvard undoubtedly would be curious about its highly competitive pool of applicants. Christina was not insensitive, but she was unwilling to defer to another girl's silence.

10

KURT SCHLEUNES, the 41-year-old head of the Marlborough math department, was a credentialed good guy. When the Middle School track club asked him to appear with them at an all-school sports pep rally, he donned a bandeau top and petticoat over his street-clothes without complaint. Every Halloween, he and his wife, Della, a Marlborough dance instructor, wore complementary costumes to school. Schleunes ran the sound system for school shows and dances and plied his students with doughnuts to keep them happy in math class. A tall, thin man who shaved his head and wore oversized black plastic eyeglasses, he was an ambassador for the unexpected—the perfect guide to a subject that traditionally gave girls trouble. No matter how much a girl disliked math, it was hard to disappoint Mr. Schleunes.

His laconic style, like his wardrobe of elegant, unconstructed suits, gave the impression of someone at ease with himself, but an endless, noisy debate raged inside him, about how best to teach math to girls. The son of two teachers, the sibling of two more, he had grown up listening to dinner-table discussions of classroom technique. He talked about it with his wife. He thought about teaching all the time.

His promotion to head of the math department this year had only increased the internal noise level. It was perhaps the most high-profile academic position at Marlborough, because math was central to the debate about how best to educate girls. In the United States, girls began their education equal to boys in terms of mathematical ability, only to falter as they approached adolescence. Their classroom and test performance suffered, and they gave up on math earlier than boys did. Although 44 percent of undergraduate math majors were women, the number dwindled to 24 percent at the graduate level.

The question was how to reverse the decline. Proponents of girls' schools blamed it on the social pressure to defer when boys were around, as well as on the enduring assumption that girls were not good at numbers. They believed that if a girl was put in an environment where there were no preconceptions about how she was supposed to behave, and given teachers who were sensitive to her needs, she would flourish.

Critics of single-sex education insisted that a number of other factors might contribute to girls' disappointing performance in math, ranging from overcrowded classrooms to unenlightened teachers; from lack of parental support to the absence of clearly defined academic goals. They said that independent girls' schools preselected girls who were expected to excel—girls whose parents were more highly educated, more supportive, and wealthy enough to afford private tuition. Success had more to do with who they were than with whether they went to school with boys.

Some researchers dismissed environmental influences altogether, and had begun to look for physiological clues. They wondered if girls and boys needed to be separated because their brains processed information in different ways—a notion that struck fear into the hearts of feminists, who hardly wanted to provide opponents of equal rights with empirical data.

While the debate continued, Schleunes and his teachers had to figure out what to do for their students. Parents who chose Marlborough expected their girls to do well in math class: If poor performance was a social issue, a function of the traditional coed classroom, then eliminating boys ought to make a difference. If biological differences were the key, Marlborough teachers had the luxury of being able to customize their approach to best help their female students.

Every math teacher at Marlborough faced some resistance, from the advanced students as well as the girls in the regular sections. Girls often anticipated trouble in math, since the notion that they could do as well as boys was at this point a theoretical one. Their mothers belonged to the generation that had stopped taking math classes, for the most part, as soon as they fulfilled their school requirements. The advanced math minds at Marlborough belonged to men, who taught the Upper School courses, while women teachers tried to entice the younger girls to get excited about algebra. Mrs. Hotchkiss, Schleunes's predecessor and now the director of the Middle School, had taught calculus, but she was the exception.

Schleunes believed that girls did process information differently than boys did, and that they would suffer as long as they were expected to learn in the same way. His experience in the classroom confirmed that they often had trouble with spatial skills and needed to visualize a problem to be able to solve it. He knew they were at a disadvantage on standardized tests, like the SATs, so he encouraged them to draw pictures to illustrate geometry problems that confused them. He was quick to remind the girls that none of his assumptions was absolute; none of his suggestions was meant to imply that there was something wrong with them. He just wanted them to know what they could do to help themselves.

Even the good students sometimes came to real understanding, what he called the "aha! moment," later in their development than boys did. Sometimes they were on the brink of giving up when it hit. Katie Tower had plodded along dutifully until the end of her junior year, when, all of a sudden, things magically began to fall into place. Sommer Louie had taken AP calculus her junior year, a class so far over her head that Schleunes offered to let her drop it without penalty—at which point she dug in and got a solid B. She went on to score four out of a possible five on her AP exam.

That experience had been a revelation for him: Great progress was possible for a willing student. Part of his job was not to give up on a girl, and not to let her give up on herself.

Too few of the girls imagined themselves as potential math majors, though he could think of a half-dozen in his AP class who showed as much promise as he had at that age. He had to bring them along—for their own sake, and for the sake of the mediocre students who needed role models. The average students needed to know girls who had moved methodically from one homework assignment to the next until suddenly they were able to think fluently in math, the way a linguist thinks in Spanish or French.

In the meantime, parents expected miracles. Schleunes's mandate to his faculty was to keep the girls engaged long enough for desire to kick in. He told the teachers what his father had told him: "'What you tell kids they are, they'll be.'"

He took for himself what he considered a difficult group: the sixteen students in pre-calculus, a class for juniors and seniors who were trying to complete the mathematics requirement with as little stress as possible. He was used to teaching an honors section, and he'd come out of the gate this year eager to get going. Six weeks later, he had slowed his pace and cut back his expectations considerably.

"I looked at some of the material and said, 'Well, they're regular-section kids, but they can get this,'" he said. "Then I realized they're missing too much. They don't remember enough from last year." He decided to backtrack and do some review work. He was still at it in the second week of October.

He was in a rut that made him uncomfortable: Every day he spent at least twenty minutes going over the previous night's homework problems, explaining the process he had already explained, analyzing wrong answers, presenting new problems to see if the concepts stuck. On a good day, he had twenty minutes left to present a new lesson, but sometimes he had only ten, which was not enough.

Schleunes often revised his lesson plan in the middle of a class if he felt he was losing the girls. He relied on his overhead projector, because it enabled him to keep looking up at the girls, who were watching the screen behind him. As soon as he saw their eyes start to glaze over in confusion, he slowed down. "I overestimate what I think they can assimilate," he said, and the only solution was to have them work more sample problems, while he walked the aisles, looking over their shoulders and answering individual questions. It was not an efficient approach. He had sworn he would not scale back the curriculum to make things easier, but that was exactly what he was doing.

"I hate to go that route," he said, "where you say, 'I'm going to chop this up and not do more than half a lesson a day.' I want to push them, but what I'm doing with pre-calc now is almost something I would do with an Algebra I class."

He knew he had to be careful. "A teacher can turn a kid off for the rest of the year with one pretty good putdown," he said. "That is not the atmosphere at Marlborough. These kids learn from the seventh grade on that if somebody has a question the teacher is going to stop and answer it. The problem is not to let the lower-ability kids start to dominate with question after question after question. They suck the level of the class down a little bit."

"Pre-calculus is an area where a lot of kids really hit the wall mathematically," he said. "It used to be a pretty traditional thing in high school, to make it to pre-calc and not do very well, because you aren't going to have to take any more math in college. But the reality now is they're making econ majors take business calculus, psych majors take calc, sometimes to weed them out of the program."

"They're going to cover a whole lot in college," he sometimes warned the girls, "and they're going to cover it fast." He wanted them to develop the skills necessary to process the information themselves, but, like tyro swimmers with inflated floats on their arms, they were reluctant to go it alone. Schleunes had to be demanding enough to prepare his pre-calc students for that environment, but supportive enough to make sure he didn't lose them. Along the way, he had to prepare them for the battery of tests they faced as part of the college-application process. He hadn't yet figured out how to accomplish all those things at once.

The advanced math classes presented different problems. Schleunes was in awe of Marlborough's top students, who, he said, "are more organized and efficient, and work harder, than most adults I know," and he had had several girls come back after graduation to report that college was relatively easy compared with the course load of a Marlborough senior enrolled in honors and AP classes. But there were pitfalls for teachers in those classes, too. College admissions had become increasingly competitive in the last few years, with an accompanying emphasis on test scores. Schleunes disliked "teaching to the test," in which the classroom became a glorified test-preparation course, but the top students demanded it. They knew their scores, they knew the other girls' scores, and those scores were too often the currency by which not only the girls, but their teachers, were evaluated.

Schleunes unhappily admitted that he taught to the test in the calculus AP section and encouraged the other upper division math teachers to do so as well. "We are a college preparatory school," he said, "but we're also in the AP business and we're in the standardized test business, and those two things don't necessarily line up that well, the college prep and the testing."

He yearned for what he called "the greatest conversations," the infrequent times when a student came in to say she had been thinking about things they had discussed in class. "It's not only what she got on her last homework," he said, "but about what's going on, sitting around talking about a problem. You can learn a lot that way." In the push to teach girls how to perform better in math, he rarely had the opportunity for that kind of talk.

Mathematics required a good dose of performance art to keep the audience paying attention. In the days before the October 10 SAT tests, Schleunes faced an anxious bunch of girls in pre-calc; though he had juniors as well as seniors, he decided to defer to the older girls' apprehensiveness and offer a few sessions of test preparation. When he handed back a quiz, he deliberately worked one problem after another so that the girls would understand where they had made a mistake. He complimented them frequently on their efforts, though no one had ever earned a test point for trying.

Halfway through a class, he moved on to the homework assignment, asking, "Okay, which ones drove you nuts?" Every girl in the room called out a number.

Schleunes saw the period disappearing, but he dutifully worked the homework on the overhead projector. It was not a good day. One girl worked the problems on her calculator along with her teacher, but one wrote in a journal, three girls in the back row whispered to each other, and another tried to see how far she could stretch her foot along the arm of the desk in front of her before its occupant shoved her away. Only the four girls in the first row paid rapt attention, as though fearful that if they turned around they would be lost, like the others.

Toward the end of the period Schleunes handed out copies of a sample PSAT test, a pre-test usually taken in the junior year, to acquaint students with the SAT format. He tried to reassure the girls: these tests tended to stress the same skills, year after year, and if they stayed focused they would do well.

"Go ahead," he said. "Try the first five problems on the test and we'll go over them."

They ran out of time before anyone finished. As soon as the bell rang, most of the girls rushed for the door—except Lindsay, one of the girls in the front row, who wanted to appeal a single point Schleunes had deducted from her quiz score. She defended her work and asked for the point, and Schleunes gave it to her, as much to acknowledge how hard she worked as anything else. Lindsay was not a kid looking for an easy grade. She struggled every day in this class. She was one of the girls he hoped to hang onto long enough to make a difference.

The point mattered more than he had realized. She pumped her arms up and down and did a little dance.

"All *right*," she crowed. "You broke the curse! A 90! *Not* an 89! I wouldn't mind a 79, or an 84, but not another 89." She walked out of the room singing, "I got a 90, I got a 90. . . ."

DR. JOANN DEAK was the sort of person who liked to lob verbal grenades into a room. A big woman with a deep, friendly voice and an outgoing manner, Dr. Deak had been at the birthplace of the study of female adolescence: The Laurel School, a K–12 private all-girls school in Cleveland, Ohio. In the late 1980s, a Harvard research team run by Harvard professor Carol Gilligan and Colby College assistant professor Lyn Mikel Brown had begun a five-year study at the school, conducting interviews and compiling information about how girls grew—and how they perceived themselves in the larger world. Dr. Deak, the school psychologist, was one of ten Laurel staff members who participated in an annual workshop with the Harvard team.

The results of that study were published in "Meeting at the Crossroads" in 1992, and the process inspired Dr. Deak to look beyond the Harvard project; to find out what other researchers were doing. At the request of the Washington, D.C.–based National Association of Independent Schools, she reviewed existing literature on adolescent girls and education, and in 1998 the NAIS published *How Girls Thrive*, a slim paperback volume that presented Dr. Deak's conclusions. This was the book Barbara Wagner had read during the past summer, the one whose credo—"Competence, Confidence, Connectedness"—she had adopted as her theme for the year. Wagner liked the way Dr. Deak integrated research on girls' emotional issues with their school experience, so she invited her to spend a day at Marlborough, talking to students, faculty, and parents.

Dr. Deak held court in Kurt Schleunes' classroom, meeting with two consecutive groups of math teachers and Deborah Parker, the school's curriculum director. She began with a provocative notion: Math ability, Dr. Deak believed, was developmental, as much a part of a girl's physical growth as the changes that accompanied puberty. But math "maturity" often came so late that teachers and parents misunderstood what was going on. They mistook immaturity for inability, and gave up on a girl before her talent had a chance to emerge. Schools set their math time-clock by a boy's development, which was why girls often performed poorly.

Early studies of brain function showed that many girls simply were not ready for the math they were being taught. Researchers believed that the left and right sides of a girl's brain operated separately until she was between twelve and fourteen. The right side was "the side of the math 'aha!'s, of the epiphanies," Dr. Deak said, "and the left side is more sequential."

Brain researchers had found that the corpus callossum, the center section that connects the two sides, was not fully myelinated—covered by a protective sheath of myelin—until the preteen or early-teen years. Dr. Deak speculated that a girl's true appreciation of math could not occur until that time, when the two sides of her brain were hooked up to each other.

A standard math curriculum could defeat a girl who was a year away from comprehending the ideas her school wanted her to learn. And rigid academic tracks that categorized a student's abilities in seventh grade were unfair to a girl whose talent might not surface until she was sixteen or seventeen. "Once she does click," warned Deak, "she's bored" by work that no longer challenges her.

She cited data on female PhDs in mathematics, who reported that they had not hit their stride until late in their high-school careers or when they were college undergraduates. "They got good grades before that," said Dr. Deak, "all those good little girls, but they didn't really understand the work until rather late in the game."

Boys often faced a similar problem with reading skills in elementary school, where typically they lagged behind the girls. The difference was in the assumptions that parents and teachers made about the gap. Elementary-school remedial reading classes had far more boys in them than girls—but adults assumed that, short of an identifiable learning difficulty like dyslexia, a boy would learn to read, even if it happened when he was seven instead of five. Girls did not get the same benefit of the doubt. Too many people looked at a girl who did poorly in math classes and figured she simply had trouble with math.

Dr. Deak told the math teachers that they had to be far lighter on their feet than if they were teaching boys. They had to distinguish lack of ability from lack of maturity and be prepared to tailor classes to a wide range of students. They had to evaluate the girls more frequently and be flexible about transferring them into a new section. It might sound like special handling, but the alternative was to consign another generation of girls to frustration and failure at a time when the culture demanded higher proficiency in math.

At least 90 percent of all students belonged to what Dr. Deak called "the instructable pool," a group for whom a good teacher made all the difference. "The biggest variable is how they're exposed," she said. "That determines whether they become enthused. It's your job to make a girl excited about math."

One of the older teachers wearily suggested that there was no one right approach for all girls. Dr. Deak shot him a sympathetic smile, but she would not back down.

"Look," she said, "some math talent is developmental. It's like getting graded for height. If you're not done developing yet, you're not going to do as well. But if you're already developed, your brain is done growing, then you're six feet tall and you get an A. I just think math teachers should get paid a million dollars apiece, because you have to figure it all out. You have to help each girl figure out where her brick wall is, and then help them figure out a way around the brick wall, or a bridge over it."

Kurt Schleunes sat through Dr. Deak's second presentation, but he was unconvinced that physiology was at the heart of the problem. He had AP students who understood whatever he threw at them and still did not appreciate their own skill. They were competent; they just did not know it.

"The societal influences are very heavy," said Schleunes. "Any girl in my AP calculus class could be a math major, but they still don't think about it; out there, in the world, it's still not something girls do. And we don't live in a vacuum. No matter what we do here, they go home, they watch TV, they talk to friends. I had two girls last year who wanted to be math majors, and that's the first time since I've been here."

"We have to crack that," said Dr. Deak. "You have to keep the lid off so it's a possibility. Keep the kids in the middle area interested. Make them competent. Otherwise we're going to lose them.

"Of course," she added, "it's still unclear how to do it. We have to get into the business of changing our culture. Good luck."

That evening, JoAnn Deak spoke to a packed auditorium of parents about the virtues of a single-sex environment. She dished out practical suggestions with the enthusiasm of a prizewinning jam maker at the county fair: Creating a successful daughter required attention to everything from hormones ("Have your daughters take the SATs at a high point in their estrogen cycle") to handling a teen's personal crises ("Negative emotions go away with action").

Her analysis of mathematics performance was enough to make even the most self-confident parent shudder. There was far more at stake in math class than an A or a C. According to her review of the research, math ability was an early indicator of a girl's overall success in school. The reverse was also true: A girl's doubts about math were usually the prelude to a host of other problems with self-esteem. And anxiety was a self-fulfilling prophecy. Once a girl started to worry about math, her performance eroded.

The key, Dr. Deak insisted, was good teaching and parental encouragement. "There are very clear emotional, psychological, and attitudinal differences between boys and girls," she said. "The adolescent female brain tends to attach emotions to almost anything, which is why, if a teacher makes a girl feel she is too stupid to live, she won't take a class in that subject again. A boy? He'll say, 'I did poorly in that course; I'll do better next time.' Or, 'That teacher's a jerk; I can't learn anything from him.' Which is why I say, 'a teacher who can grab the heart and the head of a girl will do better than a teacher who only grabs her head.'"

One of the women in the audience was troubled by the notion that girls were ruled by emotion. "How can a parent encourage her child to get over those emotions," she asked, "to not let them get in the way in class, to not let them bother her?"

Dr. Deak laughed. This was where notions of equality collided. There would always be people who defined it in terms of sameness—of opportunity, of abilities, even, as this mother did, of attitude. In her own experience, though, the only way to guarantee a girl equality was to acknowledge that she approached her life differently than a boy did. Expect her to play by a boy's rules, and the boys would always win.

"You're not going to like what I have to say," she replied. "A lobotomy is the first choice. You can teach someone to cope with their emotions, but you can't teach them not to feel. You have to achieve the magical blend: Be nurturing enough, yet always challenge her. Raise the bar, but with your arm around her. Don't *ever* lower the bar for girls."

She left her audience with the evening's one irony, which she delivered with obvious relish. Dr. Deak wanted them to know that the central character in this drama was a girl's father, not her mother. The key to raising an independent, self-confident woman was to have an encouraging, supportive father, a concept that elicited groans, nervous laughs, and a great deal of fidgeting, particularly among the women in the audience. Dr. Deak persisted. For many girls, a father's judgment carried more weight than even the most committed mother's did, down to the most offhand comment.

"I'll shoot you if you ever say anything negative about your daughters' bodies, because the evidence is clear," she warned the men in the room. "It's the kiss of death. The first thing you tease her about? It's the part of her body that she'll feel the most self-conscious about for the rest of her life. She will remember what you said. Same thing goes for grades. Evidence shows that fathers have more influence on girls' achievement than mothers do. Far more effect on goal-setting and aspirations."

Some of the fathers left the auditorium muttering to themselves, reviewing every comment they might have made about their daughters' appearance, wondering if they had already done irreparable harm. Other parents surrounded Dr. Deak to ask questions or buy a copy of her book.

There were times when life for a Marlborough family seemed completely self-conscious; every action premeditated, every comment rehearsed, any spontaneous comment subjected to analysis. Whether a parent or teacher agreed with everything JoAnn Deak said was beside the point. She had confirmed the suspicion that had drawn most of them to an all-girls school in the first place: The world was set up for boys and treacherous for girls. Despite their best intentions, parents were sure to commit grave and unwitting errors.

The objects of all this attention tended to fray as important deadlines approached. In the last days before the SAT tests, the seniors focused on the classes they worried about, like math—and as the tension level increased there, equilibrium demanded that it decrease somewhere else. The girls in Les Klein's Dramatic Literature class came in on Friday morning looking for sympathy. This was the day when symptoms began to surface: potential obstacles that could be recalled and blamed if a girl failed to do as well as she had hoped. One girl had bronchitis but was going to take the SAT anyway, because she had been sick the last time it was offered.

With perverse pride, she explained, "I have the world's worst immune system."

Another girl came in smacking a wad of chewing gum, and stared longingly at a box of doughnuts on Klein's table. She had just been in the Living Room, a lounge open only to seniors, and wanted everyone to know that she had eaten "the grossest breakfast I could think of," which included two doughnuts and three slices of lemon cake.

Klein's response was swift. "Hey, it's your mouth," she said. "You have some control over what you put in it. Why didn't you eat the melon they had out?"

"Because I have SATs tomorrow," said the girl, "and it seemed like a better breakfast for that."

"Wrong, wrong," said Klein. "That melon looked great. Are you addicted to gum?"

"It's the one thing that keeps me from putting other food in my mouth," said the girl. "Sometimes."

Klein tried to get the girls to read aloud a passage from *King Lear*, but they kept laughing for no reason. When one of them mentioned a public-television broadcast of *King Lear* scheduled for the weekend, a plaintive cry arose: Could someone tape it so that they could watch it in class on Monday? Klein knew they would be useless on Monday, as flat after the SAT as they were frantic before it.

"Maybe," she said, in a tone that meant "Yes."

11

The Young Women's Leadership
School of East Harlem
November 1998

I T DID NOT TAKE LONG for the ninth-grade algebra class that Nina Ostrov taught at TYWLS to fall apart. The textbooks arrived late, so she spent the first month writing everything out on the blackboard, waiting while the girls copied the material into their notebooks. As a result, they fell behind—so Ostrov worked through her lessons even more quickly in a frazzled attempt to keep up with the curriculum. Her effort backfired. The girls became more confused, which increased the delays. Two months into the term, they were drowning.

The language barrier only made matters worse. Ostrov was a jolly Russian émigré who favored bright colors and cheery pink lipstick, but she was far more fluent in math than she was in English. Like a tourist caught in a country whose language she did not understand, she tended to repeat the same words over and over again, more loudly each time. She did not have the vocabulary for explanations that might have eased the girls' mounting anxiety.

Most days, her class stuck to a futile rhythm, reviewing the last night's homework until the last few minutes of the period, when Ostrov scrambled to address the material for the coming night's assignment. She often had to help them through the first few homework problems in advance, or risk blank faces and blank pages the next morning. She was determined that today would be different, though. They had spent far too much time on the algebraic order of operation. They had to move on.

Girls like Maryam and Diana managed to keep up, and in self-defense they huddled at the front of the room. The rest fell into two uncooperative camps. The majority were resigned to failure. The disruptive minority, a loud knot of four girls toward the back of the room, were furious at their fate. If Ostrov did not pay attention, they would take the whole class down with them.

Ostrov wrote the homework answers on the board and waited. No one spoke. She pointed to the first answer, smiled, and got fidgety silence in return.

"I have written these on the board, not for myself, but for you," she said. "Come, I will do these, and then you. Do not be afraid to answer. There are no embarrassing answers. Or ask questions. *Please.*"

But asking questions required that the girls be able to articulate what they did not understand, and at this point algebra was as mystifying to the girls as was Ostrov's native tongue. They sat, stonefaced, until Ostrov caved in and worked the problem for them.

She was finishing a third problem when one of the girls finally spoke up.

"I don't think we should go on," she said, "because some of us don't understand this."

"But we are four lessons behind," replied Ostrov.

"But we don't *get* it," the girl whined.

"So please to ask questions," said Ostrov.

There was no reply. After a long moment, Ostrov turned back to the board and began to write.

"I think you have a formula here. There is nothing sophisticated. You have a formula, and you use it."

"We could do it better if we had books," came a voice.

Ostrov's voice rose into a frustrated wail. "We *cannot* stay in the same place," she said. "We need to move."

In an effort to clarify the lesson, Ostrov repeated the proper order of operations in algebraic equations: parentheses, exponents, multiplication and division, addition and subtraction. She wrote six equations on the board to illustrate the rules, but by now exasperation had gotten in the way of the girls' ability to grasp them. One angry girl slammed her notebook shut in disgust. Another put her head down on the desk so that her friends would not see the tears in her eyes.

Ostrov turned her attention to Diana, Maryam, and the other girls in the front, and for ten minutes, with a half-dozen students, math class ran the way she wanted it to: She wrote equations on the board and girls actually offered to work them out. Encouraged, Ostrov tapped on the blackboard and begged the other girls to join in.

"You know," she said, a pleading note in her voice "there is such *light* in my writing. I know sometimes you don't understand my words, what I am saying, but it is so clear in my writing."

"No, it isn't," came a reply from the back of the room. "You jump from thing to thing."

Diana Perez had been silent throughout the class, carefully checking her answers against Ostrov's work on the board. Suddenly she snarled at the complainer, "Just let her finish the lesson."

In the hallway after class, Diana griped about the troublemakers at the back of the room.

Maryam confessed, "I've pretty much written off math class this term. Nina can't explain it well, and the same kids are always complaining. It's so frustrating."

"The lesson was *easy*," Diana replied, "if they'd just be quiet and listen."

By November, Ostrov was gone. In her place was Jenny Long, a Chinese émigré who had come to the United States five years earlier and taught herself English. Her command of the language was no broader than Ostrov's, but Long was more able to communicate an algebraic concept. Ostrov had believed in drill, working problem after problem, and the more belligerent the girls became, the more she relied on the numbers on the board, as though she could wear their resistance down with sheer volume. Long wanted the girls always to recognize the link between a specific problem and a larger mathematical truth.

There was no point in throwing more and more work at them. Long stepped back every so often, to make sure they understood what they were doing. If they could not successfully apply a principle to a new set of numbers, she had failed them.

Anna hardly cared about Long's approach, but she was intrigued by a teacher who, like her, had come to this country without any English. Anna had begun the term at the back of the room, the refuge of the bored and confused, but lately she had been sitting at the front. Today she came in whining loudly about a homework problem that had stumped her, but Long refused to address Anna's frustration until she had completed the day's lesson. Perhaps Anna would find the answer herself, once they had reviewed the basics.

Long always began class by going over the previous day's lesson, so that the girls would have the material fresh in their minds when she reviewed the homework. Half the hour was gone before she got to the assignment, but she felt the class had been a success: no one had lost her temper, there had not been too many interruptions, and most of the girls were still paying attention. She wrote a complicated equation on the board, one that involved negative numbers and exponents, and walked the girls through it.

"Okay, look at the base," she instructed them. "Look at the sign, and think of it as a negative one. For all odd-number powers you get a negative result. For all even-number powers you get a positive result." She smiled triumphantly at the girls. "And this is true for all math teachers. Not just here, but in China, in Japan, in Mexico. All over the world!"

For once, she had them. Long managed to explain a new kind of equation without having to stop to reprimand the girls or repeat herself. She put one example after another up on the board, and the girls began to call out answers. One equation began with a negative number, and when a girl quickly volunteered that A equaled fifteen, a dozen voices cut her off.

"*Negative*," they cried.

Delighted, Long wrote down another example for them to solve. When a couple of girls in the back turned back to their gossip, she taunted them gently, saying, "Always talking, always talking; hope you get it."

Five minutes before the end of class, she allowed Anna to come up to the board to try the homework problem that had eluded her. While the other girls watched, Anna worked through the steps of the equation until she got to a bewildering row of numbers that made her step back from the board. She could not see the next step.

Long refused to finish the work. Instead, she waited while Anna stared at the board, trying to figure out what to do next. Finally, Anna found the common denominator, changed all the fractions, and looked at the equation again. She knew she could reduce the answer even further, but she did not know how.

Long stepped to the board and raised her hands to mask everything but two numbers. Then she waited, hoping that Anna would see for herself what to do. Beaming, Anna wrote the equation out in a simpler form, circled her answer, and put down the chalk. When Long picked up the eraser, Anna raised both her hands to stop her.

"*Don't* erase it," said Anna. She proudly stood next to her handiwork, feeling that today, at least, she had earned her seat alongside the smart girls.

It was 12:28, two minutes before the end of class. The doodlers and gossips at the back of the room noisily began to pack up their things.

"It's time to go," one of them yelled.

Anna stood her ground at the blackboard. "We still have two minutes to go," she said.

Fabrice Fortin wore his black sleeveless sweater, dark shirt, and black jeans with the restrained dignity of a wealthy man in a bespoke suit. A newly minted math teacher in his first year on the job, not yet accredited, Fortin had transformed room 1002 into a place where the girls were made to feel that they had been chosen for better things. He regarded hijinks as aberrant behavior, and he brought the girls back into line with silent disapproval or, at most, a quick, sharp word. He could not afford to be drawn off-track. There was too much to do.

He had achieved an almost eerie calm in his classroom. The girls, caught off-guard by Fortin's respectful air, had not yet figured out how to rile him—or whether they really wanted to. Fortin called his ninth-grade algebra students "Ladies," and rarely told them that they were wrong. He preferred to say that they were almost right, or to entreat the class to help a friend if she was having trouble at the board. He strolled the aisles between the tables and put an encouraging hand on a girl's shoulder or spoke approvingly of any student who made a sincere effort. At the back of the room, behind his desk, was an array of the best tests from all of his classes, under a banner that read MATH SUPER STARS. There was a written comment on each one: "Outstanding job." "Terrific." "Great Work."

Fortin was unique in one other way: He was black, the only minority teacher the ninth graders had. Ostrov and Long did not count; the girls considered them foreigners. Peter DeWan could tell his history students that they were as much a part of society as he was, but he was white, which set him apart. Sarah Kirkpatrick, the English teacher, was white, as were Cindy Jackson and Shirley Gasich, who taught science. The girls assumed that those teachers had enjoyed a privileged childhood that TYWLS students missed. But not Fortin. He was as close as they got to a role model, a young black man who had built a solid life for himself.

Until the Regents exam, there was no way to tell whether Fortin's understated approach would bear fruit—but most of the girls in his section paid strict attention. They sat up a little straighter; if one girl decided she had to touch up her nail polish, she was furtive about the defection—unlike the girls in Ostrov's, and now Long's, class, who liked to distract their friends from the lesson. Fortin's students figured that the usual excuses would not work with him, and behaved as though his disapproval would be particularly hard to bear.

Fortin's class was ahead of the other section. For today's lesson, he had written on the board, "AIM: How do we divide a polynomial by a monomial," and in the DO NOW box he had written two review problems for the girls to do, as a warm-up, while they waited for class to start. His straight-forward approach paid off: When he picked two girls to work the problems on the board, a third complained about being passed over. It took little to win their hearts. All Fortin had to do was treat them like the capable students he wanted them to become.

But overload was a constant threat, and as the lesson wore on, some of the girls began to fade. Amy Lopez, who had started the year at the top of this class, was stuck between two defectors, one girl who was reapplying her still-vivid lipstick, and another who was examining her manicure. Amy tried to concentrate on her notes, but she was a sociable girl, and Fortin could see that she needed help.

He counseled the others without breaking stride. "C'mon," he said, quietly, "right up here, thank you. Please pay attention," and then it was back to the equations.

When he felt that the girls had grasped the basic concepts, he asked them to work problems from the textbook. One of them looked at the first problem and moaned, "Fabrice, we're stupid children," so he stood next to her while she struggled. Amy admitted that she was unsure of her answer. Fortin read over her shoulder and congratulated her. "You got it," he said. "Keep going."

Amy was not one of the girls who volunteered to put her work on the board, though. Four other students went up, and proudly signed their board work—

"By Tanisha!!!"

"By Stephanie."

"By Peanut."

"By Jazmin."

When Fortin asked for more volunteers, Amy kept her head down and fiddled with her calculator. He leaned over to ask her if she wanted to go to the board, but she turned him down. She was uncertain about today's lesson, a fact she hardly wanted to advertise to her classmates, who considered her one of the smartest girls in the room. In truth, Amy agreed with them—but being smart was not the same as having discipline, and Amy was known for letting her attention waver. There would always be another chance to work at the board. Today, she let herself be lured into a conversation about her neighbor's newly striped fingernails.

All the teachers liked to post work. It was a good way to reward the students who made an effort and to encourage the others to try harder next time. The current exhibit outside of Peter DeWan's room was a set of timelines that the girls had drawn up to mark the milestones in their short lives. Most of them were crowded with information: birthdays, anniversaries, bits of family news. The shortest one had only a half-dozen entries, including:
"Started to go out with Frankie."
"Sister pregnant and diagnosed with HIV."

On Wednesday, November 18, TYWLS held the first parent conferences of the year. One of the things Celenia Chevere demanded was that parents show up for two mid-term conferences, one in the fall, one in the spring, to find out how their girls were doing while there was still time to salvage a semester grade. The mid-term comments and grades did not go into the permanent record. They were intended as a reality check.

Cindy Jackson showed her ninth-grade biology students their grades the day before the conference, so that they could prepare for their parents' reactions. Other teachers divulged grades to favorite students. Diana Perez managed to find out all her mid-term grades the day before the conferences, and as soon as her mother got home from work, she gave her the good news: A's in biology and biology Regents Prep, an A+ in history, an A– in English, A's in art and physical education. She got a B in Japanese, which frustrated her, and a B in math, which she dismissed. Now that she had a better math teacher, the grade undoubtedly would go up.

The Perez family lived in a twenty-story housing project in Harlem, where a sign proclaiming community pride stood next to one, in Spanish, warning about rat poison on the lawn. Maria and James Perez had grown up in projects like these, and shared a single purpose, which was to make sure that their children got out.

Maria and James had been married since 1983, and between them they had nine children—Maria's grown son and James's two grown daughters, from earlier relationships, and six daughters together. James joked that with so many girls growing up so fast, he could hardly keep track of what grade they were in. It was Maria who fought for them, since her own childhood memories were of one missed chance after another.

Her family had moved to New York from Puerto Rico in 1963, when Maria was eight. She learned English at school, and spent one happy year playing violin in a school-subsidized program, but there was no money for more advanced lessons, nor anyone to help her look for financial aid. She went to an all-girls public high school, and loved it, but never expected to go to college. Maria got pregnant at nineteen, and split up with the baby's father a year after her son was born.

Five years later, she started going out with James. Ever since they got married, Maria had devoted herself to making sure that her children escaped her fate—pregnant too young, lacking the education or money she needed to buy another opportunity. She guided James's older daughter into a special program for minority students, which led to a scholarship to a private girls' school. Linda had graduated with honors and now attended Hunter College at night. She worked for a real estate company, lived with her boyfriend, wrote poetry, and dreamed of someday becoming a writer.

She was a beacon to the younger girls and an inspiration to Maria, who vowed that none of her daughters would ever go to the local public school.

James and Maria built their lives on one immutable rule: "The girls cannot be left alone." James had to be at his job at 8:30 in the morning, so he left early, and Maria got the girls up and dressed and fed. Once the older ones had left for school, she took the three-year-old to day care in the building and went to work. James got off work at 4:30, and by five was in the kitchen starting dinner. When Maria got home, well after seven, he had a hot meal on the table. The family dinner was the high point of the day, the one hour out of twenty-four when the family was together. Then Maria cleaned up while the girls got ready for bed, and James relaxed with a cigarette.

During the week, his word was law. Even the youngest girls had a job to do at home, to teach them responsibility. Washing the nightly dinner dishes had been Diana's job, but this year her father asked her to do them only twice a week. He had done the same for Linda when she was in high school, and now it was Diana's turn to devote herself to schoolwork—as long as she understood that this was special treatment, and that she had to deliver good grades in return.

Once Friday afternoon rolled around, James shifted gears. The girls often came home from school to the sounds of Motown and the sight of their father dancing to one of his favorite groups—the Temptations, the Coasters, the Five Satins, the Tokens, James loved them all. In nice weather he took the older girls bike riding in Central Park. And every Saturday morning he took one or two of them out for breakfast, on a rotating schedule, since feeding all six at once was a fast way to go broke.

The apartment was James's territory. If he had not yet had the chance to visit TYWLS, Maria was better than he was at talking to the teachers about Diana's progress. It was his job to provide structure once the girls got home from school.

Diana was her mother's shining star. Late at night, after the younger girls had gone to sleep, they sat together on the living-room couch and talked about the future. The farthest away any of her children had gone so far was the Bronx, where Linda lived, but Maria loved to listen to Diana spin fantasies of where she might go to college. Diana went to camp one summer and met a counselor who had gone to school in London, and for weeks afterward she told her mother that that was where she would go. They talked about California and Boston. Diana shared Linda's dream of becoming a writer; she believed that talent ran in the family. She staunchly insisted that Maria was a good writer who had lacked only the chance to do something about it.

Every time Diana got a good report, the talk got headier. She and Maria savored the written comments on the first ninth-grade report. The biology teacher had written, "If she continues performing at this level, she will pass the Regent's exam in June!" Peter DeWan said she had done high-quality work in history, and suggested only that she work on her writing skills "to increase her academic ability." Sarah Kirkpatrick said that all Diana needed for a solid A in English was "a little extra preparation for spelling and vocabulary quizzes," and praised her for missing very few classes. Her mother reassured her about the B in Japanese:

"She really can't give you an A right off the bat, unless you have prior knowledge of the language," said Maria. "You get an A right off, first thing, then you get a little laid-back." Not that she expected her daughter to listen. Diana pushed herself harder than her parents did.

There was an unspoken competition among the best students at TYWLS to see who could build up the most impressive list of extracurricular credits, and this year Diana had constructed a daunting schedule for herself. Monday, the only day she came straight home from school, was her "day off," the day she allowed herself to visit a friend in the building after she finished her homework. Tuesday was ice-skating at Harlem's Riverbank Park, where a group called Figure Skaters of Harlem ran an after-school program that Diana attended, thanks to an anonymous benefactor Chevere had found who paid the prohibitive $200 equipment and entry fee. She went straight to the park from school, spent an hour on her homework, and then skated until 7:30.

On Wednesday she worked on the school newspaper afternoons, and every Wednesday and Thursday she picked up an eight-year-old boy at his after-school program and took care of him until his parents got home around 8:30. She cared for him on Fridays as well, but got done an hour earlier. Saturday morning at 9:30 she was back at the ice rink for another two-hour session. Once ice-skating was over, Diana hoped to join a mentoring program at Metropolitan Hospital.

She kept track of all her activities in her daily planner, and relished every chance to cross off an entry that she had completed. Diana took great pride in being organized. It was the one thing she believed she had inherited from James.

Maria's only concern was that her daughter not take on more than she could handle. She knew Diana's cycle. She would try to do too many things, only to find that she could not do them well enough to suit her exacting standards. That would upset her—and lead to what Maria called a "letdown," where Diana's performance began to suffer because she was feeling blue. Maria tried to help her daughter find a balance. Diana needed to do enough to single herself out, but not so much that she collapsed under the weight of her obligations.

12

ALL THE TEACHERS AGREED that Amy Lopez was a promising member of the pioneer class. In an idle moment they might debate who stood the best chance of victory, as defined by a college scholarship: Maryam Zohny, whose impeccable record betrayed a cautious obedience; Diana Perez, a more subtle thinker who was reluctant to assert herself in class; or Amy, thought by some to be the brightest, but clearly the least disciplined, of the three. Amy had an unpredictably reckless side. She would do anything to beat her classmates in sports, where winning was a clear matter of speed or skill, and her favorite after-school activity was whatever neighborhood ball game she could get in on. The teachers still talked about her climbing prowess at the Outward Bound weekend back in September, at which she had scrambled up the abandoned airfield control tower faster than anyone else.

Success in the classroom required patience and thoughtfulness, which often eluded her. Amy was her own worst enemy, satisfied with a quick answer or a last-minute cram session, when a more modulated approach was what was needed. A pretty girl, with a slender figure and huge brown eyes behind her wire-rimmed eyeglasses, she was frustrated by any activity that lacked pace, whether it was preparation for an exam or the contemplation required for an analytical report. She seemed never to be standing still.

By the time she got home after school, Amy was ready for a little TV or, more often, a nap. Lately the nap had stretched until dinnertime, which meant she rarely started her homework before 8:30. Many nights her father had to interrupt her at one o'clock in the morning to tell her to turn off the computer and get to sleep, even if she wasn't finished with her work. The next morning she woke up tired, which fairly guaranteed another afternoon nap.

The day before her parents' conference, Amy managed to collect most of her interim grades, which gave her twenty-four hours to prepare for her parents' reaction. The B in physical education would hardly concern her parents, but it was an insult to a girl who considered herself a natural athlete. She complained loudly to her friends that she would have had an A but for a single afternoon's absence.

The other grades were not what she had hoped for, either. She had gotten a B+ in art, but her academic subjects were not as strong: A B– in history, a B in English, a B in math, and a C in biology, hardly an impressive grade for an aspiring doctor. Her only A was in Japanese.

She did not know how she was going to tell her parents about the C.

"They always said, if I got a C and that was my best, they would be proud of me," said Amy, "but if I got a C and they knew I could do better—and *I* knew I could do better—they're going to be upset. Not upset. They're just going to be a little disappointed."

Amy knew where the C in Biology had come from. She had failed to finish her biology homework because her church friends from California had come to town and she had ignored her schoolwork. They were still in town when Amy was supposed to be studying for an important biology test, and when she rushed through a history report and lost what had been a solid B in the class.

She could not blame her teachers, as much as she might like to. Her science teacher, Cindy Jackson, always asked for Friday assignments on Tuesday, instead of Monday, in case a girl had a busy weekend. And Peter De-Wan had talked to Amy about how to organize her thoughts for a history report, rather than sit down and dash off a draft. It was all a matter of her own discipline. Even as she prepared to defend her mid-term report, she vowed privately to get a jump on her science homework and to spend more time working on her written reports.

Amy tried to console herself. She had met her stated goal, which was to get no grade lower than a C. She had set the goal herself, back in September, because her parents were in California on a church trip and had been unable to attend the scheduled conference. "I'm a new ninth grader," she had reasoned with herself. "I know I'm going to college soon, and it's going to be hard." With no one around to suggest that she push herself, she purposely set a standard that would be easy enough to reach. She had to admit, now, that it did not feel like much of a victory.

She had excelled at her other goal, which was to have a life beyond homework. Amy believed that there were three groups at TYWLS: the grinds, who only cared about studying; the girls who wanted a social life as well as good grades; and the failures, who clung to passing grades by their fingernails, either unable or unwilling to do the work. She disdained the failures, but she had grown impatient with girls like Maryam, who always seemed too busy to have a good time. Amy was proud to belong to the middle group, the girls who hung out at the McDonald's on Lexington Avenue after school rather than rush right home to do their homework.

Amy's father, Robinson Lopez, Tito to everyone who knew him, did not like to look over his shoulder at the past. It scared him. His father had died when he was seven, and his mother had gone on welfare to feed and clothe her six children. By the time Tito was a teenager, he was on his way to being lost. "There were gangs, there was drugs, things like that," he allowed, his sorrowful eyes averted. He might have ended up dead, from an overdose or a fight, if not for members of the Apostolic Assembly of the Faith in Jesus Christ, urban missionaries who got him into a residential program in Nebraska for troubled teens.

Three years later, eighteen-year-old Tito moved back to New York, got a job, joined a church, and started dating fourteen-year-old Sandra Calderon. Two years later, pregnant, Sandra dropped out of high school. They named their first child Robinson Lopez Jr., and when he was a year old Sandra moved out of her parents' apartment and married Tito.

He eventually found work as an itinerant minister at a couple of small churches, and in 1985 was able to take over a storefront church in Queens. Now Tito traveled throughout the United States and Central America, lecturing to teenagers about resisting temptation. They tended to listen to him, because he knew just how easy it was to stumble.

His wife, Sandra, had always felt safe. Her Puerto Rican parents had come to this country and landed jobs; her mother had taught herself English and got a bachelor's degree. After Amy was born, Sandra had gone back to school for her high school equivalency degree, and now she worked alongside her mother at the Board of Education's special education department. She also took classes part-time toward a college degree.

Sandra was a placid woman who referred to herself as "the disciplined one" in the family. She insisted that she, Tito, and Amy sit down together to review Amy's report—the teachers' comments as well as the grades.

Sarah Kirkpatrick was concerned about Amy's waning interest in English class, and had written, "Her last test was lower than her first. She must put in equal effort over time to maintain and improve her grade."

Peter DeWan implied that her B– would have been an A had she kept up with the homework. "Overall, Amy is an excellent student with good behavior and participation in class activities. . . . She has missed several assignments, and this has brought her grade down several points."

Fabrice was blunt about the B in math. "Has ability to be 'A' student," he wrote.

And Cindy Jackson wondered what had become of Amy's initial enthusiasm in biology class. "Amy had completed some beautiful work at the beginning of the year," she wrote, "but currently it is slacking off. She had a great potential for scoring an 'A'."

At the last minute, Jackson had gone back and changed the "d" in "had" to an "s," so it read, "She *has* a great potential for scoring an 'A'," but it would not be easy. Amy needed to pay attention, spend more time studying, show up for class on time, stop talking in class, and stop turning work in late.

Jackson had checked off the box next to, "Performance not meeting potential."

Tito begged Amy to do better. "You've got to do the best you can," he said. "New York City is not going to be our life forever. We need to do better than this. I don't want to see my kids do nothing with their life."

Sandra took a more pragmatic approach. She reassured her daughter, saying, "I'm satisfied *for now,*" but she was clear about her expectations for the semester grade in January. "Go up to your potential," she told Amy. "Don't settle for mediocre."

She bought Amy an organizer, to reduce the chance that she would let an assignment go until the last minute. Tito advised her to do her homework as soon as she got home and go to sleep at a more reasonable hour. Chagrined, Amy vowed to do it all; to make them proud when semester grades came out at the end of January.

Maryam Zohny got straight A's, with an A+ in Japanese and an A– in Art, so she went to the art teacher to find out what the minus was all about and was told she needed to remember her smock. Having promised herself straight A's through high school, Maryam was irked, but she swore never again to forget the smock.

Everything else was the way she wanted it to be: Sarah Kirkpatrick praised her for speaking up more often, and Peter DeWan wrote, "Her hard work and dedication will almost certainly enable her to accomplish what she needs to in this term, and during the rest of this course." Shirley Gasich, her biology teacher, said she had performed "at an outstanding level. . . . If she continues performing at this level, she will pass the Regent's exam in June." The Japanese teacher, unable to describe Maryam's achievement within the normal 100-point range, gave her an A+, 102 points, and wrote, "Maryam brings an attitude of focus, respect, and good humor to whatever she does."

Her mother, Afaf, breezed in and out of the parent conferences in record time. DeWan told her it was always nice to see her—but after all, with a girl like Maryam, there was nothing to discuss. The only advice he could think of was to encourage Maryam *not* to work so hard: to take time off and have a little fun. He spent five minutes reiterating his praise of Maryam and then sent Afaf on her way.

Afaf felt a tremulous pride at her youngest child's achievement. The only way Maryam could fulfill her dream of going away to college was if she received financial aid, and for that she had to stand out from the rest of her class. But sometimes Maryam's talk about colleges in New England, or even California, frightened her mother. She reminded her four children, again and again, that they were of a different religion, a different culture, than their neighbors. Family and church were familiar and safe. Anything outside of that circle worried Afaf. If Maryam decided to go away to college, it would break her mother's heart.

She tried not to think about it.

"I'm just proud," said Maryam's mother. "I'm happy that she's happy."

CINDY JACKSON KNEW all about dreams. She had taught elementary school for thirteen years, first in her hometown of Fayetteville, Indiana, and then in a suburb of Atlanta, Georgia. A year ago, the thirty-seven-year-old would-be actress had quit her job to move to Manhattan, the first stop on a journey that was supposed to end in Los Angeles with a regular role in a situation comedy. It began instead with a detour: Manhattan was too expensive, so she moved in with her pregnant sister and brother-in-law in New Jersey and commuted an hour and a half each way to TYWLS. She stayed in the city two afternoons a week to attend acting classes.

No one was allowed to give up in Jackson's science classes. The day after parent conferences, she began class with a brief lecture. A C was not the mark of failure. A C was a wake-up call. The girls had two months to change her mind.

"Those of you with C's can get B's and A's," she said, marching up and down the aisle between the tables. "Those of you in the cellar with a failing grade can get a C or even a B by the second week of December. You can do it. But: Do not *ever* miss an assignment. Turn them in as you breathe. Forty percent of your grade is homework, forty percent is tests. So even if you don't do so hotsy-totsy on your tests, you can get 100's on these assignments. Where does that get you? A C. Maybe even a B. Turn them in, do it well, do it on time. It's like Nike: *Just do it!*"

Jackson refused to let the girls build a grade with extra credit. They had to do the assigned work, and she promised them that in the coming weeks the load would increase. It was the only way to get them ready for the Biology Regents exam in June.

"So get ready," she said, "because I *live* to make your life harder." She sat on the edge of one of the tables, and when she spoke again there was a sweeter tone. Jackson marveled at some of these girls, like Anna, who had taught herself English and always did the work. She held out hope for girls like Amy, who had only to decide not to squander this chance. If she was tough with grades, it was because she saw no advantage to coddling them with empty praise.

"And listen," she said. "I do not want to hear, 'I can't do it.' That is not part of my vocabulary, so it cannot be a part of yours. I will not accept it. If you start to think you cannot do it, that's the time to seek help. Say, 'Self, I need help. I am learning, and part of learning is to ask for help.' That's it. I'm done for the morning. Got to get my mothering in."

13

Marlborough School

December 1998

THE STARS OF the Marlborough School sports program, the varsity volleyball players, had first call on the gymnasium after school, so Ed Sung, the assistant basketball coach, had to work his Middle School hopefuls where he could. First he had them run twenty-one sets of the stairs outside the performing-arts wing. When they were done, he lined them up on their backs to do abdominal crunches, their knees bent and their feet pressed against a wall of lockers.

"I'll never walk again," wailed one girl.

"My God," said another, "I can't move."

Alex Siegel, her face flushed from the exertion, kept her mouth shut and did more crunches.

Sung walked the line. "Raise your hands if you're feeling pain in your neck," he hollered, and three-fourths of the girls, including Alex, raised their hands. He advised them to try again, and to concentrate on using their abdominal muscles, not their necks, to raise their torsos off the floor.

Next, sets of fifteen push-ups. Sung told the girls to call out the numbers in unison. If they failed, they had to start over again. On the second set, they got stuck on number six and had to start over four times. A couple of girls started to fade, but one yelled, "*C'mon!*" knowing that the shortest route to relief was to finish.

"Oh, my arms hurt so bad."

"Look at my knees."

"Ed, do you have a Band-Aid?"

He sent them on ten laps around the perimeter of the second floor. As they ran, two girls ambled up the stairs to watch the athletes. They complained enviously about the ones who managed never to break a sweat, but they saved their real ire for a very slender girl who ran effortlessly at the front of the pack.

"Hey, you're losing weight," one of the girls called out sarcastically. She turned to a teacher who had just come up the stairs. "Do you know she can tell the calorie count of *any*thing? I can't eat an orange without her saying, 'You know how many calories are in that?' She says you can get by on three grams of fat a day."

The teacher attempted an offhanded tone. "Well, that's the very low end of a low-fat diet," she said. "It's really not too good for teenagers."

After the teacher had walked away, the girl smiled at her friend. "That's what I think," she said. "I want to grow. I want to have good hair and nice teeth, so I'm going to eat."

She waited a beat before delivering the punch line.

"McDonald's this morning, and Taco Bell tonight." They walked off, laughing, as the other girls kept running around the second floor.

Alex Siegel had started playing basketball with her dad when she was ten. Eric discovered the game in college, and he still liked to grab a pickup game when he had the time, so he set up a hoop in the front yard and taught Alex the basics.

He encouraged her to try out for the Marlborough team, even though it guaranteed a nine-hour school day during the season, not counting the half-hour commute each way. The chance for Alex to play on a team was one of the great attractions of a girls' school, as far as Eric was concerned. The girls' teams didn't have to fight for resources with a more firmly entrenched boys' athletic program. They had everything they needed: equipment, courts and coaches. Marlborough even had a "no-cut" policy for a different Middle-School sport each season, which meant that any girl who tried out got to play. This term, it was basketball—even the stragglers who hobbled through their final laps would make the team, alongside more experienced players like Alex.

Athletics provided the girls with a new way to distinguish themselves—or, as the parents of some of the older girls saw it, a new variable on the road to a college acceptance. If Alex's father prized teamwork for his quiet older daughter, Jon Tower continued to wonder about Katie's fate, without a single school sport to her credit. A girl who was not on a team stuck out as though she had given up mathematics in the ninth grade. Katie's black belt in karate might not make up for the deficit.

All the seniors knew which volleyball star had been offered a free ride at a private university and which tennis player had hopes of early decision at an Ivy League school. Their successes made some parents and staff, most notably Middle School Dean of Students Jim Skrumbis, feel that the "no-cut" policy was a mistake. Girls with more enthusiasm than ability got to play, when perhaps they ought to be directed to an activity where they were likelier to succeed. Talented athletes often felt that their efforts were diluted by their less-capable classmates. Losing in the name of community was still losing.

Skrumbis had already talked to Barbara Wagner about his desire to build a more competitive sports program. Inclusiveness for its own sake was no way to build a winning team—and no way to attract college recruiters looking for top athletes. Marlborough might be better off with a two-tiered program, with serious athletes competing on teams and the rest of the girls relegated to an intramural program. Genteel democracy did not breed sports stars.

JON AND CABEL TOWER finally issued an ultimatum on the Saturday of Thanksgiving break: Katie was not leaving the house until she had completed her application essay for the University of California, which would go to both Berkeley and San Diego. She had finished the essays for the east-coast schools, the University of Chicago, and the University of Southern California, but the UC application had to be in the mail by November 30. No matter how badly Katie wanted to go to school back east, she had to take the UC application seriously. Because she was a California resident, these schools represented insurance—and, at about $13,000 annually, a tremendous bargain compared to private tuition, which ran upward of $30,000 per year.

It turned into a day-long face-off, from 8:30 in the morning until 10:30 at night, with breaks for food and arguments. Everyone yelled. Katie cried. Her parents, both of whom had been English majors, found fault with everything Katie wrote—and the more she wrote, the more exasperated she got.

Jon Tower hated the whole exercise, because he believed it penalized kids like Katie, who were so decent and hardworking as to seem almost boring. But he never saw the point in complaining about the rules; the trick was to prevail in spite of them. He advised her, "You've got to make this thing stand out from those kids who are going to write, 'Both my parents had polio, I was sent to prison at three, and I had my prison-wall scratchings published when I was four.'"

On Monday, exhausted but finished with her essay, Katie headed for a lunchtime advisory session with her friend Lisl. The idea behind the advisory was to build little communities inside the school, groups of no more than a dozen girls who met briefly every morning with a faculty advisor. Advisories gave new seventh graders a built-in set of potential friends and a dependable adult to whom they could turn, and they provided continuity for the older girls.

The advisories met occasionally for longer sessions, which were supposed to be a time for emotional housecleaning, reflection, and quiet conversation, but with the early-decision letters a week or two away, the seniors needed to blow off steam. One of the girls in Katie's group had brought in a tape of the movie *Flirting with Disaster* and set up a monitor in the lobby of the arts wing.

The girls settled in with Chinese take-out, but as the tape started, Katie announced loftily that she refused to watch any movie in which a woman exposed her breasts to her potential daughter-in-law. She retired with Lisl to one of the photo labs, to complain about the application process.

Lisl, an early applicant to Brown University, laughed at Katie's tale of woe. Lisl had had open-heart surgery when she was a little girl. Her life was custom-built for the dramatic essay.

"Your problem," she told Katie, "is that you haven't had a traumatic life." Lisl had heard of a girl who had lied on her application, blaming her bad grades on being gay and having to care for a nonexistent ailing grandmother. "They don't really want to know who you are at all," Lisl said. "They just want to hear what compensates for the dents in your grades."

Katie was fed up with the process. There were very few dents in her grades, which were almost all A's. If her grades held this term, she would be one of a handful of seniors invited to join the school's prestigious Cum Laude society. But the game had changed. Being an excellent student at Marlborough was no longer sufficient. Now she had to convince some anonymous admissions officers that she was better than thousands of other kids who had almost all A's from good college-prep schools. It required the kind of bragging, she said, that only a "crazed ego" could produce, and she was not about to sell herself like that.

It was hard to resist, though, with everyone around her swapping rumors that ate away at her confidence. She had heard that the highest combined SAT score at one competing high school was 1430, which was higher than her score of 1400. She had heard that Harvard–Westlake, one of Los Angeles's most prestigious coeducational prep schools, had the highest math scores in the city, but that Marlborough might have higher verbal scores. And what if the Harvard–Westlake math scores belonged to boys? Had the girls there done as well in math? It was impossible to shut out all the buzz, and what she heard made her a little frantic.

"It's all about impressing the schools," she said, "or making up stories about why you don't sound impressive."

She tried to convince herself that she was not worried. "I don't feel like if I don't get into a particular school my life will end," she said. "I mean, I'd really like to go to Brown or Princeton or Chicago, but if one doesn't work out, something else will."

During the first week of December, the two college counselors, Dr. Lewandowski and Monica Ward, met to divide the list of early-action candidates in half. It was time to start calling admissions officers, to see if they could pry loose any information. Some schools, like Princeton, had a policy of not responding to such inquiries, but some schools might at least provide a hint of which girls, if any, were likely to be accepted. Dr. Lewandowski and Ms. Ward never informed the girls themselves, which would guarantee a stampede by all the other applicants, but they did share the information with Barbara Wagner.

It gave them a chance to prepare their own response to the news. "You have to be excited for the girls who are happy," said Ward, "and be prepared for those who didn't get in."

When Dr. Lewandowski called Harvard, she learned only that there might be cause for optimism regarding one of Marlborough's four early applicants. She did not know whether the committee favored Christina Kim, or the legacy applicant, or one of the other two. The other seniors might be convinced that Christina was a shoo-in, but Dr. Lewandowski knew better. Harvard's applicant pool was full of multifaceted valedictorians. It was her job to remain steady, while the girls went "absolutely nuts," as she put it, waiting for December 15.

Over the December 12 weekend, two girls received letters of acceptance from Princeton and one girl got in at Yale. They came to school on Monday, December 14, without a care in the world. They had been spared another four months of worrying. They were safe.

The other early candidates frittered the day away, knowing that there would likely be a letter waiting for them when they got home. The drill had not changed since their parents were in college. A fat envelope meant good news, because it included pages of information for the prospective student. A thin envelope was almost always bad news.

Christina lived only six blocks away, in a tiny, white-stucco house that sat behind a tired front lawn bleached from too many untended years in the afternoon sun. It was the sort of house that made privacy difficult; an alcove had been turned into a bedroom, and the kitchen extended into the living room for want of anywhere else to go. To protect herself, Christina had announced a set of rules. Starting in the first week of December, only Christina would take in the mail. She intended to march with it directly into her bedroom, and then look to see if the letter from Harvard had arrived. Whatever the news was, she would take "a minute or two to deal with it," she said, before she emerged to tell her parents. Under no circumstances were they to knock on her bedroom door.

Her parents acquiesced. No matter how imperturbable Christina seemed at school, they understood what was at stake. A Harvard acceptance was incontrovertible proof that Christina had prevailed despite severe obstacles.

She had been diagnosed with juvenile diabetes when she was eight. Managing the disease had required years of vigilance, since anything from a growth spurt to too much exercise could set off symptoms. Even a long night's sleep, one of the uninterrupted luxuries of childhood, was enough to disrupt Christina's blood-sugar levels and cause her to wake up before dawn, in pain. Youngsook quit working when Christina was diagnosed and was constantly at her daughter's side, her private nurse as well as her mother. When Christina was in fifth grade, a new insult was added: She was diagnosed with scoliosis, and had to wear a back brace until halfway through ninth grade.

At the end of Christina's junior year at Marlborough, she got a new weapon in her battle for independence—a Minimed pump, which rode on her belt like a pager and dispensed measured amounts of insulin through a tiny catheter. She could monitor herself and adjust the insulin flow as she needed it. The days of feeling ill during the last class period before lunch were over. The pump was physical proof that she could be on her own.

The world had finally aligned itself in Christina's favor. Having been tethered to home for so long, she made outsized plans. That was what Harvard meant to her: freedom.

She promised herself that there would be no histrionics. "I do a lot of stuff in my head," she said, as she waited for Monday to end. "I laugh or cry in my head. With news as big as this, I'll read it a million times."

THE SENIOR CLASS meeting provided a welcome diversion—the first discussion of this year's graduation dress. Marlborough tradition decreed that all graduating seniors wear formal white dresses, and since World War II they had worn identical gowns—a tricky proposition, since the seniors came in all shapes and sizes. Dresses were a nice, safe place to dump the collective anxiety, so the debate quickly devolved into a heated argument about spaghetti straps, which flattered the smaller girls but required girls with larger breasts to invest in a strapless bra and hope it stayed in place.

Objections started flying:

"I'm going to be falling out of that dress."

"I'm going to look slutty."

"You can't *get* a strapless bra in a D cup."

Some of the girls got so frustrated they started to cry. They said hateful things about the dress and hurled insults at each other, all the while bemoaning the way their bodies looked. Christina missed the debate, but she showed up in time to see the tear-splotched faces and hear the parting shots. It made her laugh. For all the anxiety, this was "a terrible and wonderful time," she thought, full of feeling.

Christina raced home as soon as school was over. Her mother was inside, and all the mail was still in the mailbox. Christina hesitated. She could do what she had sworn to do and take the mail into her room, or she could carry the stack into the house and paw through it with her mother, who she knew must be dying of suspense. Or she could look right now, standing on the concrete steps.

Christina found the envelope, and her heart fell. It was thin. She nursed a small hope—perhaps the rules were different for early candidates—that vanished as soon as she opened the envelope and read the first phrase, "After careful consideration." That was it, she thought stoically. They never said that after careful consideration they were delighted to say yes.

She continued to read. "After careful consideration," Harvard had deferred a decision on Christina's application until the admissions committee convened again in the spring. It was not quite as humiliating as an out-and-out rejection, but she knew that the odds on deferred applications were not good. They might as well have turned her down.

Christina walked into the kitchen and put the envelope down in front of her mother. In a forced, offhand tone, she said, "Oh. I got deferred." Then she burst into tears.

Christina had never been one for self-pity. A good thirty-second cry, another thirty seconds of what she called a "temper tantrum," which consisted of muttering "No fair, no fair" several times over, and that was it. Christina had bet on herself and lost. She was not angry, but for a moment she felt a cold regret. She had devoted six years to academics, six years she could not reclaim, and for what? She could not have done more, but she wondered, mournfully, if she would have been happier doing a little less. She decided she was bitter about one thing: "For the past six years, especially the past four years, I have totally filled myself trying to make everything run, and keep going, and balance everything. And if I had actually slept ten hours one night, and just forgotten about the test the next day, it wouldn't have made a difference."

By the next morning, she had reasoned her way to a more optimistic conclusion. Earlier in the year, her SAT scores had been mixed up with another Christina Kim's. What if no one had untangled the confusion? Clearly, Harvard had meant to accept her and reject the other girl. The deferral was a mistake.

When Christina got to school on Tuesday, she went directly to Dr. Lewandowski's office and pleaded with her to call Harvard. Dr. Lewandowski complied, not because she thought there was a mistake but because Christina was so distraught. Harvard had deferred all four early applicants, but the other three girls were far less upset. "This," Dr. Lewandowski believed, "was a goal of her life." So she called the Harvard admissions office, and was informed that there was no error. Christina Kim, class of 1999 at Marlborough School, had been deferred.

Dr. Lewandowski tried to get Christina's mother on the phone to explain that there had not been a mixup, but no one answered. Christina would have to go home again today and tell her mother for a second time that Harvard had turned her down.

This was the hardest part of the early-decision process, the terrible emotional letdown that the counselors had warned the girls about. Dr. Lewandowski leafed through Christina's folder, trying to make sense of Harvard's decision. She did have a few B's in her record, from several years ago. That could be enough to keep her out, given the caliber of students she had to compete against. She could not afford any more B's if she had any hope of being accepted by Harvard in the spring. In a few days, when Christina was feeling better, Dr. Lewandowski would remind her that there was still a chance, however small.

Les Klein wandered into the college counseling office looking for news, and when Dr. Lewandowski told her about the Harvard deferrals, Klein winced as though she were in pain. There was no way to prepare a student for disappointment inflicted by strangers. The best she could do was discourage them from turning on themselves. Klein remembered what JoAnn Deak had said about the ways that boys and girls handled disappointment. Boys tended to look for explanations outside themselves, like a bad teacher or a cold that had cost them sleep. Girls more often turned their sorrow on themselves. As the senior-class grade-level leader, Klein felt protective of all the girls. She rushed back outside, determined not to intrude, but eager to be available in case a girl was ready to confide in someone.

Christina wondered what to do. One of the other girls had managed to keep her early application to Harvard a secret from all but a few teachers and friends, and today she continued to pretend rather than confess her disappointment. Christina did not have the option of secrecy, since everyone had bought into Christina's dream of going to Harvard. Although she had told only a couple of friends about her deferment, other girls came up to her to say that they were sorry. She assumed that by now, almost everyone knew.

She did not want to be an object of pity. When she saw the girl who was going to Yale, she walked right over and gave her a hug. "Congratulations," Christina said. "You got into Yale, which is the biggest thing." She sought out a girl who was going to Princeton. She wanted them to be able to be happy in front of her.

There was nothing she could do, though, about the general level of tension. Suddenly, everyone was worried. If the best student in the class had been turned away by Harvard, then what chance did any of them have of being accepted by a first-choice school? The fact that Christina was smiling and congratulating the other girls did not help. She was proof that not everyone got what she deserved.

As she made her way from one class to the next, the question of blame kept floating into her mind, try as she might to push it out. She could not blame Marlborough, which had provided every opportunity she might have wanted. That was the whole point of a girls' school. Whose fault was it that she had not gotten into Harvard? Marlborough had not failed her. The logical next question was, Had she somehow failed?

Toward the end of the day, Christina bumped into Jeff Girion, the English teacher who had advised her on her college-application essay. She announced that she was over her disappointment. Columbia would be a fine alternative to Harvard, and much less of a long shot.

He wondered how she really felt. His experience with the Korean students at Marlborough had taught him that their community was a hierarchical culture with "absolute values placed on certain institutions and markers. Columbia will never be Harvard, and an A– will never be an A. There are no gray areas, no good-better-best. There's only best. Harvard has a truly magical aura for the Asian culture, and there is no room for failure."

But Girion had been worried, for some time, about whether what he called the "circle of power and influence" would open to let someone like Christina in. It had not, and he felt more resentment than sorrow at the decision.

"The more appropriate a candidate you are," he said, "the harder the fall is. And she *is* Harvard material. Who knows what whimsy went on once the committee sat down at the table? You get pushed into strange categories, whether they acknowledge it or not, and that includes where you come from."

"There it is," he muttered, watching Christina head down the hall to her next class. "There are lots of Christina Kims coming through the pipeline."

Privately, Christina shared Girion's suspicion that her status, or lack of it, had been one of the things that did her in, though she never confessed it to him. "I have absolutely no connections, no money," she told herself. "That's not a big factor, but those little things come into play."

The local Harvard alumnus, who had visited Marlborough and might have championed her application, was a young man in his first year of courting prospective students, and Christina doubted that he had done her any good. "He was basically everything I'm not," she said. "His strong points are community service, sports, sports, sports, and sports." She did not think he was seasoned enough to distinguish her from "a hundred people like me." In fact, she could imagine a dark little scene in which the reader, confronted by dozens of applications from overachieving Korean students, was overwhelmed by so much excellence.

In the end, humor was her only defense. Harvard must have turned her down because she was too perfect a stereotype. "I'm probably competing in the most competitive sort of applicant pool," she said, "because I live in L.A., where there are lots of Korean kids who do everything I do–and more. Plus, I play the violin, which is the perfect instrument; fits right in with the stereotype. I've got glasses and black hair and I want to go into medicine, and I did a summer internship and got a five on my AP Bio exam and a fifteen-hundred-something on my SATs. It's just perfect."

If she had done anything wrong, she decided, it was to assume that she had a place at Harvard. She had been too proud, and now she was paying for it.

She told herself, " 'You know, you sort of screwed up. You messed up.

You thought you were going, and you were too optimistic before you had a right to be.'" She had to remember that she had not lived her life solely to get into Harvard. Christina had pushed herself to see how far she could go. Her standards were her own.

"I did not do all this for Harvard," she said. "I did it for me."

14

ERICA FORNERET SPENT her waiting time anticipating how she would feel when the letter arrived from Brown. One of the other Internationals had applied early to Yale, and the two girls sought solace in the superstitious notion that their fates were somehow tied together. They agreed to go snowboarding in the mountains if they got in. If they did not, they would go paint-balling at an outdoor facility in the San Fernando Valley and shoot paint pellets at each other until they felt better. They never discussed the possibility that one of them would get in and the other would not.

Over the weekend, the Yale applicant had received a rejection letter. Erica came to school on Monday unnerved and impatient, and spent Tuesday as a prisoner of her schedule, stuck at school late for a 5:00 Drama Ensemble rehearsal. After class, she hid out in the photo studio, aimlessly noodling at her homework, a vacant look on her face. She assumed that by now the mailman had delivered her letter from Brown, but there was no way to get home and back in time for rehearsal, and she would not let her mother give her the news over the phone. She had made her parents promise not to open the letter if they were home when it arrived. Whatever the news, Erica wanted to have a moment to herself before she had to share it.

Besides, Phyllis and Rodney Forneret liked to play jokes. They might open an acceptance letter and still pull long, sad faces when Erica got home, just to make her suffer for an instant before they sprung the good news. She was not in the mood for jokes.

Everything made her jumpy. Rehearsal was normally the place where she escaped the day's tension, but today it was just another frustration. The director complained about Erica's inattentiveness, and Erica had to stifle the urge to say that she had more important things on her mind. As though there weren't six more college applications due in the next few days—USC, Stanford, Sarah Lawrence, Yale, Columbia, and Barnard—all of which might be unnecessary if she could just get home to open the mail.

Erica knew the three other girls who had applied early to Brown, and they had made a pact to call one another when the letters arrived. She wondered what it would be like to be accepted if another girl got turned down. She would feel guilty, of course, but she knew there would be "that other sense, the 'Yay, I got in.'"

She had told her friends that she did not expect to be accepted, but that was a protective maneuver, in case the unthinkable happened. "Deep down inside," she said, she assumed she would get in. The only one she confided that to was Katie Tower's friend Lisl, who wanted to study engineering at Brown, since it seemed unlikely that the two girls were competing for the same slot.

As the day slogged along, she thought about what a treat it would be to chuck all the other applications into the garbage. After all the college visits and interviews, it was hard to recall exactly why Brown was her first choice; at this point it was alluring simply because an acceptance would mean she could stop thinking about it.

"It'll be a really nice Christmas present if I'm in," she told herself. "And a lump of coal if I'm not."

When the rehearsal ended, Erica walked out to the driveway to meet her mother. Phyllis had obeyed her daughter's request and not opened the envelope from Brown, but it did not matter. She had brought it along, and as soon as Erica saw the skinny, unopened envelope lying on the car seat, she knew what had happened. Suddenly, she was in no hurry to open it. They drove home without saying a word, and Erica went upstairs, shut her bedroom door behind her, and opened the letter.

Her application was deferred until April.

All of Erica's planned reactions evaporated. She did not call the other girls, or collapse, or sulk. Instead, she came downstairs, bluntly confirmed what her mother already suspected, and proceeded to complain about everything but the decision. The senior class meeting had been childish and petty. Her drama teacher was an unfeeling tyrant.

Phyllis, who was heartbroken, listened quietly. She decided to postpone a pep talk until Erica was in a more receptive mood—but not for too long.

"I'll bide my time," she told herself, "and then I'll talk to her. First, she's in great company. Look at Christina Kim! There's nothing to be ashamed of here. Second, Erica thinks that 'deferred' means it's all over, but it doesn't. They're going to give her a second look. And we knew Brown was a stretch. Her grades could have been better."

Phyllis refused to be depressed. "She's *going* to be fine," she said, as though stating it would make it so.

That night the wind came up, a hot, spooky Santa Ana that seemed to contradict itself, gusting first from one direction and then another. The next morning, her sleepless nerves frayed, Erica went in to see Monica Ward, who told her the same thing her parents had: Brown had deferred her application, not rejected it. Brown had accepted two of the early candidates, Lisl and another girl, but Ward urged Erica not to indulge in useless comparisons. She wanted Erica to write a letter to the admissions officer who had visited Marlborough, to let her know that she was still eager to attend.

That was what it boiled down to: She had to keep her grades up, beg a little, and endure curious stares from the other girls in her classes.

She was already in her seat at the back of Dr. Morgan's classroom, immersed in a whispered conversation about the fate of some of the other early applicants, when Christina came in. She glanced over at Erica. For all their sparring in class, Christina liked and respected Erica, and she understood how bad she must feel about Brown. Christina walked up behind her, wrapped both her arms around Erica's neck, and leaned over so that their cheeks touched.

"Oh, Erica," she said, "I'm so sorry."

Erica stared straight ahead, and, with a slight shrug, said, "Hey, it's okay." After an awkward moment, Christina straightened and took her seat.

In the days that followed, Erica dutifully composed a letter that said that Brown was still her first choice and that she hoped for serious consideration in the spring. She felt it was a little "weepy and overdramatic," but she mailed it. Though she had sworn she would die if she could not go to Brown, she was distracted by the fretful issue of why the school had preferred two other girls to her. She *did* feel rejected. Defensively, she told herself that she just might be happier someplace else. If she got in on the next round, maybe she would reject Brown, and that would make things even.

"If I do get accepted," she said, "I don't know. It's '*Now* you want me, but you didn't want me then.' There's just something sort of distasteful."

Erica's close friends, the Internationals, did their best to cheer her up, which meant a lot of jokes. Her friends had long since decided that Erica would need a keeper once she departed the safety of Marlborough and her parents' home. She was the least worldly of the group, and too pretty and melodramatic to head off to school alone. Instead of fretting about Brown, she ought to be glad that at least one of her friends had applied to each of the other schools she had applied to, except for Yale.

At the end of the week, after all the early-decision letters had arrived, Les Klein watched her shell-shocked charges straggle into class, and abandoned any hope of discussing the required reading. Even Katie Briggs, that beacon of dependability, was late. One of the teachers had posted "love notes" in the Living Room—blank sheets of paper, each with a senior's name at the top, where friends could write encouraging messages. Katie was still adding comments when she should have been heading upstairs.

Klein waited until all the girls were in their seats, and then she said, "A really good friend of mine said, 'Until you get rid of hope, life really doesn't begin.'"

The girls stared at her.

"But," she went on, "the Sufis say, 'Die in life and resurrect now.'"

"I like that," said Katie Briggs.

The girl who had kept her application to Harvard a secret yearned for a way to forgive herself for not getting in. She asked, "Does your friend mean, banish hope as a means of avoiding disappointment?"

"Or don't live in the future," said Klein. "Don't do, 'I hope this relationship will improve someday.'"

The girl replied, as though she had never before considered the possibility, "Because if you tell yourself, 'I'm never going to get into this college,' then, when you don't, you're not disappointed."

Katie Briggs laughed. She could not imagine a life without hope. What was Marlborough about, after all? She had been able to devote six years to figuring out who she was and what she wanted to do. She had learned that she was a hard worker, but not a maniac: She tried her best, but her best included getting a decent night's sleep. She looked at some of the girls, like Christina, who gave up sleeping and eating and piled on the AP courses, and knew she would never be like that. Balance made Katie happy—as did forward motion. So far, she liked the nervous excitement of applying to colleges. She hoped to get into Northwestern University. She hoped to get into Washington University, in St. Louis. Hope, to her, was the payoff for all the hard work.

"I couldn't live like that," she said. "What if I started to believe it? 'God, I'm stupid.'"

Klein laughed. "It's contextual, surely," she said, "but what my friend meant was that hope had gotten in the way of her ability to grapple with the fact that things were fairly crappy. It was hope as a way to mask all pain."

They talked about hope and faith, about beliefs and delusion. Once they had calmed down a little, Klein gently nudged the discussion toward the assigned reading, Ntozake Shange's play *For Colored Girls Who Have Considered Suicide/When the Rainbow is Enuf.* Surely the black women in the play were "limited by their lives," she said. Whatever their hopes, discrimination had robbed them of opportunity. Klein used as an example the statistics on medical students, which were skewed toward whites.

This was more than the girl who was not going to Harvard could bear, since the worst part of rejection was wondering who had been accepted instead. It was hard enough to be turned down. She could not tolerate the idea that a less-qualified candidate, a beneficiary of the school's commitment to diversity, might take her place. She blurted out, "Maybe if they don't get in it should just be a wake-up call to people to work harder. I think if colleges just take who's deserving, they'll have a mixed population."

Klein knew the girl was miserable, but she could not allow that kind of comment to go unchallenged. What about a poor girl in East Los Angeles who had no access to AP classes or SAT preparation? She could be the best student in her class and still not do as well as a girl from Marlborough. "It's hard to tell them they shouldn't have special access," said Klein, "since there's no way they can compete with someone from Marlborough."

The Harvard applicant refused to budge. "But then are you being punitive to white people like us, who did the best we could at our schools? Or what if there's a black kid just like me, at a school like this, and she applies to the same schools as I do and she gets in? That's not fair."

The room was silent for a moment. In the same way that Barbara Wagner had made a commitment to ethnic diversity, colleges and universities tried to assemble a diverse freshman class—even when that meant a separate set of criteria for minorities. Sommer Louie and Erica Forneret had both been invited on special "minority weekends" at various schools, and had been named finalists for a National Achievement Award, a National Merit program that gave $2,000 awards to deserving minority students. Wagner intended to expand minority recruitment even further in the coming years. Affirmative action was easy to embrace in the abstract. It was harder for a heartbroken girl who wondered if someone else in this classroom was going to leapfrog over her—with credentials that weren't as good as her own.

One of Klein's black students was the first to speak: "Once my mom asked me, 'What's the first thing that pops into your mind when I say

CEO?,'" she said. "And I said, 'White male.' And I thought, Why am I saying that? Because it's been my experience. But here I am at a girls' school! There's no reason for me to think that."

That afternoon, the usually unflappable Katie Briggs was done in by the United States Postal Service, or maybe by the admissions office at the University of Colorado at Boulder. Boulder was one of her likely schools, and better still, it had a rolling admissions policy, which meant that the university processed applications as they were received, rather than holding all notifications until the spring. Katie could have the security of an acceptance and still pick another school in the spring, if she wanted to. She had mailed off her Boulder application a month ago in the hope that she would hear good news before the winter break.

Somewhere along the line, her application fee had gotten lost, and instead of an acceptance, she got a form letter saying that her application had been held pending receipt of the fee. Her careful plan had been for nothing, and now she had to witness other girls' disappointment without the security of an acceptance. She stomped into her biology lab and dropped her books on the lab table.

"I want it to be *over*," she moaned to no one in particular. "I am so insanely jealous of all these girls who got in and did so well."

Dr. Arleen Forsheit, who taught Upper School science classes, was quick to respond; an epidemic of jitters was the last thing the seniors needed. "Well," she said, calmly, "some did and some didn't. Some of it made no sense to me. Christina being deferred made no sense—there was nothing else you could ask for."

Dr. Forsheit wanted her students to understand that there was nothing wrong with them if they were rejected by a school. Katie Briggs was a decent, hardworking kid whom Dr. Forsheit had recommended for a science scholarship at Washington University. She would still be the same delightful girl no matter what her college letters said.

"If you have four thousand qualified applicants, or more," she told Katie, "you're going to have a lottery. There's simply no good reason to take one candidate and not the other." It was harsh comfort, but she hated to hear the girls berate themselves.

Dr. Forsheit was particularly sensitive to the limitations of the outside world, having landed at Marlborough because her intended profession could not accommodate her. In 1970, Arleen Forsheit had received a PhD in molecular biology from UCLA, and won a three-year postdoctoral fellowship at the California Institute of Technology.

But halfway through the fellowship, she had her first child, a daughter. A year later, she left for a part-time research position, and nine months and too many undependable babysitters later, she quit.

"I knew that if I left research, the chances of my going back in were slim," she said. She abandoned her career because she could not figure out any other way to sustain her personal life.

She had a second child, and for fifteen years limited herself to volunteer work for various political organizations. But her older girl entered Marlborough in the fall of 1984, and her younger daughter followed in 1988; the only way to manage double tuition was for Dr. Forsheit to return to work. She asked the Marlborough head of school if he knew where she might find a teaching position, and he hired her.

She had never intended to teach, but quickly found that she loved it. In the summer of 1995 Forsheit became head of the science department, a post she held for three years, until she decided that she much preferred the classroom to administrative work. Now she taught Upper School classes exclusively, and had introduced a new tutorial called Advanced Science: Research in the Biological or Physical Sciences, for girls like Christina, who had outgrown even the AP curriculum.

Dr. Forsheit seemed an intimidating figure, striding down the corridor in her white laboratory coat, her shoulders squared, her sensible pumps beating time on the floor. It was only when she looked up from her daily routine—when something like the Harvard decision forced her to confront the world outside Marlborough—that difficult memories surfaced. Sometimes she worried that the world was no more welcoming than it had been when she started her career; that these girls would be prepared for everything except the compromises they would have to make. There was no way Dr. Forsheit could control that. The best she could hope for was that they would graduate with their confidence intact.

So she coddled the seniors. It was the funny thing about life at Marlborough: the oldest girls ended up wanting the same kind of emotional support they had had as seventh graders. She wrapped an arm around Katie's shoulder and gave her a hug. "The nice thing about the end of the process," she said, "is that you'll get into several schools, all of which will be right. And you'll have a wide choice."

Katie confessed that she had had a dream in which two of the colleges she was applying to took her early because they wanted her so badly, even though she hadn't applied for early decision.

"It's so exciting," she said. "But it's so tiring."

Katie Briggs's life was an anomaly, in a world of step-families and executive moms, indulged kids and overstuffed schedules. Jeff and Debbie Briggs, their daughter, son, and dog lived five minutes from school in a stately old home with buttercream walls and big flowered couches. Their lives looked like a postcard from the 1950s: the family relaxing on the patio behind the house, sipping iced tea and eating too many homemade chocolate-chip cookies, the kids taking a dip in the pool while the dog scrambled for attention. An alumni interviewer for one of the colleges had sunk happily into a couch and chatted his way through brownies and coffee before he remembered that he was supposed to talk to the applicant at a neutral location. It was his first year on the job, and coziness had clouded his brain and made him forget the rules.

Jeff Briggs was an earnest, soft-spoken lawyer who lived to provide for his family. His wife, Debbie, was a tiny, antic woman with short red hair and an easy laugh, who worked part-time in a neighborhood bookstore, close enough for Katie to drop in on her at lunchtime. Jeff and Debbie considered themselves dependable, not indulgent, parents—an important distinction, when some of Katie's classmates drove their own cars to school and wore designer clothes on free-dress day. Katie had always found it fairly easy to be happy—she was quite literally a buoyant child, who had been on the swim team at Marlborough since seventh grade. She had smooth, pale skin and fine, white-blond hair; even at eighteen, there was something of the little girl to Katie.

This year, happiness took a little effort. When Katie listened to some of her friends list their extracurricular activities, a little internal voice said, "'Why didn't I do that? Oh, I only have five out of the eight slots filled in.' But then I think, 'Well, five out of eight, that's not too bad.' There's always the voice that says 'I'm not good enough,' that weird voice. And then I say, 'Oh yes you are. *Shut up.*'"

She was applying to a dozen schools, a list, she said happily, that had "no cohesiveness to it," and included Duke University in North Carolina, Boston University, the University of Colorado at Boulder, Washington University, and three of the UC campuses: Berkeley, Los Angeles, and San Diego. As far as Katie was concerned, it was too early to have a single vision of the future.

"I don't know what I want," she said, "if I want to stay here, if I want a big school or a small school, what I want to study. I'm really all over the place."

She did not envy girls like Christina and Erica, who had been turned away by the one school they wanted. "It's good, in a way, that I don't have my heart set on some place that's impossible," she said. "I guess in a way I am letting the process decide."

In the meantime, she was determined to enjoy every moment of her senior year. There were things about Marlborough that Katie disliked—she felt that she would be more comfortable around boys if she had been in class with them—but she was not so foolish as to think that life would have been perfect somewhere else. "I have my unhappiness here," she said, "but if I went somewhere else, I'd have a different kind of unhappiness." What she imagined she had missed mattered far less than what she had gained: the feeling of "teamwork" in class; the friendships; the fact, she said, that "I'm not afraid to shout out the wrong answer in my math or physics class."

She was not afraid of much: Katie Briggs had made her mark at Marlborough on her first Halloween there, when she came to school dressed as

Barbara Wagner, with a platinum pageboy, a good wool suit, and the head of school's ever-present can of Tab. She wanted to spend her senior year having an equally good time, even as the world tugged at her sleeve and asked her to hurry along.

Katie had looked forward all term to the annual Winter Choral Concert because she was the lead soloist with the Chamber Choir. She had an elaborate set of anticipatory rituals that included wearing a favorite scarf to protect her neck from a chill, sipping hot tea for days in advance, and, the day before a performance, indulging in a hot bath and a massage.

When she walked onstage this time, though, she felt a tightening in her throat. It wasn't stage fright; she had sung in public for years. The problem was that this was the last Winter Program. Today had rushed up on her too fast, and she had the terrible feeling that it might be over in a blink.

She looked out at the audience. She found her mother, and tried to focus on Debbie's face, but that only made Katie feel worse. Her mother was such a staunch ally; if Katie looked at her she would start to cry. She could not look at her father, who worked ridiculous hours to make good on his promise to send her to whatever school she wanted to attend. Her best friends were in the crowd, but where would they be in eight months? Scattered, relegated to her e-mail address book or the occasional long-distance call.

She fixed her gaze on the clock at the back of the auditorium, the only safe place in the room, took a deep breath, and began to sing.

15

ON KATIE TOWER'S first day back to school after the winter break, Cabel was the first one in the kitchen, making coffee and waiting for the kids to come downstairs. She looked like the sort of woman who might startle easily—porcelain skin, fine white-blond hair, delicate bones—but Cabel traced her Virginia family back to the Civil War, and prided herself on a steely ability to cope. She was often emotional but rarely rattled.

A new thought ambushed her as she padded around the silent kitchen: This was the first day of Katie's last semester at Marlborough, the first day of her last season at home. By this time next year, home would be the place Katie visited on her vacations. Cabel had remarked on the finalities of the semester before—the last first day of school, the last Halloween, the last senior-mascot ceremony—but this time it felt heavier.

Katie might never need her to make lunch again.

Cabel walked over to the refrigerator and took out the ingredients for a sandwich for her daughter. She would not allow herself to fall apart in front of Katie, but she was not quite prepared for the coming separation. She wanted to grab Katie back, just a bit.

Cabel Tower was not the only mother who felt wistful. Phyllis Forneret had begun to cry at television commercials, so she did what she always did when sentiment threatened to overwhelm her—she got busy. The best way to endure the coming semester would be to celebrate it. She would hunt for a fabulous prom dress for Erica at her favorite resale shops, and she would plan a graduation tea for family and friends. Not just food and good company, but a proper garden party with special invitations and her collection of vintage china and tablecloths.

Phyllis Louie and Youngsook Kim expressed less ambivalence about their coming emancipation. Phyllis Louie defiantly announced that she would never, ever cook another meal once Sommer was out of the house. When her oven had gone on the blink three years earlier, she had instructed Robert to fix it as well as he could, but not to even think about buying a new one. She had calculated the distance to graduation: three more years of three meals a day—just over 1,000 meals—and she would be done taking care of her daughter. Let the oven limp along until Sommer left for college. After that, she and Robert could get by on take-out, and Phyllis would have a little free time for herself.

Youngsook Kim insisted that Christina would be better off on the East Coast; that the intensity of their relationship over the last ten years had not been good for either of them. She and Christina agreed, she said, that it was time for them to be apart. Youngsook had come to the United States twenty-five years ago, when she was thirty, imagining a life of happiness and comfort. Her story had ended in the house on North Plymouth Boulevard, where her husband fought to establish his house-painting business with only marginal success. Christina would be the one to see the world, while her mother stayed behind to raise Christina's younger sister. Youngsook did her best to get used to the idea by insisting that she had meant it to be this way.

Even Debbie Briggs felt unsettled, though there would be no sharp break with Katie. Her daughter still sought out her advice; theirs was the gentlest of transitions, just a gradual, inevitable shifting away. Debbie knew that Katie was excited about going to school in another part of the country, but it was hard to imagine her far from home. Debbie preferred to think that Katie might land as close as San Diego or Berkeley—and made sure not to say so. The most important thing was Katie's happiness; her parents would have to get used to the rest.

The second semester at Marlborough began quietly, in what passed for winter in southern California. The seniors hunkered down, biding their time. They were allowed to duck out for lunch to the Larchmont business district, three blocks away, and early in the year they had paraded their privilege, swaggering back onto campus with a half-empty iced blended mocha or a fruit smoothie. Now it was too cool or damp to walk, and no one wanted to relinquish a parking space.

Katie Tower, Christina Kim, and a dozen other girls colonized Myranda Marsh's history classroom and spent their lunch hour talking or watching videotapes. They had to conserve their energy for the long wait until the college letters came in April. All the busy work that had occupied the fall was over. Like a trapeze artist in mid-air, they were suspended between effort and outcome.

It was waiting season for seniors at high schools around the country. The difference at Marlborough was the level of expectation. A Marlborough senior believed that she had given herself the edge over other girls. Marlborough was supposed to save Erica Forneret from distraction and keep Katie Briggs happy within herself. It was supposed to nourish Katie Tower's sophisticated intellect, and put Sommer Louie on the fast track to a college scholarship. It was supposed to catapult Christina Kim into an elite college.

These girls had entered Marlborough as seventh graders in the fall of 1993, in the wake of all the publicity about the inequities of the coeducational classroom. They basked in the belief that they had made the best choice, as confirmed by educators, researchers, and the American Association of University Women's 1992 report. They amassed their own anecdotal evidence, based on coeducational summer workshops they attended, or friends they had talked to. Sommer Louie marveled at the changes in the girl who had been her best friend in elementary school, a girl she still saw around the neighborhood once in a while. Now it seemed to her that they had very little in common.

"In elementary school you couldn't tell us apart in terms of our focus, our state of mind," she said. "We were on the same track. Now she's a different person. Her mind is not in the books. She has a boyfriend this week, a boyfriend that week. She doesn't have the same drive." The only difference between them, as far as Sommer could see, was where they had gone to school.

Barbara Wagner liked to think that most parents saw their daughters' senior year "holistically" and defined a good education in broader terms than a college acceptance. She did not deceive herself, though. Plenty of parents were interested in the academic equivalent of a designer label. They had invested a tremendous amount of time and money in their daughters, and they expected to see a profit.

"When we define ourselves as a college prep school," Wagner said, "there's always a tension about that. There's a drivenness. It's a rare parent who says, 'You know, it really doesn't matter to me where she goes to college. I really just want her to be happy.'" Wagner believed that Katie Briggs and her parents truly felt that way. Katie was not made of ice; she would feel bad if she got turned down at a favored school. But she was not the sort of girl who based her preferences on what looked good to anyone else. Her parents seemed fairly calm about the process, which made it easier for Katie to get through it.

Not everyone was as easygoing. "The majority of them, if they told the truth," Wagner said, "really have different aspirations. Not 'as long as she's happy.'"

On January 29, just before lunch, the girls were herded into Caswell Hall for an impromptu assembly. Wagner took the podium, looking grim, and the girls whispered to each other, wondering what they possibly could have done to make her look so stern.

It was all a front. Wagner had worked hard to protect today's surprise until the last minute, and now she sprang it on the unsuspecting girls. There were several buses lined up outside, ready to transport the entire student body and faculty over to Pan Pacific Park, where an afternoon of much-needed fun awaited them.

A sanctioned ditch day? The girls raced out the door, and within twenty minutes everyone had reassembled at the park's central field, which Marlborough had reserved for the afternoon. Five employees of a place called Pie n' Burger flipped hamburgers, cooked French fries, cut fruit pies, and set out tubs of iced soft drinks. One of the history teachers was ready to organize games. Les Klein and a member of the yearbook staff ran around the field shooting photos. Kurt Schleunes climbed to the far northeast corner of the field as though he were out for a stroll, to make sure that no one tried to leave school early. Wagner presided over it all, sporting a red fleece pullover like the ones the seniors wore.

The central field was shaped like a bowl, with trees along the rim and the playing field and picnic area in the middle. The youngest kids, amazed at their good fortune, clustered around the picnic tables, while the seniors filled their plates and retreated to the shade of the trees. They lolled on the grass and debated who had constructed the sloppiest sandwich.

Christina Kim, that emblem of dignity and achievement, walked over to the rim of the bowl, stretched out on the slightly soggy ground, and rolled sideways down the hill. She climbed up and did it again. An equally restrained friend joined her. After a few more rolls, the yearbook photographer, incredulous, asked them to do it one more time, for posterity. Christina trudged up to the top and rolled down again, her navy polo shirt flapping. Several of the teachers watched approvingly. If Christina was inspired to be silly, then this outing had been a success.

MYRANDA MARSH had come to Marlborough intending to revolutionize the history department, but more and more she felt mired in a bureaucracy whose demands she took as a personal affront. Her teaching

life, she said, involved "putting twenty pounds into a two-pound sack," because the history department refused to give her the freedom she felt she
deserved. She was told not only what she had to teach the Middle-School
girls, but how she had to teach it—and acceptable method did not yet include the things that mattered most to Marsh: the games and projects she
devised to engage her students.

She complained at department meetings, but she lacked powerful allies. One of her male colleagues considered her "provocative, pedagogical,"
and wondered whether her techniques in fact backfired and intimidated
some girls who might otherwise be willing to speak. Marsh replied that she
was teaching the girls to stand up for themselves, to abandon their fear of
being wrong and realize that there was no such thing as a wrong argument,
only a lame one.

The old standbys of history class, memorization and drill, were fine for
learning facts, but they did nothing to teach a girl courage. Marsh could turn
a classroom numb reciting a chronology of conflict in the Middle East. She
preferred to explain the essentials of the conflict and ask the girls to come
up with a solution. She wanted to produce girls who knew how to think.

If she had to weigh the three elements of this year's slogan—"Competence, confidence, connectedness"—she would emphasize connectedness
over the other two. According to JoAnn Deak, physiology played a big part
in competence, and there was no way to rush a girl who wasn't ready to
learn. Even if she was, she might clash with a particular teacher and never
discover her real abilities. As for confidence, it was always under attack—
from the media, from girls who were prettier, taller, thinner, richer, or had
a higher grade-point average—and new research suggested that self-esteem
was not something that could be supplied by well-intentioned parents and
teachers. It had to be based on a girl's own feeling of accomplishment.

Connectedness was the key. Marsh had come to that conclusion not
just from her reading but in her own life. She had felt at sea for so many
years, alienated from her family, lonely at school. She intended to make
sure that these girls felt a sense of community, even if it meant doing the
extra work that her games and projects required.

She worried that she overwhelmed the girls in her classes with what was essentially a double workload, but she refused to budge. If the department was not willing to incorporate her ideas, she would have to add them to the existing curriculum.

By February, Marsh had almost given up on the senior members of her department, and she assumed that they felt the same way about her. She turned, more and more, to a handful of women teachers she occasionally saw outside school, women who respected her priorities. Once in a while they met for a drink on a Friday night, or sought each other's company at lunchtime. Marsh saw the beginnings of a network, so she invited her colleagues to her classroom for lunch, for what she hoped would be the first of a monthly series of meetings to discuss teaching technique. She gave the group a name: "Insidious."

She got to her classroom before any of the others, only to find that Katie Tower and her friends had staked out the room for their lunch. They complained loudly about having to relocate, which only made Marsh laugh.

"Solve it!" she cried. "You can't solve it? You have no problem-solving skills?"

One of the seniors shot her a wicked smile. "We'll just kick out some younger girls from somewhere."

When they left, Marsh set out a bag of cookies and waited, with all the enthusiasm of a child waiting for her birthday-party guests. She had big emotions—anger, outrage, glee, nothing tentative about her heart. Soon, her friends arrived: Barbara Gobus from the English department; Margarita Soriano, who taught Spanish; Leigh Hansen, who taught Latin; and Sandra O'Connor, who taught Middle School math. They were seasoned teachers, but they were fascinated by what Marsh had to say, and aware of her growing sense of alienation. This was an opportunity to learn about some of the newest educational research and at the same time to show a colleague that her efforts were appreciated.

Mrs. Soriano happily reported that she had used her own version of talking chips in Spanish class, with excellent results. Since participation was more important to her than whether a girl had the right answer, she collected a chip each time a girl either asked or answered a question. She also tried to encourage cooperation. "When somebody said something wrong, I didn't give them the answer," she said. "I said, 'Oh, who can help her? Who can help her?' And it worked out *so* nicely.'"

"That's the goal," said Marsh. "To take yourself out of the equation and let them help each other more and more." She encouraged Soriano to divide the girls into smaller groups next time, and to have them check each others' work.

Dr. Hansen was not sure if anything could make Latin conjugations and grammar a friendlier process. Working in groups might only compound the girls' confusion. "Half of the girls don't get it," she said, "but they don't know they don't get it until they go over the homework."

Marsh would not give up. "It's *perfect* for the Socratic method," she said, savoring a cookie. "Everyone either has to explain something or get it explained to them."

Dr. Hansen wasn't convinced. Translating educational theory into the classroom could be difficult; the techniques that made Marsh's seventh-grade history class such a lively place might not apply in every class. Dr. Hansen was not interested in change for its own sake. "Sometimes it's just memorization: Did you do it or not?" she said. "Either you learned the conjugation 'puella, puellae' or you didn't. What can I do with that?"

"Put them in pairs," said Marsh. "It creates an investment, on the part of the girl who does know it, to drill the other girl. Or the other girl, the one who didn't get it—this is especially true with girls—even if she won't learn it for herself, she might be 'guilted' into learning the words to help her partner."

Dr. Hansen was skeptical. A lot of girls missed *puella,* the singular of the word for "girl," because they left the 'e' out. *Pulla* meant chicken. There was no way to make that interesting, and no way to keep a girl who made the mistake from feeling foolish.

Marsh would not be denied. "Then make it the bonus question!" she said. "Tell them, 'I'll give an extra point to anyone who can tell me how to turn a girl into a chicken.'"

If the youngest girls had to learn control, the oldest girls had to learn to relinquish it, at least as far as Les Klein was concerned.

"I've had this epiphany in my life," she told her Dramatic Literature class, "That everything in life is about hanging on or letting go. Whenever there's a crisis in my life, it always comes down to one of those two things. When I was in graduate school, I had a saying from Buddhism that read, 'We cling because we suffer because we cling because we suffer,' all in a circle. The point is, whether we cling to something because it's good or bad, it doesn't matter. As long as we cling we are not living in the moment."

"Except the only way to live in the moment *is* to cling," replied one of the girls, "which is kind of contradictory."

Klein held her ground. The most important thing in life was to take chances. "Before you can fly," she said, "you have to let go."

"And fall," said another girl.

"Well," said Klein. "Maybe."

16

The Young Women's Leadership
School of East Harlem

January 1999

WINTER WAS HARD for Diana Perez. There was an epidemic of asthma among Manhattan's poor, and the cold months were the worst. The world conspired to make it hard for her to breathe: Outside, a damp chill hurt her lungs, and inside, the air was dry and stagnant, the windows always closed against bad weather. Her father, James, chain-smoked and could not stop—did not want to stop, given the paucity of indulgences in his life, and dismissed the idea that cigarettes aggravated Diana's condition. His smoking was a daily habit, and she did not have asthma attacks every day, so logic absolved him. Besides, he had had asthma as a boy, and had outgrown it. There was no reason to think that the same thing would not happen to his daughter.

His wife Maria was on him about it all the time, as were the girls, but she despaired of getting him to stop. "He says it's the only bad habit he's got," she said, helplessly. "It's his stress release."

Diana's first asthma attack, in sixth grade, had landed her in the intensive-care unit for a week and scared her so badly that, by her own estimation, she had "never been really, really healthy since then." She had sinus problems and allergies on top of the asthma, so she used two inhaled medications to keep her breathing right.

Even so, Diana had several attacks over the Christmas holidays, and her life developed a new rhythm, spiked by attacks and treatments, with lulls—maybe days, maybe a lucky week—in between.

By the time school started again in January, her usually stoic nature had deserted her. "I feel buried," she said. Final-semester exams were at the end of the month, so she looked for ways to conserve her strength. With her mother's permission, Diana started staying home from school if it was terribly cold outside, rather than risk getting sick. On the mornings after an asthma attack she slept late, past the start of the school day. Diana was a good enough student to skip a few days or show up late and still catch up.

She ended up missing more than homework. With all her absences, Diana got confused about the schedule for the Earth Science Regents written and laboratory exams. She had left school for the holidays thinking that both parts of the test were scheduled for June, as they had been the previous year, when she had failed by two measly points. She returned in January to learn that the exams were three weeks away, at the same time as final exams.

Celenia Chevere had set up a schedule of mandatory extra study sessions after school on Mondays and Wednesdays, and on Friday mornings. Diana, overwhelmed, told her teacher that she could not adjust her own schedule "on such short notice." It was impossible for her to get to school earlier than she already did for the morning session, and she babysat after school on Wednesdays. She managed only one Wednesday review, and had to settle for studying her old notes whenever she had a moment.

As the exam got nearer, the science teachers abandoned the regular textbook in favor of two Barrons Regents Exam Review books. There was time only for drill. Diana and Maryam's teacher, Shirley Gasich, strode back and forth at the front of the room rattling off terms: "Chordates, arthropods, c'mon, study these classifications, they *will* be on the test." All the girls took notes. Fear had accomplished what the teachers could not; the ninth graders were silent unless they had a question that pertained to the exam. Diana tried to keep up, but all she wanted to know was, did they have to memorize *all* the terms? She was short on time and energy, and needed to conserve her resources. She could not afford to study extraneous information.

Gasich gave the girls the last ten minutes of class to study quietly, and Diana and Maryam immediately turned to their books. Their two tablemates preferred to discuss the plot lines of their favorite television soap operas. One girl had missed an episode of "Guiding Light," and despaired of finding out what had happened to a young couple on the show.

"You have to buy Soap Opera Digest," counseled her friend.

"I want Nicholas to get back with that girl *so bad*," said the first girl.

N EXT DOOR, Cindy Jackson stood at the front of her classroom with her hands on her hips. With the Earth Science Regents and end-of-semester finals just days away, it was time for another lecture. One day last week, more than half the girls had been absent, a luxury they could not afford. They were not going to pass unless they got serious about the work, and that meant showing up for class on time, every day.

"There are germs *everywhere*. You can come up to my desk and use some of that sanitizer," she said, pointing at a pump bottle of antibacterial wash. "I wash the desks with Lysol every day. But I can't get everything. *So watch out*. Take care of yourself. If you feel you're getting sick, stay off milk products. Don't wreck your diet, just do it for a day or two, because milk products retain toxins."

The girls were fascinated; someone would likely go home today, full of self-importance, and announce to her parents that she had to give up milk because it was toxic. Jackson was clever about advice. She could berate the girls, but she knew that would alienate them. Instead, she flattered them— told them they mattered and gave them tools to get by.

She paced the center aisle, addressing individual girls. "You pull yourself together, bundle up, and get here. Because that's what happens in the adult world. You keep on. Otherwise, you don't get paid. So unless you've lost a limb or you're dead, you be here. Now, I'm going to sound cold when I say this, but I don't want to hear any more, 'But I was sick.' Bring in your medicine with you *and get here.* The show must go on. That's it."

Woven into Jackson's lecture was the implicit assumption that these girls were destined for the adult world of college, jobs, and paychecks. TYWLS might be one large, institutionalized lucky chance, but no professor or boss was going to cut them slack because they had grown up poor. The special treatment ended on graduation day.

She paused for breath and grinned.

"So thank you for being here," she said. "I'm glad you're here."

The girls waited to see what Jackson would do next. The younger teachers might have ideas about how they wanted to teach, but after twelve years, Jackson had a practical bag of tricks. Right after winter break, she had introduced what she called the "*esprit de corps* quiz," a spelling quiz with a prize at the end. If the whole class got a perfect score, they received bonus points, which could mean the difference between a C and a B by the end of the term. She told them which words would be on the quiz and gave them plenty of time to review—but if a single girl missed a single word, there would be no bonus points for anyone.

At first the girls whined that the test was too hard, but when they failed to talk Jackson out of it, they tried another approach. They cornered the weak spellers at lunch and drilled them on the words. They quizzed each other on the way to the subway in the morning. They passed their first quiz, which satisfied their teacher on three levels: They knew the terminology, they felt good about themselves as individuals, and they believed in themselves as a group. No one wanted to be left behind.

Today, Jackson was going to let them play Jeopardy, a classroom game modeled on the television show. She knew she was taking a chance, letting the girls spend precious time on a game, while next door Shirley Gasich fired review questions at them straight through the period. She knew Chevere held the science teachers responsible for the girls' performance. But every one of these girls had failed the science Regents last year, and Jackson worried about the pressure they were under. They loved Jeopardy. Perhaps they would learn more if they had a chance to blow off a little steam.

She divided the girls into four teams and reviewed the rules. Each team started out with ten points. Jackson announced a category, and the teams placed bids based on how confident they felt about the subject. Then she read off a question, and the girls had thirty seconds to write down their answer. The winning team got a homework pass for the evening's assignment.

Jackson purposely divided the girls so that the strongest students were scattered throughout the room, and gave each table a small grease-board, a marking pen, and an eraser. The first category was the digestive system. Each team bid ten points, and Jackson gave them the first question.

"Name the part of the digestive system responsible for absorbing water," she said.

There was a great riffling of papers as the girls searched for the right answer, followed by whispered consultations and frantic scribbling on the grease-boards. When Jackson called "Time," the team captains held the boards up. Team one guessed "kidneys," and lost ten points. The other three teams doubled their points by getting the correct answer, either "colon" or "large intestine."

As they placed their bets for the second question, one of the girls swore under her breath. Jackson stomped over to her table and barked, "Okay, thirty minutes, Monday or Thursday, you choose. I'm not kidding. *No more cussing*—you potty-mouths are through. You're going to do time—and I have plenty of things to do."

She called for bets: One point from a humbled Team One, 13 points from Team Two, 10 points from Team Three, 8 points from Team Four.

"I'm eating an orange," said Jackson. "What's the first enzyme that starts digestion? And here's a hint: You have to know what kind of food it is, and then look at your chart."

Team One lost again, and their total sank to one point, while the other three groups hovered near thirty. It might be all right not to win, but it definitely was not all right to be eliminated before the game was over. The next category was digestive disorders. Team One bet its one remaining point and waited to hear the question.

"I've gone to the bathroom three times this morning," said Jackson, to barely suppressed giggles from the girls, "and had extreme cramping. You know the name of this disorder. What is the cause?"

Team One guessed "constipation," and protested loudly when Jackson said that the disorder was diarrhea and the problem was a failure to absorb water. The question, as she had phrased it, had not mentioned what *happened* when the subject went to the bathroom. They thought all she had was cramps, so they ought to get some points.

Jackson asked if any of the other teams wanted to lend Team One some points. That was another reason for the game—to make the girls feel that they were in this together. Team Four shifted four of its 18 points to their less-fortunate friends, and the game continued until the end of the period.

Once a week—not nearly enough time, by Jackson's estimation—the girls stayed in biology for a double period and spent the second hour preparing for the Regents Laboratory examination. The first order of business was taking attendance—counting not only the girls but their textbooks. It was hard to get some of the girls to remember their books every day, and one student, sitting behind Amy Lopez, had forgotten hers for the third day in a row. Jackson assumed that she had lost it but was too embarrassed to confess. She instructed the girl to bring money for a new one and moved on to the next table.

The girl turned sullen, dropped her head and muttered about how else she might get into trouble, since that was clearly her destiny. She stretched out her leg and poked at Amy's long ponytail, which hung down below the back of her chair.

Amy bristled. She knew she had not studied enough for the upcoming exams, and for the first time she felt vulnerable. Failure suddenly seemed contagious. "Don't do that," she snarled at the girl. "It's not funny."

"So what," said the girl.

"That's why you won't go to college," said Amy, loud enough for everyone to hear.

Amy continued to tell her friends that she planned to become a pediatric surgeon, but sometimes, when she talked about the future with her parents, she spoke instead of becoming a physician's assistant. Final grades for the first semester would be released at the end of January, and she did not anticipate much improvement over her mid-term grades. At the beginning of the year, she had been flattered by the notion that she was smarter than her grades showed. As she headed for a disappointing report card, everyone's expectations began to feel like a burden.

Amy had made a stab at keeping to a schedule after mid-term grades, and for a few weeks in November, she managed to get to bed at a decent hour. But napping, watching television, and staying up late was more fun, and by Christmas break, she was floundering again. Her parents had scheduled a church trip to California over the holidays, and Amy begged to go along. That meant missing the first two weeks of school, in January, and when she got back she had to scramble to catch up.

Her public reputation as a smart kid was starting to crumble. Usually the girls on her Jeopardy team deferred to her; Amy could retire any debate by voting for the answer she thought was right. Today, for the first time, the girls had challenged her. When she disagreed with an answer, they asked for proof, and sometimes she did not have it. She had to riffle through the textbook, just like the other girls, looking for evidence to support her position.

Not that she was worried. She had made an effort to do better, even if she had been unable to sustain it, and she was, after all, a smart kid. Amy did not need straight A's to prove that. For a girl who hated to lose, being a student with untapped potential was far safer than giving her all and falling short.

On January 22, Cindy Jackson called the girls up to her desk, one at a time, and showed them their final semester grades. Their parents would not find out for three more days, but as usual, she wanted the girls to have a little advance warning. Thanks to a high score on her semester exam, Amy ended the term with a B+, but Jackson was far from satisfied. She had come to think of Amy as lazy, a girl who "likes to take it to the edge and challenge the system, see how far she can push it." Jackson tried to encourage her privately, writing notes on Amy's tests, praising her answers and her writing. So far, she had not gotten the reaction she wanted.

Jackson was irritated—but not yet worried. Amy's performance was fairly typical for a ninth-grade girl. This year and the next were all about figuring out just how responsible a girl had to be. By the beginning of eleventh grade, when college suddenly appeared on the horizon, these girls would turn into "horses running for the barn," focused on their goal.

Diana Perez dug in, in the days before finals, hoping that her exam grades would eclipse weeks of spotty work and absences. She still clung to an A in English, but she had failed to turn in her most recent book report, and she needed to do well on the final to guarantee her semester grade. Sarah Kirkpatrick's policy was to penalize the girls for every day they were late with an assignment, and she badgered the bad girls incessantly. So far she had not confronted Diana, who liked to think that her performance up until now had bought her a little leeway.

On the day of the English final, Diana took her seat without speaking to a soul. She wrote in her blue book at a furious pace, never once looking up to see how others were doing. Two groups of girls finished early—the ones who were prepared, and the ones who didn't care—but Diana wrote past the bell. Maryam hovered, waiting for her friend, and when Diana finally surrendered her test she complained that she had not had enough time to do her best work.

They hurried to Peter DeWan's history classroom and another final, and halfway through the period, Diana began to tire. She stared at one essay question that refused to make sense to her, stabbing at the words with her pencil. Then she took a deep breath and began to write again.

By the time she and Maryam lined up outside the science lab for the Earth Science Lab Regents exam, Diana was in a trance of anxiety and exhaustion—a blank stare on her face, her pencil clutched in her fist, wanting only to survive one more challenging hour.

Suzanne Kerho, the sunny young science teacher who administered the lab exam, assigned each girl to a lab station. Kerho did not like the exam. Of the six problems, one was an exercise in hand-eye coordination, and another was pure mathematics; she worried that the girls would not do well simply because they were caught off-guard. But they had to pass to get a Regents high school diploma, so she showed them how to use the stop-watches that had been set out for them and began timing the first question. They had six minutes to answer each one.

Silently, the girls moved from one station to another. Maryam easily got the answer to a measurement question at Station 3, but on a day like this she did not trust her eyes to read a ruler. She counted off the number of centimeters between two points, one at a time. Only then did she write down her answer, close her test booklet, and fold her hands in her lap.

Diana seemed far more jittery. Her first task was to time a ball as it sank in a long, narrow tube filled with blue liquid. She glanced over at the teacher twice, her pencil in her mouth, and then stared at the tube. She wrote down an answer, closed her booklet, and sat, her eyebrows knit together, her mouth stern. When it was her turn to sit out a cycle—there were seven girls and six seats, so everyone got to rest once—she chewed her fingernails.

But she was not suffering from nerves; it was adrenaline. Diana could not believe her good fortune. When the test was over, she burst out of the room laughing and gleefully shoved open the stairway door, as though she had rediscovered her own strength. She told Maryam that she had done very well because these seemed to her to be the same questions that had been on the test last year, when she had failed by only two points. One Regents test out of the way, and the week's weariness was forgotten.

First-semester grades came out on January 25. Maryam Zohny got straight A's, with an A+ in Japanese and in her Biology Regents preparation class.

Amy's best grade was the B+ in biology. She held steady with B's in math and English, though both Fabrice Fortin and Sarah Kirkpatrick urged her to work even harder during the second semester. Fortin suggested that she spend more time studying, or consider after-school tutoring. "Whatever the case," he wrote, "I expect her to do much better next semester." Kirkpatrick merely asked that Amy take the work more seriously, "take time to think about our reading on a deeper level and demonstrate this thinking in more thoughtful journal entries."

Amy slipped from a B– to a C in history, a generous grade, given that she had received a D+ on the semester exam and a C– for the second half of the term. DeWan was blunt. "Amy can be one of the best students in the class," he wrote. "However . . . she seems to have some difficulty with tests and is perhaps not studying enough."

The consensus on Diana's first term was clear: She was a very bright girl who needed to come to school more often. Diana had kept her B in Japanese and her A in math but had faltered in her other classes. Sarah Kirkpatrick was very concerned about her chronic absence, and gave Diana a C in English for the second half of the term. Diana had turned in her book reports late and had not submitted a reading log. The only reason she got a B for her semester grade was her strong performance at the beginning of the year.

Diana got an A– in history, down from an A at the middle of the term, but DeWan felt compelled to issue a warning. "Diana has been an excellent student overall," he wrote. "However, her absences seem to have taken a toll on her grades. . . . I understand these absences may be unavoidable, but they still are bound to affect her progress in the course."

Her B in biology reflected C-level work in the second term. Under "Additional Comments and Suggestions," Shirley Gasich had checked off "Student failed to make up work due to absence," and scribbled beneath it, "5 homework assignments incomplete." She checked "Missing major assignment" because Diana had failed to turn in a project.

At the bottom of the page, under *Recommendations,* Gasich checked *Parent/Teacher Conference.* She had requested a conference with Maria and James right after the break, on January 4, but so far had not received a reply. She wanted to remind the Perezes that she was still waiting to hear.

Like Cindy Jackson, Celenia Chevere preferred to take the long view when it came to her star students. Maryam was her shining light, Diana's grades were excellent despite her asthma, and Amy was irrepressible Amy. The semester grades went into their records, nothing else. Maryam and Diana looked great on paper, just the kind of candidates that a college with a commitment to diversity would want.

Chevere did not deceive herself; there was plenty of work yet to be done. "They have come a long way," she said. "Have they met my expectations? Not yet." The best way to motivate them, she believed, was to advertise a bright future. She encouraged Holly Simon, the guidance counselor, to talk to the tenth-grade girls about their college dreams, and over the holidays had contacted the college counselor at the school her younger daughter had attended. He had encouraged Chevere to send Serena away from home for college, helped them find the right school, and then guided them through the process of applying for financial aid. She hoped he would volunteer to help set up a college counseling program at TYWLS.

TYWLS graduates going to college: That single idea kept Chevere going despite the day-to-day problems she faced. She had already identified a quartet of eighth graders who would likely not return for ninth grade, girls who were failing their classes while their parents complained that the school was somehow failing them. She was prepared to replace any teacher who did not seem to be bringing the girls along. Jenny Long was an improvement over her predecessor, but her lack of language skills made her a limited resource; she could hardly serve as a student advisor when all she could talk about was math. And Chevere had her eye on both of the science teachers, to see how well their students did on the Regents exams.

She pushed the girls, the parents, the teachers. She pushed herself. "I live with the school," was how she put it. Chevere thought about TYWLS in the shower in the morning, and at home, alone, in the evening. She made the ninety-minute commute to work by train and bus, and try as she might to think about anything else, she thought only about school. In the morning, it prepared her for the inevitable problems of the day. In the early evening, it helped her "reflect on the goings-on."

She knew that some of the families complained about her. They said she was demanding, strict, rigid; that she was too hard on the girls. On the ride home, Chevere reminded herself that she was doing the right thing. She was not here to be beloved; she was here to get results. "This is not the time to be loose," she told herself. "We need to do this, and I have to be this way."

17

Marlborough School

February 1999

PRINCE CHARMING PROVED to be as disruptive a force in real life as he had been in Cinderella's. Marlborough teachers were used to casting girls in boys' parts for plays and dance presentations, but sometimes the cheat did not work, and they had to import the real thing. Della Schleunes had choreographed the story of Cinderella as the centerpiece of the annual dance recital, and she needed a credible prince. If she put a girl up on stage, romancing Cinderella, the piece would lurch dangerously close to parody. She asked a friend who had danced with the Dance Theatre of Harlem to help her out.

She had worked hard all year to make the girls comfortable with themselves. Her profession was known for its harsh aesthetic—an impossibly skinny body was the ideal, and the rounded assets of womanhood, full breasts or curvy hips, were considered detriments. But the girls in Dance Dimensions were not professional dancers, and Schleunes told them time and again that what mattered was how they danced and how they worked together. How they looked was beside the point. When the year began, Schleunes had lined all of them up in front of the floor-to-ceiling mirror in the main dance studio. "Find one thing about yourself that's pretty okay," she said, "and decide that whoever sees you sees *that*."

The arrival of the prince changed everything. Edward Alan Jenkins was tall, handsome, and an authoritative presence onstage. He was accommodating and not at all arrogant, which disarmed the girls completely. He showed them how to help him during a lift; he reassured the bigger girls that he would have no problem getting them off the ground. They giggled and shrugged and, in private, swore to lose five pounds immediately.

Schleunes overheard them and posted a sign in the performing-arts hallway, reminding the girls that it was a dancer's responsibility to be well-fed and well-hydrated. She called a group meeting and informed the girls that she expected them to function "on a non-apologetic basis."

Sommer Louie worried about Prince Charming's lift, despite his reassurances. She worried about her own choreographed piece and the routines she had to memorize for her friends' dance numbers—eight pieces in all, which had to be ready for the second week of February. She stayed at school every night until six o'clock, when her father came to pick her up.

The whole time she was there, she worried about the mail. It was too soon for acceptance or rejection letters, but there were all kinds of other official documents: financial aid forms, invitations to visit a campus, acknowledgments of applications, notices about missing bits of information.

With Sommer out of the house until dinner time, her mother succumbed to temptation and opened the college mail. She remembered Dr. Lewandowski's warning at the start of the year, about how parents needed to step back and let their girls take responsibility for the application process. It meant nothing in the context of seventeen years of yearning.

Sommer complained about the intrusion, but her mother did not stop. Finally, after getting home late from a dance rehearsal, Sommer lost her temper.

"*Don't open my mail!*" she screamed at her mother. "*Don't. Don't touch it.* Just leave it out there for me. Don't say anything about it. Don't touch it."

"I just thought it might have been about financial aid things," Phyllis replied. For all the talk of trust and responsibility, Phyllis felt that she was the only one in the family who was being realistic about college. But Sommer saw it differently: To her, there was a big difference between staying on top of things and nagging. After the blowup, Phyllis forced herself to wait. She did not open the envelope from Rice University, so her daughter had the pleasure of being first to read the special invitation to visit the campus, all expenses paid. The whole family was invited, but Robert deferred to his wife about who should make the trip, and Phyllis had her job and an ailing uncle she visited every night. They decided to send Sommer on her own.

Phyllis asked Sommer to tell Monica Ward about the invitation, to see what the college counselor thought about it, and Sommer came back with a report. "Monica said that this is a really good indication," she informed her mother. "A strong indication."

Phyllis tried not to get too excited. Like an athlete at the end of a long race, she felt she had to conserve her strength. "I don't want to start packing yet," she told herself. "So we'll see. Or should I? I don't know."

Sommer got a letter of acceptance from USC and a call from the alumni association there about a scholarship, but she indulged a new optimism and insisted that she was not interested. Phyllis backed her up. "SC," she announced proudly, "is not a stretch for Sommer."

When Phyllis brought in the mail on Saturday, February 20, there was an envelope from Tulane University, one of the schools on Sommer's short list of favorites. Phyllis handed it to Sommer—who, despite her angrily stated intention to open all college mail while alone in her room, tore open the envelope in front of her mother. The illogic of apprehension had vanished. Now that she had real news in her hand, Sommer needed her mother at her side.

Sommer opened the envelope and broke into a huge smile. "I got accepted to Tulane," she said.

"Let me see this letter," her mother replied. She had to read it for herself.

"I do like Tulane," said Sommer, though they both knew it was not her first choice. "At least now I can go somewhere. Someone wants me."

In a daze, she called Erica and two other Internationals, but no one was home to share her good news. She left messages on their answering machines and wandered outside to tell her father, who was working in his garden.

When Phyllis had recovered a bit, she had a question. "Sommer," she asked, "did you apply for any of the scholarships at Tulane?" Neither of them could remember, so they pulled her Tulane folder from the box of college files. There was nothing on their copy of the application about financial aid, but when Phyllis read more closely, she realized that Sommer had qualified automatically, based on the general financial information her parents had provided.

Phyllis felt better. Sommer didn't care. As much as her mother worried about which school would provide the most aid, Sommer refused to think about it. This was no time to discuss limitations.

As her mother said, "Sommer doesn't give a damn. She wants to go where she wants to go, and if she has to work for the next hundred and fifty thousand years to pay off her student loans, then that's what she's going to have to do."

They both were invited to a tea the next day for prospective Stanford University minority students, hosted by an alumna. On her second try, Sommer had raised her combined SAT score to 1310–a substantial increase from 1260, but still below Stanford's supposed cutoff of 1340. It was important for her to make a good impression at the tea, so she and her mother turned to the question of what to wear. They debated, into the afternoon, about whether the shoulder pads in Sommer's good green jacket were too assertive.

Erica Forneret got in at the University of Southern California, but she did not want to go to a school so close to home, hemmed in by familiar landmarks and family dinners. She still held out hope that Brown would take her–and if not, that she would get into Columbia or Sarah Lawrence. She never thought much about Yale, or Stanford, which were long shots;

she just wanted to leave Los Angeles. College was supposed to be an adventure.

Erica was ready for a change. Her self-diagnosed case of "senioritis" had flared up in January, when she suddenly found herself unable to focus and unwilling to care. First she dropped out of Dr. Forsheit's special science-research group. Lab work never went quickly enough to sustain her interest, and the prospect of spending the second semester doing research put her to sleep. She felt guilty for letting Dr. Forsheit down, and she felt like a quitter, but she dropped the research project anyway. She auditioned for a production of the Anita Loos play *The Women,* and won the part of a scatterbrained, independently wealthy woman who drinks her way through multiple marriages.

She learned her lines and showed up at rehearsals, but that was the extent of Erica's discipline. She dashed off her homework assignments during a free period, or never did them at all. If she had resented Dr. Morgan last semester for failing to help her take part in English class, now she depended on her teachers' benign neglect to keep her out of the spotlight. When it was sunny, she might wander over to Larchmont for ice cream during her free period, or for lunch with her friends. After school, she liked to head home and watch old movies on television. Some days, she never even opened her backpack to see what she was supposed to be doing.

It was "so pointless," she said, to push herself. Schools decided before they saw this semester's grades. She wasn't going to flunk out. There was lots of room to maneuver, between her usual behavior and what she needed this term to get by.

Her parents did not push her. They left Erica alone to watch TV, catch her breath, and ponder the one important social event of the school year— the prom, which was held at the end of April. Phyllis had already found a prom dress for her daughter, a shimmery silver one with a little train. Erica loved the dress. The only issue was who her escort would be, if she found one at all. Erica Forneret had had only one date in her life, because of what her mother called her "very high standards." She would rather be alone than be with someone she did not like, so at the moment there was no candidate for prom date.

She and her friends usually went to school dances together, because none of them had much of a social life, but the prom was different. Sommer and another friend of Erica's both knew boys they wanted to take, but the boys claimed so far to be more interested in friendship than romance. They might be telling the truth, or that might be code for wanting a romance with someone else. They might be playing hard to get. The girls anticipated weeks of effort ahead of them.

As far as Erica was concerned, figuring out what a boy really meant was often more trouble than it was worth. For now, she would have to settle for a good part in the school play, a beautiful dress, and possibility. Another month or two of languid waiting, and maybe she would hook up with a college, and a boy, she liked.

Katie Tower got home on the afternoon of Tuesday, February 23 to unexpected good news: a letter of acceptance from the University of Southern California. Like Sommer and Erica, she had no intention of attending USC. It was her insurance policy in case the entire east coast, the midwest, and the UC system turned their backs on her. Yet she was amazed at how happy she felt. Her mother was pleased. Even her usually undemonstrative father was excited.

She had also been invited to join Marlborough's Cum Laude society, which was restricted to the top five percent of the junior class and the top ten percent of the seniors. When she thought about it, she probably had been crazy ever to worry about being accepted somewhere. But there were two levels of reality these days: getting into college, and getting into the right college.

Two days later, at a senior class meeting in the Living Room, Katie stood in front of her classmates in a sample graduation dress alongside another girl who modeled a different style. Katie's sample, which was a size too big for her slender frame, had a boat neck that threatened to slip off her shoulders, so a classmate stood behind her and held the dress tight from neckline to waist. The other model inhabited her sample perfectly—a dress with wide straps, a fitted bodice, and a slightly flared skirt.

Katie hoped that today's meeting would go better than the last one had. She had begun to wish that "girls like me, who could wear anything," would stop arguing, and try to be a little more understanding. "They're resisting just because they don't want anyone to tell them what to do," she said, "but since they *could* wear anything, why don't they go along?"

The opposing contingent—the girls whose figures were not as adaptable as Katie's—spoke first. Her friend Tai, who was short and plump, asked the other model, "Are you wearing a bra?"

"Are you?" asked Lisl, a strident voice in the pro-bra faction.

"What *about* bras?" wailed a tall, heavyset girl.

"No problem," said an athletically-built girl who was one of the senior class officers. She turned to the two mothers who were in charge of graduation dresses and pronounced, loudly, "You have to be mindful of bras."

"She's not wearing one," replied one of the women, reassuringly, "but with those straps it will be fine."

Everyone was trying to keep the peace. Les Klein encouraged the girls to take a vote right now, even though several seniors, including Sommer, were away visiting colleges, but the group was evenly split. Katie and the other girl swapped dresses—and in the name of compassion, Katie confessed to one problem that might bother the pro-bra faction.

"The straps are set very wide," she said. "You kind of feel insecure."

"Like they're going to fall off?" asked the mom.

"No," said Katie. "Just—insecure."

Given this new information, Klein called for another vote, and got only ten girls in favor of the dress with straps. No matter. Class loyalty decreed that they wait until Monday for a final vote; they could not make a decision when so many of their friends were away.

Lisl waited while Katie changed back into her uniform, and the two of them headed for their next class. Katie was amused by the extended debate, but Lisl was incensed. She reminded Katie that she had spent the night before last year's graduation consoling a friend who was in tears because the graduation dress had a low-cut back that exposed her acne. Lisl thought it was "sexist" to require the girls to wear dresses, proof that "the feminist bullshit everyone talks means nothing." If Marlborough wanted to celebrate academic achievement, they ought to put the girls in caps and gowns.

That was a tradition worth perpetuating—not this silly argument about who was going to look prettier in which dress.

M ARCH WAS women's History Month, and in the wake of the graduation-dress debate, Marlborough confronted self-image with a special all-school assembly featuring Dr. Joan Jacobs Brumberg, a professor at Cornell University. Dr. Brumberg had written two books about the collision between cultural pressures and a girl's sense of herself, *Fasting Girls: The History of Anorexia Nervosa,* and *The Body Project: An Intimate History of American Girls.* The title of her speech was "From Corsets to Body Piercing."

She was a pugnacious woman in her fifties, and she attacked her subject with a fervor characteristic of women who had come of age in the first wave of the women's movement. Unlike the girls in the auditorium, who grew up assuming opportunity, Dr. Brumberg vividly remembered a time when most women accepted the roles of wife and mother as their destiny. She wanted these girls to understand that society was used to telling women what to do—and that even seemingly independent young women like them were vulnerable to outside influences. She started out with a rattling set of statistics: By the age of seventeen, according to her research, 78 percent of American girls reported that they disliked their bodies. Girls as young as eight and nine complained to their pediatricians that they were fat and needed to go on a diet.

Teenage girls had become "appearance junkies, valuing their appearance over creativity, intelligence, generosity, kindness," said Dr. Brumberg. "And there's anecdotal evidence, though it's not yet established in the literature, that it's worse in southern California than anywhere else in the country."

There was in this country an epidemic of what she called "bad body fever," and she believed that the only way to eradicate it was to confront it. To bolster her argument, she read excerpts about New Year's resolutions from two different girls' diaries. The first spoke purely in terms of personality traits she wanted to improve, while the second girl wrote about how she wanted to look and what she hoped to buy.

"One diary projects good works," said Dr. Brumberg. "The other projects good looks." The first diary, one of the ones she had collected for *The Body Project,* was from 1892; the second, the one that focused on appearance, was from 1982. The implication was that today's young woman had replaced moral concerns with a narcissistic set of desires. "So what's happened?" Dr. Brumberg asked her audience. "Can we blame it all on Calvin Klein, on advertising? Can we blame Hollywood? MTV? Are you the first generation to feel this way? What was it like in the past to get your period, to develop acne, to start to feel sexual?"

She presented a slide show of 20th-century photographs and advertisements, designed to illustrate how the media defined femininity. She wanted the girls to see just how aggressive the message was, how pervasive the cult of physical beauty. If they understood the pressure they were under, they would be better able to defend themselves against it.

There were two theories about the role that single-sex education played in a girl's self-image. The majority view held that girls grew up with a healthier attitude about their physical appearance, because good looks held no currency during the school day. Marlborough and TYWLS were meant to be vanity-free zones, where the only part of the anatomy worth advertising was the brain. The one nod to a girl's physical identity was an expanded sports program, which enabled her to define herself in terms of fitness, not beauty.

That was the ideal. In reality, the absence of boys could have an unintended negative effect. With no one around to "leaven" the conversation, as one girl put it, girls sometimes indulged in an almost obsessive analysis of their physical attributes and flaws. Several of the seniors recalled ninth and tenth grade as the most difficult time, when an entire lunch-period conversation might revolve around the relative merits of someone's thighs.

Dr. Brumberg called that phenomenon "the hothouse effect," an ironic consequence of separating out a bunch of intelligent girls. "The brightest girls are often the ones who are the most highly perfectionist—and there's also the issue of mimetic behavior among girls," she told her audience. Isolate a group of teenage girls, and inevitably the talk turned to an often-scorching appraisal of those physical attributes they believed they could control—particularly their weight.

The solution, she felt, was for a school like Marlborough to acknowledge the issue. "I don't think that simply by being in a girls' school you're protected," she said, "but I do think that you're getting other kinds of things that help you cope with this. A single-sex school can put emphasis on other things besides reading *YM* and *Seventeen*. It's also more likely that the school will have a course like Gender and Sexuality or Women's History, where a teacher who wears some feminist lens herself will have the girls going through their magazines and cutting out ads that are offensive. Developing some critical-thinking skills."

Girls' schools offered "great freedom," she believed, because they provided a girl with "the opportunity to be herself." But seven hours a day without boys was not enough to guarantee a healthy adolescence—and anyone who thought otherwise was, in her estimation, naïve.

Dr. Brumberg had agreed to stay on campus for lunch with any student-government officers or seniors who wanted to meet her in Dr. Morgan's classroom. Erica decided to go—not because she was particularly interested, but because she was loopy with exhaustion from the rehearsal schedule for *The Women*. Erica felt herself exempt from modern ideas about beauty. She had a timeless, theatrical sense of style that had nothing to do with fashion trends. Erica liked a signature necklace of heavy, round silver beads or a skirt made from a vintage tablecloth, regardless of what everyone else was wearing. Still, being occupied was better than giving in to fatigue.

Christina came to lunch because she was interested in the intellectual debate about body image and women's role in society. Between her fight with diabetes and her stint in a back brace, she had never had the luxury of fretting about her looks. She was curious about girls who came at life from the opposite direction.

The class officers came because they felt it was their duty.

Katie Tower and her friend Lisl came because they were furious. To them, all this talk of "bad body fever" was a colossal insult, no better than a racial or religious slur. What right did a stranger have to suggest that every girl in the auditorium was neurotic about her appearance?

For the first ten minutes, the lunchtime session was a polite round of agreeable sentiment: Several girls wanted to talk about advertisements they hated, and one devoutly embraced the idea of "being more aware of ourselves." Dr. Brumberg referred to herself as "unlean," and the girls chuckled. Dr. Morgan and Les Klein hovered in the background with a parent who had offered to serve as Dr. Brumberg's chaperone for the day.

Finally, Lisl could stand it no longer. She had strict criteria for true gender equality, and she saw insidious threats where most of her friends did not. She believed in hygiene—her long, straight strawberry blond hair was always shiny and clean—but beyond that, she took an almost belligerent stance about her appearance. She rarely bothered to tuck in her uniform shirt, and she preferred dark slacks to the more popular short skirt over boys' boxer shorts. She often wore a school blazer, as though happy for the extra camouflage, and favored heavy, lug-soled shoes.

To her, all this talk about looks was somebody else's problem. It had nothing to do with her life. She was going to Brown University and intended to become an engineer. Gender and looks were irrelevant to that. In fact, she found Dr. Brumberg's presentation to be condescending—a double standard masquerading as a commitment to equality.

"Using the terms like bad body fever and stuff, I think you're really emphasizing negative aspects," Lisl said. "Putting all this emphasis on how the female appears, and what the teenage girl appears to be. My question to you would be, Do you think you're adding to it? When you speak so fervently about how we have to stop this, or look at the impact—don't you think you're simply adding to it?"

Dr. Brumberg was startled by Lisl's question. She picked her words carefully. "I'm a historian," she said, "and I'm reporting on what the clinical establishment is saying. Do you follow what I'm saying? I didn't do the research. The data show—and it may not be your problem, all right?—that women in America are dissatisfied with themselves, and that they're more demanding about physical appearance than any other aspect of their lives: their creativity, their athleticism, their sociability, their relationships."

Her voice tightened up. "I didn't make that up, okay? I'm trying to explain why we might have come to that position. I'm not chastising you."

Lisl refused to yield. "Doesn't dissatisfaction create change, though? So wouldn't that be a beneficial change? Maybe we're in sort of a time of change."

Dr. Brumberg cut Lisl off. How could anyone consider a negative self-image to be a tool of progress? "Dissatisfaction about your body," she said, incredulous. "You think that is going to generate social change?"

"About whatever," said Lisl. "Any dissatisfaction moves people to change things." She accused Dr. Brumberg of acting as though beauty were a bad thing, and attention to hygiene and athletics, evidence of a superficial nature. Perhaps girls were simply being practical about how the world worked. She brandished a magazine ad that touted yogurt. "Look at this," Lisl said. "It says, 'You need yogurt or else you're not going to get a date.' In some ways, isn't that *true?*" The girls Lisl knew who had boyfriends were slimmer and prettier than the other girls. Maybe the ads were merely a reflection of reality, not an attempt to define it.

Dr. Brumberg and the teachers had hardly expected such antagonism, and Lisl was not finished. What really infuriated her was the implicit suggestion that Marlborough girls were no different than anyone else.

"We heard you say that external appearance came in lieu of good deeds and actions and stuff," she said. "I don't think you can say that vanity has totally disappeared from Marlborough's campus, but we're *heavily motivated people here.* It's hard for us to look at somebody who's omitting that part of our life and saying—"

Dr. Brumberg cut her off. "You're taking the thesis of my book somewhat as an insult," she said.

"I'm not," said Lisl. "I'm just explaining to you, since you seem rather surprised—"

"You regard it as a charge that women of your generation are shallow."

"It's *personal*," said Katie. "Maybe I feel *better* in makeup or certain clothes."

"What's wrong with enjoying it?" chimed in another girl.

"There's nothing wrong with enjoying it," replied Dr. Brumberg.

"That's the way you're coming off," said Lisl.

Dr. Brumberg appealed to Dr. Morgan, who had arranged for her visit. "In fairness to me," she said, "have these people read my book?"

Dr. Morgan sighed. One assigned chapter.

Dr. Brumberg decided to make her case one last time. "The book is about the way in which in the twentieth century, not just young women but everybody, regards the body as perfectible," she said. "That's a change in our intellectual psyche. If you deny that the body is a critical piece of your self-identity, I think you're being pretty defensive. Your parents watch their cholesterol. Your grandparents may be counting their fat grams. This is the kind of culture in which we live. My charge is not that you're shallow and you don't have other interests. What I'm telling you is that if you looked at these diaries the way I have, from the 1830s to the 1980s, you'll find there is a big shift in the way girls think about themselves."

Her stern tone of voice was a warning. As the session drew to a close, she would not tolerate interruption.

"This is not an argument against makeup, against earrings, against getting dressed up and taking care of yourself," she said. "But you are a little blind and a little defensive if you can't admit that there are people in this culture who become appearance junkies. *I'm not saying that you all are like that.* I'm not saying that you don't do wonderful things. . . . I'm just telling you that girls beat themselves up today about appearance in ways they didn't in the nineteenth century. That's the thesis. If that is threatening and upsetting to you, I'm quite surprised."

She reminded them that boys were not immune to similar behavior; there were "gym rats" who spent all their free time working out, and there was steroid use, which to Dr. Brumberg was the male analog of anorexia.

Her audience was plainly skeptical. For six years, they had lived in a world that considered them capable. The last thing they needed to hear, as they waited out the final weeks before the college letters arrived, was that they carried an internalized flaw, like a damaged gene, that rendered them not quite good enough: lacking in depth, concerned with frivolous things.

Their nerves were too raw to appreciate Dr. Brumberg's study. All they heard was a middle-aged woman telling them that they were narcissists. She was the universal bad mother, wagging a disapproving finger in their faces, and they simply did not want to hear what she had to say.

Erica's friend Chrissy, a gracious, soft-spoken girl, tried to lower the temperature in the room with a confession. People were always telling her she was not thin enough, or needed more makeup, or ought to color her hair, "and they say it's not for yourself—it's so a boy will like you."

One of the other girls cut her off. There was no way to rid the world of people who said stupid things, but a smart girl refused to listen—and surrounded herself with like-minded people. A Marlborough girl did not need instruction. She just needed other girls who understood.

"You need a friend to say, 'No, no, you're plenty thin,'" said one senior. "Girls need to say that."

When the bell rang, the girls fairly stomped out of the room, leaving the teachers to offer their abashed apologies for the seniors' behavior. They had never imagined such a defensive response. Dr. Brumberg said it was far worse than anything she had seen on the east coast, and she wondered: Did the teachers think that girls in Los Angeles were worried about other people's assumptions about the west coast? Were they afraid of being considered "flakes" by everyone else?

The parent volunteer suggested it was something else—a good thing, in fact. The girls' response proved that Marlborough had done what it set out to do, and produced a group of independent young women. "The girls really see themselves as better than everyone else," she said, "because they've been allowed to go to Marlborough." If the idea behind a girls' school was to make the girls feel sure of themselves, then of course they would resist the idea that they were hamstrung by vanity. That was something that happened to other girls, at coed schools.

"They will find out that life's not like this," said the parent, "but at least

Marlborough postpones that realization until college." Perhaps they would be better able to cope with "bad body fever" for having had shelter from it, if only for seven hours a day.

As for the adults, they had to face the unexpected consequence of their efforts: Girls who were raised to believe in themselves might well grow up to disagree with their teachers.

18

THE AMERICAN ASSOCIATION of University Women started the stampede to girls' schools with its 1992 report, "How Schools Shortchange Girls," which enumerated all the ways in which the coeducational classroom denied girls an equal education. Parents who could afford a choice responded by seeking out single-sex schools for their daughters—and that new wave of interest revived girls' schools like Marlborough, which embarked on a program of self-improvement designed to make them competitive with the best coeducational college-preparatory schools.

Had supply and demand been an issue only for wealthy families who chose to opt out of the public schools, the trend would have been of less concern to social critics or policy makers. But many parents could not afford to buy their daughters a way out of the coed classroom, and they looked to the public schools to eliminate inequality. The AAUW report demanded a response, so public schools stepped gingerly into the business of creating an equitable place for a girl to learn.

TYWLS was the first of a new generation of public schools to give girls their own classes. Other public school systems, mindful of the challenges TYWLS had faced, devised programs that stopped short of complete separation. Districts in Maine, New Hampshire, Illinois, and Virginia split up girls and boys for math or science classes, while in California, Governor Pete Wilson devised an experimental plan that neatly sidestepped any accusations of preferential treatment for girls.

Starting in the fall of 1997, Wilson awarded $500,000 grants to seven schools around the state as part of the Single Gender Academies Pilot Program, a two-year experiment designed to provide a supportive environment for at-risk boys and an intensive math-and-science program for girls, in a shared facility. One of the most ambitious schools, in Fountain Valley, south of Los Angeles, catered to seventy kids the system had already spit out: dropouts, drug casualties, pregnant teens. Boys went to class in the morning, and girls went in the afternoon.

The AAUW had inadvertently opened a Pandora's box of problems. Critics insisted that the separation of public-school students by gender was as unacceptable as the exclusion of blacks had been before the 1954 Supreme Court decision in Brown v. The Board of Education. Inclusion had been the guiding principle of American public education since then, and girls' schools sounded suspiciously like a return to an exclusionary policy. The goal might be the same as it had been in the 1960s—to achieve parity with white male students, who continued to set the standard for achievement—but this time, separatism was being touted as the solution, not the problem.

In TYWLS's case, though, the objections had generated a tower of documents and no action, and one of the school's main adversaries had frankly lost interest in shutting it down. Norman Siegel, the director of the New York Civil Liberties Union, said that he had "more important things to do" than pursue a little school in East Harlem. He was far more concerned about the incendiary activities of the New York City Police Department. The officers accused of brutalizing Haitian immigrant Abner Louima were about to go on trial, and in February, four other officers had killed a young African man, Amadou Diallo, as he reached for his wallet to show them identification. There was no time to pursue a school that wanted to improve the math and reading skills of disadvantaged girls, even if he disagreed with its tactics.

On March 12, 1998, the AAUW issued a new report, "Separated by Sex: A Critical Look at Single-Sex Education for Girls," based on a one-day forum the group had held in November 1997. They concluded that although inequity still defined the coeducational classroom, the data were not compelling enough to support an endorsement of single-sex schools. Independent and parochial schools could continue to do as they liked, but the only fair solution for the public schools was system-wide reform.

If this sounded like a reversal of the group's 1992 position, the AAUW insisted it had been misunderstood from the start. The 1992 report was supposed to lead to reform of existing classrooms, not mass defection. In 1995, the AAUW had endorsed what it called "short-term experiments in separate schooling, emphasizing the need for further assessment." Now it was time to evaluate the data.

AAUW executive director Janice Weinman told *The New York Times,* "A lot of things pushed people toward single-sex alternatives; some people were looking for easy solutions. . . . We went in with an open mind, and what the research shows is that boys and girls both thrive when the elements of good education are there, elements like smaller classes, focused academic curriculum, and gender-fair instruction."

The AAUW's review of the existing literature proved primarily that the study of gender in the classroom was still a young science, vulnerable to second-guessing and structural flaws. What two authors called the "statistical nuisance" of selection bias kept getting in the way: It was impossible to randomly assign students to single-sex or coeducational classrooms, so there was no definitive way to tell whether gender affected outcome. It might simply be that the best students in a given location preferred one type of school over the other. The bias was a particular obstacle in the United States, since private single-sex schools attracted students who already enjoyed the benefits of economic and social privilege.

Most of the studies the AAUW reviewed focused on quantifiable measures of achievement—test scores, grades, the percentage of girls enrolled in advanced mathematics and science classes—and disagreed on whether a singlesex class or school made a difference. Two Irish studies ignored achievement and instead addressed the issue of self-esteem, with provocative results. A 1990 study concluded that a single-sex school did in fact benefit a girl's selfesteem. A 1993 study found that levels of self-esteem might not vary with the school environment, but the source of that self-esteem did. Girls at coed schools tended to evaluate themselves on the basis of appearance, while girls who attended single-sex schools were likelier to base their selfesteem on academic achievement.

That single finding might seem to be a selling point for an all-girls school within the public school system, given the short shelf-life of physical beauty in a culture that idolizes young women. The AAUW took a more cautious stance, calling for more and better research.

The four papers presented at the conference suggested that consensus was a long way off. One researcher admitted that her findings were inconsistent, but believed that single-sex schools represented "short-term and seemingly easier reforms [that] often deflect effort from the more difficult changes. . . ." Another study implied that researchers were asking questions based on questionable assumptions about gender and behavior. A third called for further research, but admitted to finding "threads . . . that suggest some possible positive effects of these classes for girls."

Cornelius Riordan, a sociology professor at Providence College, was the strongest voice in favor of single-sex education. His complaints about coeducation hearkened back to the writings of David and Myra Sadker: Equality was "a scarce commodity" at coed schools, which he considered "male-dominated and male-controlled cultural institutions"; the best hope for the poor, for minorities, and for girls was to get out. The girls who went to TYWLS stood to benefit most from a single-sex school, according to Riordan, because they belonged to all three categories.

"Single-sex schools provide an avenue for students to make a proacademic choice," he wrote. "Single-sex schools should not be expected to correct the gender-equity problems that exist in society and in coeducational schools. Nor should anyone fear that their existence would detract in any way from efforts that should be made to provide greater gender equity in public coeducational schools."

But Riordan's endorsement was lost in media coverage of the AAUW report, which focused instead on the group's apparent change of heart. Weinman said that the AAUW would support single-sex experimentation in the public schools only if it was accompanied by more research. What girls really needed was the equivalent of clinical trials for new drugs—studies designed to isolate the effects of sexual segregation on a randomly selected group of girls.

Ann Tisch told *The New York Times* that TYWLS was not interested in becoming a laboratory in some long-running experiment. Data were useless to current TYWLS students, who could not wait while researchers compiled more information. They would have graduated by then—or they would be out on the street without a high school diploma, like many of their peers at local coeducational high schools. The school existed to offer families an escape. Tisch was not about to surrender TYWLS; she would not punish the girls for not having the money to buy their way out.

The day after the AAUW report was released, *The Wall Street Journal* ran a blistering editorial that accused the group of misrepresenting its own latest findings. The AAUW had "tanked its own study. . . ." the *Journal* complained. "The [press] release is more categorically negative than virtually anything you will read in the study's text."

The editorial said that a careful reading of the report showed far more enthusiasm for single-sex education than the AAUW was prepared to admit: "It is at worst uncertain about the school's benefits, and in many places says all sorts of positive things about them." The *Journal* blamed "political partisans" who were afraid of strengthening the school choice movement and drawing the best students away from public schools.

Neither side addressed Ann Tisch's dream of a network of public schools like TYWLS. The *Journal* failed to mention it at all, while the AAUW made only glancing reference to "a strategy . . . that has questionable legality and questionable evidence of success."

———

For the teachers at Marlborough, the AAUW report was noise in the far distance, an intellectual exercise that had nothing to do with daily life. Barbara Wagner dismissed it as a political document, a careful retreat from the first report, which had been widely interpreted as a call for single-sex schools. Coed schools were guilty of neglect, whether conscious or not, and girls' schools were there to compensate. Wagner did not need any more studies to convince her.

She was concerned with a different problem. Girls at coed schools often suffered from too little attention—but girls at single-sex schools sometimes felt that there was too much. Marlborough students were surrounded by other girls who were just as determined as they were to live up to everyone's expectations. The challenge for the faculty, the girls, and their parents was to identify the point where striving deteriorated into stress. The girls had to do their best without tipping over.

Three years ago, the eighth graders had been casualties of too much work and too little feedback. Part of the solution had been to postpone some of the academic pressure until ninth grade, but this year the ninth grade had rebelled in what Wagner called a "work hysteria." They complained about too much homework, too many tests and quizzes, too many projects, too little preparation. They knew that they needed to do well in their classes, but they needed sports, they needed boys, they needed fun as well.

In the early years of the women's movement, equality came dressed in a man-tailored suit and a foulard silk tie. It took years for women to think about what they might want beyond the same opportunities men had. In the first decade of the new girls' school—when "separate but equal" was redefined as an advantage—administrators like Wagner struggled to find a balance between working the girls as hard as a boy had ever worked, and creating a more enlightened environment in which they could learn. Sometimes, as in Dr. Forsheit's advanced research tutorial, it was possible to do both. Sometimes it seemed a tug of war.

The debate crystallized for Wagner in the spring, when Susanna Jones, the director of the Upper School, informed her that she was leaving to take the job of head of school at Ethel Walker, a Connecticut boarding school. Ms. Jones had come to Marlborough six years earlier, with the current graduating class, and her tenure had been successful on every level: The girls' academic performance and record of college acceptances had made Marlborough an increasingly popular choice for new families, and the students adored Jones, often seeking her out as a confidante. She left a legacy of more AP offerings, better test scores, and happy girls. Wagner had to find someone who could build on her accomplishments without destroying the Upper School's equilibrium.

Wagner intended to begin a national search for Jones's replacement, but before she did anything she asked Jim Skrumbis, the Middle School dean of students and a member of the history department, if he intended to apply for the job. At thirty-six, having had what he called "just about every lower-level administrative job you can have," Skrumbis had arrived at a critical point in his career. A year ago, he had been a candidate for the job of director of the Middle School, and when Laura Hotchkiss got that job, Wagner had invented the dean of students position for Skrumbis. He had already begun to chafe in the role. A short, trim man with an athletic stride, always available for a pickup basketball game at lunchtime, Skrumbis was a competitor. He wanted a new game.

Skrumbis loved the school. He had started as a part-time teacher in 1986, "petrified" and thrilled at the prospect of working with Doc Langdon, the legendary head of the history department. Since there was no opening for a full-time teacher, Skrumbis went into self-imposed exile a year later and spent nine years at another private school. A chance encounter with Langdon brought him back to Marlborough, this time as the older man's colleague. He and Doc taught sections of Ancient Civilization, a class Skrumbis described proudly: "It's the rite-of-passage course. Old-fashioned rigor, lectures, discussion. It's incredibly popular with the parents and the kids, but there's a lot of work. It's a college-level presentation."

In a way, Ancient Civ symbolized Skrumbis's philosophy: he wanted to help build a school where the girls worked hard and never backed down.

He had to submit a statement of educational philosophy as part of his job application, and to do so he referred to the statement he had prepared for the Middle School job. He had disagreed with the then-head of the Middle School, who saw it as a separate entity. The incumbent had pushed for "a middle-school environment that is not content-driven, that is a unique experience," according to Skrumbis, "a very gentle approach as relates to homework and curriculum, a nurturing, humanistic—some would say anti-intellectual—approach. That's where the rub is, that's where the argument comes."

Skrumbis felt that this approach lulled the younger girls into a false sense of security that vanished when they hit tenth grade. He believed that Marlborough ought to acknowledge seventh graders' wobbly self-image, but not pander to it.

In his statement for the Upper School job, he reiterated his commitment to academic excellence.

> Providing an intellectually rigorous experience that produces independent thinkers and self-reliant problem solvers must be at the core of Marlborough's academic experience. The dramatic challenges and opportunities that these young women face must be addressed by continuing to offer curricula that are sensitive to their particular needs and, perhaps more importantly, by developing a sense of community wherein our girls know they are supported and encouraged by parents, teachers, and administrators—whether that be on the field, on the stage, or in the classroom.

He knew that his emphasis on six years of strenuous academics might raise the collective stress level, but as dean of students he had already come up with ways to alleviate pressure. Skrumbis prided himself on being a guy who knew how to have "pure, unadulterated fun," from the all-school picnic he helped to organize to an assembly featuring a hypnotist who put willing volunteers in a trance. Hard work was at the center of his vision for Marlborough, but there would be plenty of time to blow off steam.

"We don't claim that this is going to take care of all the problems of feeling overworked and overwhelmed," he said, "but it's a start."

By March, Skrumbis was one of four applicants to have survived the initial screening, and like the candidates from outside the school, he spent a day being interviewed by students and faculty. He told them all the same thing: Reducing the work-load was not the way to reduce stress; often it was the girls who put pressure on themselves, pushing to do more as a way to prove their abilities. He was mindful of what he heard from "a substantial portion of the parents," he said. "They tell me, 'We've chosen this school, we're willing to pay fourteen to sixteen thousand dollars a year, and we're willing to trust that all this homework is legitimate, because we've got this college priority.'" Some parents might have been concerned about losing their daughters under an avalanche of work, but they were in the minority.

LES KLEIN GAVE a lot of thought to applying for the job Skrumbis wanted. Her passion for the school was probably her greatest attribute; her lack of respect for the rules, her greatest weakness. "I'm really bad at enforcing the rules," she admitted. "I haven't given a demerit slip since I got here. And I'm a process person. I like to throw out creative ideas, but I'm no good at follow-through. I'm not good at it, and I don't like it."

Still, this was probably the one opportunity she would have to affect Marlborough's future; the job of Upper School director might not come up again during her tenure. She approached two girls she had had in her classes, one already in college and the other still at Marlborough. She wanted their advice. Did they think she ought to apply for the job?

"Essentially they laughed in my face," she said. "You're a *teacher*," they told her, which was far different from being an administrator. She decided not to apply; she would put her energy into the selection process instead.

Klein liked Jim Skrumbis, but she worried a little about all his talk of more competitive sports and a Middle School that truly prepared the girls for the academic demands of the Upper School. Some of the struggles that plagued the Middle School were developmental; it was a time when girls tended toward emotional outbursts, no matter what adults did to make their lives easier. But many of the girls labored under what Klein thought was a dangerous misconception: that suffering was somehow a measure of accomplishment.

"Had I gone forward with the job," she said, "the one thing that would have been my top priority is that stress does not equal quality. Spinning your wheels doesn't necessarily mean a quality education. It's the single most devastating aspect of life here."

She had recently seen three girls, "bright seniors," she said, who were copying one another's math homework—a violation of the school's honor code. Klein asked them what they were up to, and "One said, 'Hey, in seventh grade we just erased the name and handed in each other's work.' They very quickly learn to get around superfluous work."

She saw seventh graders drinking too much coffee because they needed to stay awake. Her junior-year students complained that they had four tests scheduled for next week, and a big English paper due right before spring break, when many of them hit the road to visit college campuses.

Sometimes Klein wondered if it would be a better idea "to allow the kids to go a bit more slowly." She remembered one student of hers who had gone to Harvard, only to come home before the end of her freshman year, too exhausted to keep up. "She was just *fried*," was Klein's recollection. Yet only last week Klein had found herself suggesting that her department add a tenth-grade honors English section. The department had resisted the idea for years, because it required even more work of the girls, but "colleges do want those scores and grades," said Klein, and starting honors in tenth grade might enhance verbal SAT scores and improve a girl's grade-point average, because of the weighted grade. She was caught between instinct and good intention, and she could not come up with a satisfactory answer to the question that plagued her.

"How do we provide a quality education," she wondered, "and have them not feel like they're just struggling to survive?"

When Skrumbis spoke to the faculty, he reiterated his position: School was not the place to back down. Like Barbara Wagner, Skrumbis thought about Marlborough in a larger context, as a big-city school in a high-pressure urban environment. There were other reasons the girls were stretched so thin.

"I don't think that's just a function of Marlborough," he said. "I think it's life in the nineties, on the west side of L.A., with all the demands of being a girl in an affluent family. I think we give these girls a great education and get them into great colleges. I also think it's hard to be sixteen years old and growing up in L.A."

THERE WAS POLICY, and then there were brush fires. Klein was one of two dozen teachers who sacrificed their lunch break on March 18 to talk about the seniors, who lately had begun to show up late, skip class altogether, and regard exams as an opportunity to use their bargaining skills. It might be "typical senior behavior," according to one physics teacher, but it set a bad example for the younger girls. The question was whether or not to ease up on the seniors, and the teachers, who had gathered around a big work table in the art studio, were divided into two camps. Klein belonged to the group who thought the girls needed a break, while other teachers took offense at the seniors' defiance.

One teacher had come up with a compromise that enabled him to acknowledge how tired the girls were without abandoning his agenda. At the start of the quarter, he had announced that he would give four scheduled tests. If a girl felt she needed more time, she could choose to delay a test for one day. A French teacher who had heard too many excuses said she was not about to reward the girls for falling apart.

"They are learning to play dumb," she complained, "so I just say no. This is the day you take the test. And so they do."

Arleen Forsheit thought that trying to get out of scheduled tests was only a symptom of a larger problem. She was tired of girls who acted as though they could negotiate a customized education. Marlborough was supposed to give girls a greater range of options than they might find in a coed school, but with that opportunity came responsibility. If they cared enough about their education to come to Marlborough, they had to be prepared to do the work.

"There's a culture that's developed in the Upper School," said Forsheit. "It's best symbolized by the student who said to me, 'I would like to take my test on this day.' And I said, 'Excuse me. This is not a matter of, I would *like*. If you need to change it, that's one thing." She had set the tone for her classes the previous fall, when she told her Anatomy and Physiology students that anyone who missed a test would lose one-third of her grade for every day's delay. The next day, almost 90 percent of the girls took the test.

One of the men at the table dismissed the girls' complaints. The workload was perfectly reasonable for a responsible girl. The problem was one of attitude. "They're manipulating the system," he said.

Klein resented the accusation. The faculty needed to talk about why the girls were behaving this way before they debated how to stop them. "To say that the kids are lying is offensive to me," she said. "They've fallen behind because they're ill? Why are they ill? I think these kids are stretched so far that they're susceptible. I know one kid, a junior, a very good student, and she's been so angry and in tears all week because she's got the first draft of her English presentation next week—*and* four tests. Why does she have four tests at the beginning of the quarter?"

The teachers who had scheduled those tests protested, in chorus, that they had already delayed the tests a week. One of the math teachers suggested that the faculty was to blame, for encouraging girls to take on more than they could handle. Perhaps the answer was not to push them to sign up for so many honors and AP sections.

Upper School director Susanna Jones broke in. "But the college counseling office is going to ask you for more," she said. As the application process grew ever more competitive, a girl needed those advanced credits to stand out.

"And some kids ask for more frequent assessments," said a physics teacher, "because they don't want to go for too long without a sense of how they're doing."

One teacher suggested setting a limit on the number of papers or tests a teacher could require, but Myranda Marsh did not want to hear any more talk about tactics. "These little things are nibbling away at the problem," she said. "I want to address a larger, structural problem: What are we obligated to give these girls by the time they graduate? We can only fix things if we know what the end point is we have to reach." In the past couple of days she had been told both to reduce the number of special projects she assigned, and to make sure that she adequately prepared the Middle School girls for the demands of the Upper School. She could not figure out how to do both.

Jones smiled gently, because she knew that Marsh would not care for her answer. No one was going to abandon the basic curriculum. Some of those added assignments might have to go.

"Myranda, to address your question, the college counselors will tell you that we're dealing with a baby boomlet," said Jones. "In the eighties, the colleges were empty, and they went on huge marketing campaigns, and now they're reaping the benefits—it's a very competitive environment. You're going to be surprised by a lot of the decisions you hear about in the next few weeks—and they won't be happy surprises."

She let that prediction sink in for a moment. "Our reputation rests, to great extent, on where our graduates go to college," she said. "For that, we have to make sure they do well on their SATs. Their parents' expectations are not going to change. I'm sorry to deliver such bad news, but we're operating under a lot of pressure."

The bell rang, and the teachers scattered without having agreed on what to do. Marsh stalked off, muttering to herself. The brave move would have been to eliminate some of the traditional aspects of the Middle School curriculum, like the endless memorization of historical facts, all of which were now available at the touch of a computer key. Better to emphasize some of the tools she used to help the seventh graders learn to be independent thinkers. She wanted more emphasis on how to think, not what to think. She wanted a little healthy upheaval. That was the best way to lower the stress level for the girls.

Marsh knew that she was unpopular in the history department, but there was a fine line between being a rabble-rouser and being an obstructionist, and lately she felt that her colleagues had stopped listening to her. Even her allies outside the department had other priorities; despite the best intentions, they had never been able to align their schedules for a second "Insidious" lunch to discuss teaching techniques. She had to settle for lunch with a loose group she had dubbed "The Malcontents," teachers who preferred grumbling to anything like the strategic planning Marsh enjoyed.

She wondered if she ought to go back to law school.

"If I'm going to be this miserable," Marsh said, "why shouldn't I make a hundred thousand dollars a year?"

A few days later, she got a call from a high school principal who hoped to start a charter school a year from the coming fall, and wanted Marsh to help him run it. Charter schools were autonomous public schools, part of the system but independent of it, with their own curricula and budgets—just the sort of reform agenda Marsh was after.

Marsh had heard of two jobs for the coming fall, but the charter school held the most appeal. It promised what she had told herself she would find at Marlborough: a progressive environment that welcomed her theories about the right way to teach. She decided to keep quiet, bide her time, and make a move at the end of the next school year.

19

SCHOOLS WITH ROLLING admissions policies were a nice distraction for some of the seniors at Marlborough, but the bulk of the letters would not arrive until early April. Jeff and Debbie Briggs wondered what they could do to help Katie keep her balance. One night at dinner, they asked her to tell them what she liked about herself, as though they could weave those traits into a kind of armor to protect her.

Katie enjoyed the exercise. The first thing she said was that she did not let her grades define her. Back in tenth grade she would have been devastated by a C, but somehow, over the last two years, she had gotten past that. She was comfortable with herself. A bad grade was a bad grade, and nothing more.

She competed against herself, not against the other girls, and she was happy as long as she felt she had done her best. Katie had taken the SATs for the first time as a junior, and scored just above 1100, which would have sent some girls scurrying for a test-preparation class. She did not go. She bought a prep book and did not open it. Early in her senior year, she took the test again and scored in the low 1200s, and on a third try hit a high of 1390.

The last time, she had tried a technique she devised herself: She started at the end of the math section, with the hardest questions, because it felt better to go from tough to easy than the other way around. It worked so well that she did the verbal section backward as well. She was proud of herself, she was happy with the score, and she had avoided sacrificing her weekends to prep classes.

She wanted her parents to know that she was pleased with them, too. Katie said that a lot of the girls used their parents to intervene on their behalf whenever there was a problem at school. Katie's parents preferred to let her work out her own problems. They listened to her complaints, but they only got involved if she could not get results. She appreciated that. She liked to think she was better at solving problems because of it.

Marlborough had made it difficult to meet boys, but Katie had decided simply to postpone a social life until she hit college. She felt awkward dating. Surely it would be easier when with no effort at all she found herself sitting next to a boy in English class, or standing in front of one in the cafeteria line. She knew one thing: She would not trade the last six years with any of her friends who went to coeducational schools, not even if it meant she were better at small talk.

She recalled that dinnertime conversation frequently in the days that followed. It became a little meditation that she could use to steady herself as the tension level increased. Katie Briggs looked back on her career at Marlborough and felt she had done the best job Katie Briggs could do. Other girls had higher scores and more AP credits, but Katie was satisfied with what she had achieved and confident that her efforts would be rewarded.

On March 19, Christina Kim and two other girls found out that they, along with an early applicant, had been accepted at the Massachusetts Institute of Technology. Christina went home, found the fat envelope, and had a moment of giddy delight.

"So I'm going to college after all," she joked to her mother, as though there ever had been any real doubt. MIT had never before accepted a girl from Marlborough, so Christina had the chance to experience all the feelings she had been denied when Harvard turned her down in December. She was going all the way across the country, which was what she wanted, to an elite college, which was what everyone thought she deserved.

Christina had had plenty of experience finding joy on the far side of disappointment, from her childhood struggle with diabetes to the self-imposed challenges of her junior year. She had a knack for putting bad news in a box and walking away from it. As of March 19, Christina was a scholarship student at MIT. She ordered her school sweatshirt and accepted everyone's congratulations.

Looking back, Jon Tower realized that the early days of senior year had been a relatively easy time. He and Cabel had invested their nervous energy in the application process and stayed away from the kind of comparative gossip that would have driven them crazy.

By the end of March, it was almost impossible to maintain that kind of distance. Katie's fate was tied up with everyone else's, and as he heard each new bit of information, Jon adjusted his analysis of Katie's chances.

On March 22, the day of the Cum Laude assembly, all the talk was about the four girls who had been accepted at MIT. Jon was already so proud of Katie, who was one of nine seniors being inducted into the academic honor society that morning. The timing, just days before the college letters arrived, seemed a good omen.

"Of course, the MIT girls are all probably saying, 'Well, I guess I'll go if I don't get into Harvard,'" Jon said to Cabel. "The joke will be if Katie's the only one to get into Harvard. She'd probably rather go to Princeton. But *four girls at MIT.* Maybe it's going to be okay. Katie'll get in somewhere."

Seven juniors and sixteen seniors sat onstage, including the seven seniors who had been inducted last year, along with faculty members who had joined either Cum Laude or Phi Beta Kappa during their school years. Cum Laude was modeled on the Phi Beta Kappa society, with its emphasis on honor and character as well as academic achievement. It had begun ninety-three years ago, for the students at seven independent boys' schools. The first all-girls school joined the group in 1920, and Marlborough had been a member since 1970.

The girls onstage were in perfect uniform: white shirt with collar, navy pullover, gray skirt, white socks, and white sneakers. One by one they stood, as their names were called, and walked over to the podium to collect a certificate of membership and a hug from Barbara Wagner. When they were done, she asked all the new members to rise. The front rows erupted with flash cameras, as everyone in the hall rose to sing the Marlborough alma mater.

After the assembly, the Cum Laude members and their families walked over to the Living Room for a reception. The Towers dropped in only briefly. Jon was off to work, and Cabel was more interested in the alterations schedule for the graduation dresses. If Jon focused on what was coming next, Cabel tried as hard as she could to attend to the present. Though she was eager for the suspense to be over, she was in no hurry to find out where Katie was going to college. Knowing would somehow make it more immediate—and it would come soon enough.

The closer graduation got, the more concerned Cabel was that she would miss one of the last, irreplaceable moments of Katie's senior year. It was difficult to juggle school activities and work, but Cabel would have plenty of chances to relax next year—probably more than she wanted. Teaching a girl that she could do whatever she wanted had its disadvantages, especially if she believed you and took off across the country.

The seamstress would take up residence in the college-counseling conference room during the week of May 10, which gave Cabel enough advance warning to be able to schedule her life around Katie's fitting appointment. The sign-up sheet had just been posted, ten minutes for each senior, and Cabel wanted Katie to sign up right away.

"It's my last chance to help my daughter get dressed," she said.

In the days before spring vacation, Katie took refuge in routine. She joked that an "ingrained fear of reprimand" kept her going, but Katie genuinely liked to work, so she continued to hand in her homework and complete her required reading. She got bored without enough to do. Other girls planned to travel over spring break or do nothing at all. Katie intended to read her entire Art History text over vacation, which was one way to keep from being preoccupied with the mail.

Her parents tried to keep their anxieties to themselves, but the optimism they felt on Cum Laude day was fragile. Cabel's mood changed when she saw an article in *The Wall Street Journal* that said that Harvard accepted almost half its freshman class from the early-applicant pool. True, Katie had not had a single favorite school, but Cabel confessed to Jon that perhaps they should have picked one; should have forced the issue a bit.

ARLEEN FORSHEIT KNEW what to do with girls like Christina, who were driven by their own idiosyncratic curiosity. They needed a guiding hand to help them channel their energy, and they needed a mentor, like the UCLA researcher who had given Christina an early glimpse into the workings of a medical laboratory.

The more difficult question was what to do with girls like Katie Tower and Katie Briggs, who loved science but had not yet figured out what they wanted to do. The research tutorial demanded more of a time commitment than they were prepared to make, but by senior year, they had worked their way through the standard curriculum. Dr. Forsheit did not want to lose them, so she taught a new Upper School elective called Science and Society. For spring term, almost a dozen students, including Katie Tower, signed up for the class.

The idea was to take science out of the lab and into daily life. Dr. Forsheit took inspiration wherever she could find it: The reading list included Jonathan Harr's *A Civil Action,* about a small community's suspicion that its water supply had been polluted by industrial solvents, and Richard Preston's *The Hot Zone,* about an outbreak of the Ebola virus. One class session was devoted to a segment of the television series *Law and Order* that addressed the legal rights of an estranged, infertile couple.

Despite her best efforts, the seniors were having a hard time concentrating. The classroom discussion of *A Civil Action* ground to a halt, so Dr. Forsheit gave up and turned the girls loose on a lab assignment. For all her talk of schedules and penalties, she knew when to back off. College letters were coming. She would be satisfied as long as the girls were doing something.

They had kept daily logs of products they used, from deodorant to diet soda, and now Dr. Forsheit asked them to pair up at the computers and search the Web for information about various ingredients in these products, in the hope that having something to do besides turn pages would keep them awake.

Katie prided herself on avoiding processed foods, so she chose to research something she refused to use: packets of instant hot cocoa. She rattled off the ingredients to her partner: sugar, sweet dairy whey, corn syrup, solid cocoa, partially hydrogenated soybean oil, nonfat dry milk, cellulose gum, dipotassium phosphate, mono- and diglycerides, and artificial flavor. "Cocoa's supposed to be chocolate and water or milk, that's all," Katie complained, "not these other things." Her partner was perfectly happy to drink cocoa. What scared her were food products that contained yellow dye.

The girls called out their results, the more disgusting the better. "The fourth ingredient in Coke gets rid of rust stains and mineral deposits," one girl reported. "Aaaaagh!" Another girl insisted that Coke was better than certain clear soft drinks, which contained bleaching agents to remove the brown color of some of their ingredients.

"Have you seen the warning on Carefree gum?" Katie asked.

Her lab partner stopped in mid-chew. "Katie, give it up."

Dr. Forsheit weighed in. "I don't chew gum."

Encouraged, Katie persisted. "I just find it amusing that even little packs of gum have the words 'lab rats' on them."

She and her partner wandered over to listen to more of the soft-drink results. The next ingredient on the cola can was titanium dioxide, and Dr. Forsheit helped the girls locate a Web site for a company that produced the chemical. "Titanium Dioxide," read the corporate slogan. "Something We All Need!" A partial list of products included paints, enamelware, photography, and some feed stocks, which only convinced Katie that anyone who drank soft drinks was crazy.

"Eccch!" she squealed. "You're drinking *metal*. You know how rust is iron oxide? This is like—titanium rust."

They kept reading the titanium dioxide product list, which included deodorants, ibuprofen, and, to the girls' horror, lipstick.

"It's a pigment," said Dr. Forsheit, who rarely wore makeup.

At that, Katie sobered up. "But isn't it true that if you just use a little bit it's okay?" she asked.

SOMMER LOUIE'S LIFE was going so well that she could finally afford to be choosy. She had so far been accepted by Tulane, USC, UC San Diego, Emory University, and Vanderbilt University. Thanks to a need-blind admissions policy, some colleges and universities accepted students without knowing their families' financial situation—and then were obligated to offer assistance to the students who needed it. The Louies did not have to worry about whether Sommer would receive financial aid. The only questions were how much she would get, and from what sources—grants, loans, work study, or a combination of the three.

She was set, except that she had not yet heard from her favorite school, Rice University. Sommer loved everything about the place. She had a cousin in Houston, so she felt safe going there; away from home but not cut off from family. At about $20,000 a year, Rice was cheaper than many private schools, rated fourth nationwide in a *U.S. News & World Report* analysis of quality and cost.

Most important, Sommer had enjoyed her visit there. Rice seemed to her a "diverse and accepting" place. She saw black students and whites walking together on campus, unlike one of the other schools she had visited, where the black students confided that it was easier to avoid the white students than to figure out which ones might tolerate their presence. A Rice admissions officer who already seemed to know all about Sommer had made a point of introducing herself during Sommer's visit. When she sat in on classes, she told her parents, even the teachers knew her name.

Sommer rattled off all the advantages of Rice as she strolled up to the

Marlborough technology center with another girl, a junior, a rapt student of the college-application process. Lately, Sommer had taken to checking her e-mail from school. She had met a student who worked in the Rice admissions office, and hoped she might get advance word of her status once the admissions committee had made its decision.

Today there was an e-mail entitled "Good News."

"Oh, my God," whispered Sommer. It was a message from the girl at Rice. Sommer was in.

She logged out immediately, ran downstairs to hug Monica Ward, and then used the college counseling office phone to call her mother at work.

Phyllis, who had already splurged on a bottle of Dom Perignon champagne to celebrate if Sommer got into Rice, was speechless. The campaign she had waged from the day Sommer was born was over, and they had won: A girl whose family could not afford the college application fees was going to a good private university. Eighteen years of determined effort, Phyllis's eye always on that goal, and suddenly she did not have to strive any more. Sommer was on her way.

"*Yes*," Phyllis said, finally, not trusting herself to say much more without losing her composure. She told Sommer that her father would be very proud, and then she went back to work.

Monica Ward spent the week before spring break calling her friends in college counseling at other private schools, to demand her rightful portion of awe. Four girls accepted at MIT. "It's incredible," she told her friends. "Tell me if you don't think this is incredible." Three of the girls were in Arleen Forsheit's advanced independent-study class, which Ward credited for their showing. "There are a lot of students out there interested in science," she said, "but very few of them have the background in research that Arleen provides."

Ward congratulated the girls who had good news and comforted the ones who were still waiting. Some of them came into her office crying—not from disappointment but from uncertainty. Ward dispensed hugs and told them it was better if they found out at home, over the break.

"You can concentrate on yourselves," she said. "Focus on whatever happens. Deal with whatever emotions you experience, in private." She told them to call her office, even though school was closed, and leave a message on her voice mail. She promised to check in, and to call anyone who didn't leave a message, to find out what was going on. By the end of the second week of vacation, it all ought to be over.

Not that her life would be any calmer. The first day back from spring break was always "pandemonium," she said. The seniors had news and needed either solace or help making a choice. The juniors would be back from their first trips to look at colleges. The sophomores, who had to choose their classes for next year, would want to know who got in where, and what classes the successful candidates had taken, so that they could map a similar course. It never stopped.

Barbara Wagner waited for an all-school assembly to announce that Jim Skrumbis was the new director of the Upper School, and the ensuing riot of foot-pounding, applause, and whistles confirmed that she had made a popular choice. Most of the students considered Skrumbis to be their candidate; the outside candidates were educators, unknown commodities, but Skrumbis was their ally. As the girls headed off for spring vacation, the world was in alignment—some good news from schools, and a replacement for Susanna Jones who already knew what Marlborough was about. The seniors left feeling hopeful; the younger girls, safe.

20

The Young Women's Leadership
School of East Harlem
March 1999

IT WAS 9:30 in the morning, the time when the sleepy girls in Cindy
Jackson's ninth-grade biology class were just starting to come to, and the
fidgeters were already thinking about lunch. Normally, Jackson had a
hard time keeping the lid on her class. Today was different. She sat on the
table at the front of the room and faced a rapt audience. If Amy and her
friends had been this attentive up until now, Jackson thought, the Regents
exam would be a snap.

What had them hypnotized was sex—specifically, their teacher's description of a man's erect penis. From a scientific point of view, it was a simple
phenomenon: a stimulus caused an increase in the flow of blood to the
penis, and that, in turn, "caused tension," as Jackson put it. But the day's real
lesson was how to respond to that physiological process, and she wanted
the girls to understand the difference between science and a sales pitch.

"Now, it is *not* a life-or-death situation," she said, as she got up and paced back and forth. "Do not *ever* let a boy convince you that he's got to do something about it. It will go away. He will try every line on you. But he *will not die, he will not get an infection. He will not have some permanent erection.* You need to know that a guy's body will take care of itself—no matter what they may say to young ladies. Boys, in their own genuine ignorance, may not know their own bodies."

Jackson could have taught reproductive biology out of the Regents exam prep book, which was what she was supposed to do. In fact, she owed Celenia Chevere a memo listing the topics she intended to cover between now and the end of the year, since she, like everyone else, was running behind—but this morning she had decided to take a detour. Like the school's benefactor, Ann Tisch, Jackson believed that pregnancy was one of the biggest threats these girls faced. The teenage birth rate had declined every year since 1991, but not fast enough: Almost one million teenagers got pregnant every year, about five teens out of one hundred, and about half of those girls gave birth. The rate was higher among minorities and the poor, with one in five black teenagers and one in six Latinas getting pregnant every year.

The girls at TYWLS stood at a dangerous intersection: Many were ignorant about sex and birth control; their parents, because of religious or cultural restraints, often were reluctant to discuss it; and abortion was out of reach, because of shame, money, religion, or a simple inability to find the right doctor. Many of the girls' mothers had been teenagers themselves when they got pregnant, and plenty of the boys in the neighborhood were more eager than they were informed. Jackson's students needed help learning to say no. Failing that, they needed to be safe.

All the schoolwork in the world meant nothing if a girl had to drop out because she was pregnant. Tisch often repeated her story about the teenage mother she had interviewed in Milwaukee, and Jackson, for one, had taken the message to heart. She wanted to provide a forum where the girls could ask whatever questions they had—without fear of embarrassment, and without risking their parents' disapproval.

She assumed that many of her students were already sexually active. There was no point in preaching abstinence to them, because Jackson was, after all, an outsider: white, educated, a professional, a woman who had it made, as far as the girls were concerned. They would dismiss her as just one more lecturing adult. Instead, she offered them a deal. They could write down any question they wanted her to answer, without signing their names. She would read the questions aloud in class and provide a straightforward answer.

As long as the girls kept quiet and paid attention, Jackson was prepared to tell them whatever they needed to know. Having dismissed the idea that a girl was somehow obligated to relieve her boyfriend's aroused state, she glanced down at the next question, from a girl for whom the concept of refusal had come too late.

She read without looking up. "'If sperm gets into your eye, can it cause infection?'"

Everyone in the room began to giggle.

"Okay, look," said Jackson. "Your eye is a prime candidate for infection. It produces a lot of fluids. Sperm is a bodily fluid. If he has a sexually transmitted disease, and say a sore at the tip of his penis, and the sperm passes over that sore, sure, you can develop an infection."

"But not AIDS," came a voice from the back.

"Sure," said Jackson. "AIDS. Your eye is a bodily opening. Sure it's possible."

Emboldened by the mention of AIDS, another girl spoke up. "I read you can get it by kissing," she said.

The girls responded with a loud chorus of "No"s.

"*Oh, yes you can,*" said Jackson. "Not by saliva. Only blood by blood. But if you have a cut or sore in your mouth, sure you can. There's research being done about saliva's protective quality, but nobody knows yet."

The girls were silent. Jackson had not yelled at them, laughed at them, or been offended by their questions. She was not acting like a parent. She was acting like a smart older sister.

One girl called out a question she had forgotten to write down. "Is sperm good for your skin?" she asked.

"As a lotion? That's what I'm assuming," said Jackson. "Sperm is protein. Most skin lotions are fatty acids. So no, not as a lotion."

She read the next question aloud. "'Can sperm substitute for breast milk?'"

"Who *wrote* these?" yelled someone at the back of the room.

"Hey," said Jackson, "it's a question. But remember, what is sperm? Protein? Mother's milk contains protein, but it also contains water, fats, and in the first couple of days, colostrum, which is vital to the child. So no, sperm won't substitute. And besides, there's so little of it produced compared to mother's milk. Now, what's next? 'Could a girl get pregnant by sperm being on the hand and being finger-popped?'"

Everyone laughed and waited to see what Jackson would say. She had hoped the girls would be this frank about what they were doing, but she had to be careful not to chastise them for what she might consider improper behavior. That would be the quickest way to shut them up.

"Now, this person is referring to a kind of intimacy," she replied. "But first the sperm is exposed to the air, which is a killer. Second, it's cooled down. And third, even if a boy has sperm on his hand and then manipulates the female internally, there isn't enough force in his hand to propel the sperm up to her fallopian tube."

She glanced up with a look of stern triumph on her face.

"Next," she said, "'Can a girl get wet enough to show through her pants?' Yep."

She looked at the next page and hesitated, just for an instant. So far, the questions had sounded like the kinds of things a teenager might ask, but someone in the room clearly had need of more serious information. "Now here's a question," she said. "'When a fetus is aborted, is it coherent? Does it feel itself dying?'"

Cindy Jackson's nephew had been born on October 5, and she loved being even a peripheral part of her sister's and brother-in-law's new family. That was who was supposed to have babies—stable couples who had gone to school, found jobs, and were ready to start a family. Not kids who ended up pregnant because they did not know any better. One student had left TYWLS last year because she was pregnant. One of the girls in this room might already be pregnant, or she might have had an abortion and was trying to come to terms with what she had done. Jackson briefly reviewed the abortion process, and then addressed the "political issue" of the fetus's viability.

"Now, coherency, that issue of consciousness, is the gray area that divides right-wingers and left-wingers," she said, "and somewhere down the line you need to decide how you feel. No decision is right or wrong, but you need to know how you feel. Staying on the fence is weak. You need to take a stand."

"Now, I have my opinion," she went on, "but don't ask me to share it. I won't. I don't want to influence you, and I don't want you to think, 'She's my teacher, I ought to agree with her.' Yes, a fetus in the first three months has nerve endings, but is that the same as you or me? A fetus does respond to a saline solution—if you watch an ultrasound you see it pull away. But is that feeling?"

A few girls quietly murmured, "Yes."

"Or is it just nerves reacting?" Jackson asked them. "Ask yourself: Could you watch an ultrasound of a fetus dying? If you could, then maybe you're okay with abortion. If you couldn't, then maybe that tells you something. Can I imagine my baby dying? Can I imagine a fetus passing through me? These are all facts you have to think about."

The girls who whispered "yes" were too young to drive a car or help elect a president. Jackson was hard-pressed to decide which was worse—a child bearing a child, or a child terminating her pregnancy. She figured that one of the best ways to discourage these girls from becoming sexually active was to remind them of how high the stakes were: They could keep a baby and forget about the tantalizing future that TYWLS advertised, or they could end a pregnancy and bear the emotional weight of that decision.

"I will tell you one opinion of mine," she said. "I think every potential parent ought to have a license. Go through a class, get a permit. Think about it. You have to have a driver's license, all the other things you have to have a permit to do. There are so many babies having babies."

She moved on to the next question. "'What should you do about peer pressure to have sex?' Okay. First of all, sex has to be consensual. You may love this fellow more than anything, but if he's got to pressure you, there's something wrong. *Just say no.* Tell him, 'When we're ready.' How do you know when you're ready and it's the right guy? That's the million-dollar question. *Think about the consequences of sex.* 'Can I raise a baby? Are we going to stay together? Can I handle this without having a diploma or a job?'"

Three-quarters of the way through the hour, and the girls had barely moved. For once, they wanted Jackson to get through the entire lesson. "'What do you do,'" she read, "'when you're pregnant and afraid to tell somebody?'" She pursed her lips. There was something so sad about this. Teachers were supposed to teach lessons, and with luck the best ones inspired their students. These girls ought to have someone else, parents or older sisters or neighbors or aunts, to ask about sex. Jackson was friendly, but she was hardly their friend. She had not expected such intimate, urgent questions, and she wished the girls had someone to talk to besides her.

"Take responsibility for that baby," she said, wondering if one of the girls was pregnant. "Tell someone—your mom, a teacher you trust. You've got to tell somebody, because you're not just thinking about yourself now. Tell somebody. Get to a doctor. Take care of that baby."

"Now, 'Where can I go to get protection if I don't want to tell my parents?' Okay, there are two people here at school who are certified to talk about condom protection—Shirley and Holly—and you can go to either of them. It has to be for yourself, not a friend, and I think you have to sign something, and I don't think they will tell your parents."

She hurried on. "'What happens if I get pregnant a couple of months after an abortion?'"

At that, she lost any semblance of cool. Her mouth formed a tight, disapproving line, and her gaze darted from face to face, as though daring the girl who had written this question to step forward.

"First off," she said, a note of anger creeping into her voice, "you are incredibly ignorant. You need to find out about what a second abortion will do to your body in terms of scar tissue. You need to investigate other options, like maybe putting the baby up for adoption. And you need to figure out how to keep this from happening again."

At that moment, Celenia Chevere walked in the door. She had a question about the paperwork on a textbook order, and she needed Cindy to find something in her files. The girls looked away, abashed, as though the principal had somehow overheard the topic of the day's class as she walked down the hall. The bell rang and they began to pack up. As they left, they made overlapping jokes about what they had heard:

"Can you feel *wet*. . . ."

". . . *wet* . . ."

"*WET!*"

Amy left without speaking to anyone. In her household, sex before marriage was simply taboo. Her father, Tito, worried every time she had to walk home alone, even the short distance between school and their apartment building, at 102nd Street and First Avenue—not about Amy, but about the boys she encountered along the way.

He did what he could to keep her safe. He wore a pager, so that she could call him and punch in the time she expected to be done at school. If he could get there, he showed up to walk her home. He encouraged her to help him out at the church and made sure she was there for services every Sunday morning. His frequent out-of-town speaking engagements might mean that she missed more school than she should, but Tito wanted to expose Amy to teenagers who cared about religion. In a home devoted to faith and ambition, there was no room for early sex; if he could not control the outside world, he could be close by as Amy made her way through it.

Cindy Jackson did the same question-and-answer session with Maryam's and Diana's section, and Maryam was aghast at some of the questions she heard. It was not a moral issue. She simply could not understand why her friends allowed themselves to be so easily distracted.

After class, she said to a couple of friends, "What is this? I mean: Do your homework, and don't think about it."

Maryam would never do anything to jeopardize her school record. While the other girls worried about boys, she worried about her mid-term progress reports. They were very good, as always, but Maryam felt she deserved better, and she was not afraid to say so. She cornered Sarah Kirkpatrick to find out why she had received only a 90 in participation in English and not the 100 she had expected. Her teacher explained that she never gave a perfect score so early in the term. Maryam had received the highest grade in her class.

"I don't give a one-hundred lightly," she explained. "In participation, that's if you never, ever do anything you shouldn't do, and nobody's like that in class, totally focused. Most kids got seventies."

Maryam did not want to hear about most kids. She resolved to get a perfect participation grade by the end of the term and reminded Sarah that her goal was a straight-A record for all six years. Next, she headed for Cindy Jackson's classroom. Maryam had scored in the high 90's in her previous biology section, but Jackson had given her an 87 on her initial report. Maryam wanted an explanation, because she was doing the same work she had done in the last term. She wanted to know what had happened to her A.

Jackson was happy to explain. She had started to add Regents review questions to her quizzes and tests, and they were more difficult than the simple recall questions she usually included. Maryam had received B's on too many quizzes and tests to warrant an A. If she wanted it badly enough, she would have to work harder between now and the end of the year. Maryam could not become complacent. Jackson told her that even the best student in the class had to stretch sometimes.

CINDY JACKSON HAD begun to wonder if TYWLS was the right place for her. She put tremendous effort into her classes. She tried to establish a bond with the girls, and today she felt that she had succeeded in reaching them. They worked so hard to be cool, when in fact they were young kids with lots of questions. They needed an ally as much as they needed a teacher.

She was proud to have earned their trust, but the feeling had vanished as soon as Chevere walked in the door. Jackson knew what the principal would think if she found out about today's lesson—that she had shirked her responsibility to prepare the girls for the Biology Regents exam. She was not sure that TYWLS appreciated her efforts. She did know that she was tired of the school's teach-to-the-test philosophy, even though she understood the urgency behind it.

As the end of the school year approached, rumors cropped up about which teachers were staying and which were leaving. So far, Jackson had heard that one humanities teacher and one library aide would not be asked to return, and that Chevere planned to make changes in the math and science departments. Her future hinged on the girls' performance on their Regents exams—unless she decided on her own to look for another job. She had heard from a colleague at another school about an opening for a chemistry teacher and had contacted the principal there about an interview. The High School of Health Sciences offered her a job, and she wondered how long she could hold them off without losing the opportunity. Making a living as a public-school teacher in Manhattan was a joke; at a first-year teacher's salary of $28,000 a year, she despaired of ever being able to afford an apartment. If Jackson was going to live on a shoestring, she wanted at least to feel that someone appreciated her hard work.

When she got back to her sister's home that night, she called her parents in Indiana.

"I want to feel respected," she told them, "and I don't, here."

Chevere had little interest in her teachers' emotional health. As far as she was concerned, satisfaction came from getting results. She was not about to hold a teacher's hand when there was so much to do, and she expected her teachers to understand that.

Girls came to TYWLS for discipline, and the progress it promised, and after three years there was more demand than ever. New York's public-school students applied to the city's specialized high schools for ninth grade, listing the schools they wanted to attend in order of preference. The eighth graders at TYWLS had to go through the motions, and this year, the quartet Chevere had identified had done so poorly that they would not be allowed to return. Even with those openings, TYWLS had room for only fifteen new girls in next year's ninth-grade class. Chevere had just learned, to her great pride, that more than 875 girls had named TYWLS as their first or second choice.

She took their enthusiasm as a vote of confidence. TYWLS had earned a reputation as the place to send an ambitious girl, and Chevere was determined to live up to that public perception. If any student—or any teacher—was unable to keep up, there were plenty of candidates eager to take her place. She already had a private list of teachers she did not intend to ask back.

This was English teacher Sarah Kirkpatrick's last year at TYWLS, but she had not yet decided when to tell the girls the news. New York had not made life easy for Kirkpatrick and her new husband, an aspiring music producer. She was so tired after a day at work that she usually fell asleep by ten, while he often worked through the night at a sound studio. Sometimes she got home from school with papers to grade, only to find him waiting, eager to go out with her for the evening, and sometimes she left for work in the morning before he got home from an all-night session. Producing music would always interfere with a normal life, so they decided to return to Louisiana, where Kirkpatrick's husband could study electrical engineering and try to establish himself as a designer of audio equipment, and she could continue to teach.

She worried about the effect her decision would have on her students, particularly the ninth-grade girls, who had been with her for two years. Maryam would be fine, because Maryam was determined to be fine. In fact, Maryam's attitude about her scores and grades had begun to grate on Kirkpatrick's nerves just a little. She had imagined Maryam standing over her, arguing, as she wrote up her progress report, and was not surprised when Maryam came in to challenge her grade.

At least Maryam had an independent sense of her own ability. Too many of the other girls linked their success to Kirkpatrick. They liked themselves in part because she liked their work—and when she found fault, they lost faith all too quickly. When she left, some of those girls would blame themselves, as though their behavior, and not her private life, had hastened her departure. Their self-confidence was very tenuous. She decided to delay telling them for as long as possible.

This morning, she gave her classes two writing assignments to complete over spring break, as well as a "peer review editing form." One of the assignments was a book report, and Kirkpatrick wanted to get someone else in the family involved in the process. "Ask someone to help you," she explained, "a parent, a neighbor. Not your six-year-old brother, but someone who'll have some insight, and not say, 'Oh it's great' or you'll beat them up."

The girls had spent their Christmas break preparing for final exams, and now they saw their spring break slipping away. Chevere enthusiastically endorsed the idea of homework during vacation. Most of these girls had at best a tentative hold on their study skills, and she worried that their school muscles would atrophy without daily exercise. She encouraged the faculty to make bridge assignments, but it was hard to follow her mandate without demoralizing the girls.

"If you're feeling overwhelmed," said Kirkpatrick, "remember, you can use one of the books you're reading for science—except that you also have to read twenty-five books this year. You'll really have to think about managing your time. Maybe read a certain number of pages every day. I have book reports and essays to grade over break, and I have a friend arriving on Thursday, not leaving until Tuesday, and I'm not doing a thing while she's here. So I have to manage my time."

Kirkpatrick insisted on approving in advance every book the girls read for their reports, so she walked around the room passing out permission slips. When she held one out to a girl seated at Diana's table, the girl refused to put out her hand.

"I don't know what to read," she muttered.

Kirkpatrick leaned over with an exasperated look on her face and made a great show of consulting her watch. "Did I hear you say 'I don't know what book to read?'" she asked. "When is this due? Thirteen days? How long ago did I tell you to pick a book? Two, three *weeks*?"

The girl, defeated, put her head down on the table. "I don't know what book to read," came the muffled reply.

The other girls sat, frozen, waiting to see who would back down first.

Kirkpatrick said, loudly, "Well, you have to pick one by the end of to-morrow. Or you can go to the public library over break, but then I can't ap-prove it in advance. And what if I don't approve it?"

The girl refused to pick up her head, so Kirkpatrick left a permission slip on the table next to her and moved on.

The second assignment was to take a chapter from the Bible and recast it in the present day. Kirkpatrick had written a list of suggested biblical pas-sages on the blackboard and had handed out photocopied excerpts. She ex-pected everyone to choose one by the end of the period.

Diana already owed her teacher her last two essay-length book reports, in addition to her reading log. She quietly reviewed photocopied pages of the Bible, her pen tight between her teeth, her foot jiggling nervously. She was tired and feeling overworked, but she hoped to get caught up over spring break. Some of the girls simply skipped assignments. Diana never considered it. The worst thing Diana could say about another girl was that she was lazy. No matter how much the asthma got in her way, she had no intention of letting herself, or her parents, down.

Diana liked to tell a joke on herself, that she had never been farther west than Harlem. It was true, and when she thought about it seriously it was too sad to endure. She wanted to see somewhere else, and if wearing herself out doing schoolwork was the only way to get there, that was what she would do.

It was six o'clock, and Maria Perez was late getting home from work. James had five minutes before he had to start making dinner, so he played with the baby while her two middle sisters ran around the apartment and Julia, a sixth grader, did her homework. For once, Diana had a night off from responsibility. As soon as her mother walked in the door, they were going to an awards banquet for the Figure Skaters of Harlem, over at River-bank Park.

Diana nursed the private hope that she would win an award this year. She loved ice-skating. She loved every afternoon she got to spend at the rink: time to skate, time set aside for the skaters to do their homework, no noise, no sisters, no babysitting, no responsibility to anyone except herself.

On the ice she felt graceful and capable. She had already written an essay to apply for the summer program, which took only a half-dozen girls in her age group, down from fifteen during the school year.

She got dressed for the party in a tank top, a fitted black jacket, a short black skirt, pale hose, and ankle boots. She combed her long bangs into place, darkened her eyebrows, and chose a pale lipstick. Maria still wasn't home. Diana added blush and a little eye shadow.

Maria walked in the door fifteen minutes before the banquet was supposed to start, said hello to everyone, and walked right back out again with Diana. There was no time to put on a fresh shirt or even to splash water on her face; the most important thing was to get Diana to the banquet in time to enjoy herself. As they left, James called out from the kitchen, "A woman's work is never done." It was unclear whether he meant Maria or himself, since he still had to serve dinner, clean up, and get the other girls ready for bed.

Diana and Maria cut quickly past a tangle of apartment buildings and followed the train tracks up to 138th Street, where a long pedestrian overpass crossed Riverside Drive and deposited them at the park entrance. They still had a long way to go, past a new soccer field and track, past the indoor and outdoor swimming pools, through the gymnastics building and past the outdoor ice rink. The banquet was being held in the main hallway of the skating center, a narrow, high-ceilinged room that had been transformed for the evening into a banquet hall. There were balloons on weighted metallic bases, several large, round tables, and, in the middle of the hallway, service tables stacked high with pizza boxes and liter bottles of soda.

Diana wanted to go up to the front and sit with her friends from the skating program, but all the seats were taken; some girls had brought enough family and friends to fill a whole table. For a moment, she and Maria hesitated, unsure of what to do. Since Maria had a full-time job, she was exempt from doing volunteer work for the group, but as a result, she did not know any of the other parents. She did not know whom to approach for help, and Diana was suddenly shy about asking. They were edging toward the back of the hall when one of the volunteers noticed them. She showed them where the extra folding chairs were stacked and directed them to an empty table, while another mom got them a cheese pizza and some Cokes.

The ceremony began almost immediately, hosted by the group's director, Sharon Cohen, who presented awards for participation and scholarship to several girls, including Diana. After Diana collected her prize, she and Maria lingered near the service table, waiting to hear who had won the more competitive awards.

There were forty-five girls in the program, but only three would be recognized for what Cohen called "outstanding performance in terms of commitment and attitude." The first two winners, seated at crowded front tables, jumped up when they heard their names. Then Sharon Cohen called, "Diana Perez," and Maria raised her hands high above her head, applauding loudly. Diana, flushed and trembling, walked to the front of the room to receive her trophy, then stopped at the other tables on her way back to receive the congratulations of the other girls. Maria watched, beaming, thinking about how hard her daughter had worked.

Each girl received a program that contained photos, a history of Figure Skaters of Harlem, and plenty of blank spaces for autographs. Diana moved from girl to girl, getting them to sign her book and signing theirs, while Maria waited where she stood. She did not feel comfortable walking up to strangers to start a conversation, but she was happy enough just to watch Diana having a good time. When her daughter was ready, they headed for the overpass and the walk home, two of the last guests to leave the party.

Diana strode along proudly, clutching her trophy in front of her. As they got to the far end of the overpass, a group of three teenage boys walked toward them, on their way to nothing more pressing than a late night on an empty athletic field. They sneered at Diana as they passed.

"Ooh, look at that," said one. "Look at the fancy prize she's got."

"At least I'm doing something," she muttered under her breath. She walked a little faster toward home.

21

Marlborough School

April 1999

K ATIE BRIGGS HAD not told her parents that the University of
California at Berkeley was her first choice, but as spring break approached she decided, privately, that that was where she wanted to
go. It was the perfect destination, no matter what criteria she used—academically challenging, the most prestigious UC campus, economical compared to private schools, far enough away to feel like leaving home and
close enough to reassure her.

She and her parents planned to spend the second week of spring break
visiting Northwestern University, Washington University in St. Louis, the
University of Colorado at Boulder, and UC Berkeley, with a detour to
Duke University or Tufts University if she got in. Unlike some of the girls
who had started visiting schools last spring, Katie had yet to travel. She had
seen Berkeley two years ago, and that was it. Her parents preferred to wait
until the last minute, in case Katie got rejected anywhere. That way, they

could delete the school from their itinerary rather than spend unnecessary time and money.

The early letters promised a busy travel schedule: Katie got in at UCLA, UC San Diego, and the University of Colorado at Boulder. She got in at Boston College and rejected it as too small. Tufts put her on a wait-list, but Katie was philosophical. Tufts had always been a reach for her. On the Friday before she and Debbie were supposed to leave, they scheduled a shopping day to help them both forget about envelopes and suspense.

Katie's defenses were not in place when she got home and found the "little letter" from Berkeley. She sat down with a thud and read what she would come to describe as a "really nasty letter," explaining that she could enroll in a community college and transfer to Berkeley as a junior, once she had amassed sixty credits. She was not used to being treated like an anonymous also-ran.

"All of a sudden," she said, "the one place that I'd seen and liked was just whipped away from me. And I was just lost."

When her father got home that evening, her parents said all the things parents are supposed to say: If a school doesn't want you, too bad for them; we're on your side; you were accepted at a lot of great schools. Katie listened from what seemed like a great distance. The next morning, her mother misjudged how much comfort Katie was prepared to accept, and Katie blew up at her.

"I just want to be *alone*," she screeched. "Don't touch me. Don't hug me. Don't— I'm *fine*, you know." She retreated to her bedroom until guilt overcame her, and then she came out to search for her mom. Debbie was in the laundry room washing clothes for their trip.

"Mom," said Katie. "I'm sorry if I was being kind of, you know, snotty. I just— I don't know what to do."

Her mother looked up and waited.

"I feel *lost*," Katie wailed, and Debbie hugged her, hard, while they both cried.

They left on Monday without Jeff, who had too much work to be able to join them. It was not an easy trip. They got to Chicago first, spent the day at Northwestern, and went back to the hotel to call home, only to learn that Northwestern had rejected Katie's application. Duke had turned her down as well, which eliminated the need to travel to North Carolina.

Katie saw Washington University and liked it. She saw the University of Colorado at Boulder and loved it. Katie had been invited to join the honors program there, 125 students who lived together and took advanced courses. It seemed to her like the best possible choice—a school big enough to have a football team and strong school spirit, but with a specialized academic program to challenge her.

Katie was ready for a "concrete feeling," ready to make a commitment, but on the phone that night her father warned her not to give her heart away. He was concerned that while UC San Diego cost only $13,000 per year, Boulder cost $23,000—a price he was prepared to pay, but only if he believed his daughter would get a better education for the money. He worried that Katie would not have much in common with the 90 percent of Boulder students who did not qualify for the honors program. Jeff reminded her of what he had said before she and Debbie had left home. "It will take a really good case," he said, "to convince me that Boulder is a better school than San Diego."

Once she and her mother got home, they drove down to San Diego to take a look around.

By the time school started again, Katie had almost regained her equilibrium. She prided herself on her ability to withstand pressure of any sort: She had never been one to get carried away with what the crowd was up to, and college acceptances were no exception. She was not about to participate in the circus of shrieks and tears.

Two days before school began, she announced to her parents, "I have one day of vacation left. I don't want to see anybody or talk to anybody." She set to work at feeling better. Though her parents insisted that she could choose the University of Colorado at Boulder if she preferred it, Katie Briggs expected to end up at the University of California at San Diego. She felt good about saving her parents lots of money, and about being able to get home in two hours if she ever felt the need. San Diego had a great science department. Buoyed by the practicality of her choice, she embraced her future—and chose to forget, slowly, that it had been imposed on her.

Not even Europe was enough to make some of the seniors forget about college letters. As soon as school let out, Erica Forneret and her sister, Martine, left on a breakneck week's tour of England, France, and Italy, thanks to the mother of one of Erica's friends, a teacher who arranged affordable group tours through an educational foundation. Erica made her parents promise not to open a single envelope while she was gone, but her friends lacked that kind of discipline. Chrissy got a call from her mother at four in the morning, telling her that she had been accepted at Georgetown University, her first choice. Another girl called home daily.

Erica, still stung by the early Brown rejection, decided not to let college intrude on her trip. She had her acceptance at USC, as well as at UC Santa Barbara and UC Santa Cruz, so she knew she was going somewhere, even though she told her friends that she had no desire to attend any of those schools. What she wanted, far more than news, was just to have a week off, to lose herself at an art museum or gelateria.

She found that she liked being away. She liked not knowing.

Back home, her parents obeyed the edict about the mail. "It wasn't hard, though," said her mother, "because I know thick and thin." Phyllis was the one who got home first every day, so she took in the mail. When the envelope came from Brown University, she called her husband.

"It's here," she said, "and it's thin."

Sarah Lawrence and Barnard sent thick envelopes. When Erica and Martine finally did call, just to say hello, Phyllis told her older daughter that there were two thick envelopes waiting for her at home. She did not say from where, and Erica did not ask.

The girls got home on Friday, April 2. Once Erica was settled in her room, her mother brought her the batch of letters.

"Here," Phyllis said. "Open your stuff." And she walked out, to give her daughter some privacy.

Erica did not really need to open any of the envelopes; their size took away all the surprise. But she opened each one, "going through the motions," and tallied up: She was in at Sarah Lawrence, Barnard, USC, UC Santa Barbara, and UC Santa Cruz. She was rejected by Brown, Columbia, and Stanford. Perhaps the biggest surprise was the rejection from UCLA, since Erica did not recall having applied there.

Erica had taken her first trip to look at colleges during spring break of the previous year, so these letters marked the end of a year of anxiety—almost. There was still Monday morning back at school. After spring break, seniors were allowed to wear sweatshirts from the schools they planned to attend. Come Monday, everyone would know which girls were happy about the future, based on their just-out-of-the-package sweatshirts. The seniors who had had their hearts broken, like Erica, might not bother with a sweatshirt from a second or third choice.

She looked at the stack of letters and realized that she did not care where she went to college. She did not feel "attached" to these schools, the way she had to Brown. Any of them would probably be fine.

She told herself, "It doesn't matter that much, one way or another," but she did not say that to her parents.

There was one more week of vacation, but on Saturday Erica had a day-long drama rehearsal. She was not home when Phyllis took in the mail and started to scream. Martine and Rodney came into the kitchen to see what the fuss was, and found Phyllis holding out a big, fat envelope from Yale University.

"We have a surprise for Erica," Phyllis announced, breathlessly. "Should we call her?"

"No," said Rodney. "Let's keep it a secret." He wanted Erica to be home, with her family, when she found out.

So Phyllis drove over to school to pick Erica up, and said only that she had a surprise for her daughter at home. Erica figured her mother had baked something nice for dessert.

When she got home and saw the envelope, she bristled, just for a moment.

"Don't you think you should have opened it," she snapped, forgetting that she had made her parents promise not to, "*before* you told me I had a surprise?" She had dismissed Yale as a possibility when Brown turned her down for the second time. As far as she was concerned, that second thin envelope had killed her chances at any Ivy League school.

She sat down at the kitchen table and opened the envelope. The fat-and-thin rule held: Erica Forneret had been accepted for admission to Yale University. Yesterday she had faced a series of second-best choices. Today she was one of the girls whom everyone else would envy.

Her parents and sister hugged and kissed her, and then, giddy with relief, they reviewed every step of the process. Phyllis gave Erica all the credit for this surprising good news. She replayed the night of Erica's interview with a Yale alumna, when what was supposed to be a brief coffee date turned into an hour-and-a-half conversation. Clearly, Erica had made an advocate of that young woman, who in turn might have encouraged the admissions committee to pay special attention to her application. Rodney congratulated himself, in hindsight, for not calling a colleague who was a Yale graduate. Getting in was great, but getting in without anyone's help was even better.

Erica had no time for analysis. She wanted to get on the phone to her friends, now that she finally had news worth sharing. Her parents got to work adding a quick trip to Yale onto a planned visit to Barnard, which had offered to fly Erica in to see the campus. Phyllis, who was terribly afraid to fly, wanted Rodney to meet up with Erica in New York and go on to New Haven, but he insisted that she go instead. Rodney had made his peace with Erica leaving home. He felt that she had "good moral values, a level head, and she's going to be okay. I want Phyllis to see the environment, and to have her comfortable with the idea of Erica going away."

The Fornerets' only concern was how Erica would handle the world they had managed to evade for six formative years. It wasn't boys that worried them; Rodney and Phyllis expected Erica to be as foolish as any other girl with a strong romantic streak and no experience. They had no doubts about the strength of her self-confidence, not after six years at Marlborough. What they worried about, instead, was how Erica would react to being treated as a "black girl" for the first time in her life.

"One of my concerns is that Erica has had this freedom to do and be whatever she wants," Phyllis said, "in a very open and loving environment at Marlborough. My concern is the perception of those who will perceive Erica as a black child, and she hasn't come across that yet." Thanks to Barbara Wagner's aggressive commitment to diversity, girls of every race heard the same message. The real world was not like that.

Martine watched her parents and sister scurry around, as ebullient as they had been depressed barely a week ago. In this household, the promise of an all-girls education had been borne out. Marlborough had catapulted Erica into the Ivy League, despite a disappointing performance in math, despite a consensus that she was a girl who never quite worked up to her potential. Phyllis sometimes thought that Erica was her own worst enemy, but Marlborough had given her the chance to be her best self, an actress, a reader, a writer. The Yale acceptance was a seal of approval. They had done the right thing.

That night, Phyllis wrote in her journal, "Someone lifted that basket and saw the light." For weeks after, she cried whenever she talked about it.

The optimism Jon Tower felt on the day Katie was inducted into the Cum Laude society was too strenuous an effort for a hardened cynic, and as spring break approached, he settled instead into a more familiar fatalism. "She'll either get into everything or she'll get into UC San Diego and USC," he said, and either way it would have little to do with who she was. Colleges were no more a meritocracy than, say, Hollywood.

"It's possible that she's not going to get into these schools," he told Cabel, "but I'm not worried that she's going to have a bad life. One way or another, she'll find a way to do what she wants to do."

The schools on Katie's list were predictable enough targets for a member of the Cum Laude society: Harvard, Princeton, Yale, Brown, Brandeis, Columbia, Stanford, Berkeley, UCLA, Johns Hopkins, and the University of Chicago, with USC and UCSD as the safe choices. Though Katie was careful not to identify her favorites, her parents believed that she preferred Princeton, Berkeley, and the University of Chicago, which she had never seen. Once all the letters arrived, they would figure out which schools to visit, even if it meant pulling her out of Marlborough for a few days. It was the only sensible approach.

They waited, and tried not to talk too much about what they were waiting for. Jon, who seemed to have memorized the fates of all the early applicants, reminded his wife that Christina Kim was the "poster girl" for the unexpected. Given her fate at Harvard, there was no such thing as a sure bet. Privately, he tried to prepare for the worst case. What if all the prestigious schools, the name brands, turned down his daughter?

As for Cabel, she cared far more about Katie's feelings than the news itself. "My anxiety is not that she is not going to get into a good college and her life will be ruined," she said. "Katie's a fabulous person. But I don't want to see my baby girl go through disappointment. I don't want to see her be hurt."

He and Cabel had talked themselves into being ready, only to spend spring break staring at a numbing assortment of skinny envelopes. At the end, Katie had come perilously close to her father's doomsday prediction: She was accepted at UCLA, USC, and UC San Diego, and turned down by Stanford and every school east of the Mississippi, save Brandeis and the University of Chicago. The worst blow was UC Berkeley, which deferred Katie's acceptance until January. She could take extension classes on campus during fall semester, or she could take classes at Santa Monica City College or UCLA. She was so astonished that she did nothing at all.

During morning break on Monday, April 12, the seniors huddled in little groups in the Living Room, the one place where they were safe from the prying questions of the younger students. The girls who did not want to talk lingered at the edges of the room, under the photographs of past student body presidents, or found a happier classmate to whom they could listen. Some of those girls were easy to spot; the ones who had heard early enough had already ordered and received their school sweatshirts, and they stood out like tour guides in a sea of travelers. Some, like Erica, had been ambushed by good fortune and would have to settle for their uniforms for a few more days. She was surrounded by the other Internationals. None of them wanted to insult Erica by suggesting that she was anything less than Yale material, but even she admitted that serendipity must have played a part.

"My mom thinks it's because I've read books all my life, that's her theory," she said, her laugh floating above the quieter conversations.

Sommer Louie was just as pleased, with twelve out of thirteen acceptances. Stanford University had turned her down, but as the financial packets began to come in, she distracted herself comparing offers. Her parents had retreated slightly from their initial position, that Sommer would have to go to whichever school gave her the best deal. The financial-aid officer at Rice University told Phyllis that the Louies could expect approximately $16,000 a year in aid, between scholarship money, loans, and work-study, which meant that they would have to come up with $4,000 a year. Other schools had offered more, but not enough to break Sommer's heart. Phyllis and Robert would stretch their budget to accommodate their daughter's first choice.

The funny thing was, Sommer did not feel as thrilled as she wanted to feel. How strange, that the process had been more exciting than the end result.

"It's just weird, to send in the confirmation," she admitted to her friends. "It's so *final*."

Katie Briggs stayed away from the Living Room on Monday. On Tuesday morning, before class, she stopped by the College Counseling office to talk to Monica Ward. When Katie had first heard from Berkeley, she had left a plaintive message on her college counselor's phone machine. Now she wanted Ward to see that she had recovered. It was something of a test for Katie. If she got through this conversation all right, she would feel ready to talk to the girls about where she was going.

"Are you okay?" Ward wanted to know.

"Yeah," said Katie. "I'm happy with my choices. They're really similar schools, San Diego and Boulder, and they have a lot of the same strengths, the same weaknesses."

Ward got up from her desk, put her arms around Katie, and began to cry. She had spent the last twenty-four hours bouncing off the walls—laughing, crying, jumping up and down with the happy girls, sitting in a sorry puddle with the sad ones. A few of her colleagues had suggested gently that for the girls' sake Ward might try to present a more controlled demeanor. She could not do it. Monica Ward got emotionally involved with the girls, and Katie was one of her favorites. She had been a friend of the Briggs family before she ever became their college advisor because, before she came to Marlborough, Ward had worked alongside Debbie at the bookstore. She knew how disappointed the Briggses must be. She hated the fact that she could do nothing to make Katie feel better.

"I just want you guys to be happy," Ward sobbed. "You've worked so hard."

Katie sighed. She had reviewed all of Ward's predictions—which schools were likely acceptances, which ones were a stretch. Her counselor had been right about every one. The only reason Katie had felt so bad, at first, was because she had allowed herself to get caught up in the generalized dreaming. It was a relief to get back to reality.

"I love you, Ms. Ward," she said.

The rest of the day was fairly easy, since the seniors knew better than to pry if a girl looked like she did not want to talk. But that afternoon Katie got on the swim-team bus to go to a meet, and the tenth graders descended on her and the other two seniors on the team. The younger girls wanted to know everything: Where had the seniors been accepted? Where were they going? What were their SAT scores?

Katie replied, "I don't care to share that information," but the tenth graders persisted. If Katie wouldn't confide what her SAT scores were, would she say what classes she had taken? How about some advice on curriculum choices?

"This shouldn't be happening at this stage of your life," was all Katie would say. "Live a little."

She told herself the same thing. She was going to go to a good college. She had to focus on that rather than on the schools she would not have the chance to attend.

"It happened for a reason," said Katie Briggs, "and I'm not going to sweat about it."

Katie Tower did not get back to school until Thursday of that week, having taken hurried trips to Brandeis and the University of Chicago. She came home certain that she did not want to go to Brandeis, even though the school had offered her $11,000. She loved the University of Chicago, but did she love it enough to spend three times what a UC school cost? Perhaps the temporary indignity of extension courses at Berkeley would be the best solution after all.

She yearned for the letdown of an obvious choice, but had to settle instead for listening to the girls who had already made their decisions. She was surprised at how proud of them she felt. As a ninth grader, Katie had joked rather derisively about all the activities designed to encourage school spirit, and talked about "bondage" instead of bonding. Three years later, she took some comfort in her class's successes. "*We* got into MIT," she said. While she pondered her own options, she took solace in the other girls' good news.

Katie had no concerns about parental hardship, since her parents had set up a college fund when she was born. The money was Katie's to spend as she chose, but the more she thought about it, the more she liked the idea of spending less on college and having money left over at graduation. She could spend a year in Europe. She could start graduate school without taking time off to work and save money. The University of Chicago held a strong appeal; as Jon said, it offered the kind of "intellectual community" that they all thought Katie would enjoy. But UC Berkeley was a terrific place, and if she went there, she could prolong her education, in graduate school or on the road, without having to worry about how to pay her bills.

It would be a little weird, taking extension classes for a semester, but Katie would figure out ways to make herself feel that she belonged. She asked her parents to send in the registration check for Berkeley's extension program and started to tell people of her decision.

A week later, Cabel called the extension office to make sure that the check had arrived and that Katie was all set, only to learn that the extension program had already filled up. They had waited too long. Katie Tower was number 101 on the waiting list for the fall term, which essentially meant that she could not take any classes until she enrolled in January, long after the other freshmen had made friends and learned their way around. Her only other options were to attend classes at a two-year college, try to get into UCLA for one term, or go somewhere else.

Katie could not stand the idea of waiting until January, working while all her friends went off to college. She did not want to go to a junior college for one term. Freshman year meant picking a school and going there in the fall, but that required her to make a choice she had never considered. She could go to the University of Chicago, which she had already decided not to do, or she could go to UC San Diego, which had never been part of her plan. Berkeley and the University of Chicago had reputations. UC San Diego had what Dr. Forsheit considered to be one of the best science programs in the country, but no one else regarded it with the reverence they reserved for the two schools that had tied Katie's future in a knot. It was one of Katie's safe schools, and now she had to figure out if there was a way to choose it without feeling that she had settled for second-best.

22

THE SENIORS WORE their college identities like stiff new shoes, proud of themselves but prone to the occasional wobble. Spring fever had been a sporadic problem before the letters came, but now the girls had no reason at all to behave. There were so many more important things to think about than classwork: graduation dresses, the senior trip to Hawaii, the prom, the perfect shoes, hair and makeup for each of those occasions; it was time to indulge all the aspects of teenage life that they had ignored for six years.

The teachers' challenge was to maintain a semblance of order among the younger girls, who had yet to earn the right to flaky behavior. Susan Cope, one of the Middle School English teachers, had been wrestling all term with a particularly incorrigible group of seventh graders. She had asked another teacher to sit in and observe. She had tried everything from extreme empathy to extreme discipline, but no single tactic worked. There were real animosities in this class, girls who did not like each other and did not mind saying so, as well as girls who would not sit still. If Cope managed to get one corner to behave, a problem erupted across the room. The good girls, like Martine Forneret, were getting lost in the shuffle.

In exasperation, Cope offered the girls a deal. If they were good for a solid week, she would give them bonus quiz points. By Thursday, they were still being obedient, but Cope could see cracks starting to appear in the smooth surface. She decided to give them permission to act out. As they entered the room she shoved a sign-up sheet at them, so that each girl could pick a character in "Romeo and Juliet," which they would read aloud in class.

The move had an unintended advantage: One of the girls who arrived late got what she considered to be a bad part, and announced loudly that she was going to get to class early next time. The girls started to read with a minimum of trouble, and the energy Cope had been trying to tame for weeks slid into a more productive mode. They tried funny accents, they mugged, they waved their arms, they pointed imaginary swords. Romeo sighed for Rosaline, the object of his affection before he met Juliet.

Cope had them. In the second scene of the first act, Romeo picked up Benvolio's rhyming style, and Cope interrupted the readers to ask what they thought that meant. One girl spoke up immediately: Clearly, Romeo was trying to communicate with Benvolio on his own level. Several of the girls knew what that was like. One complained that her mother was always after her to talk more slowly. One griped that her friends never had much to say.

Cope let them go on for a little while—seventh graders liked to relate what they read back to their own lives. But she did not trust the new peace, which could fall apart in an instant, so she soon guided them back to the text. Romeo told Benvolio of his lovesick yearning for Rosaline, and the seventh graders started speculating about Rosaline's appearance. Cope interrupted them, confused. There was absolutely nothing in the text about how Rosaline looked.

"It says she's beautiful," protested one girl.

Susan Cope smiled and took her time looking around the room. There was Martine's little olive-shaped face, with doe eyes behind her glasses and a mouth full of braces. There was a big girl chewing bubble gum, despite

Cope's repeated prohibitions. There was a moon-faced girl with frizzy blond hair, and an Asian girl with a chic, shiny bob. Some of the girls had reached puberty, and some had not. Some of them had already achieved the sleek look the magazines were selling, and some never would. The seventh graders were always a wild assortment.

Yet they assumed that Rosaline was beautiful, if for no other reason than that Romeo was in love with her—and like as not, they defined "beautiful" in some way that did not include the way they looked. Cope was one of the more worldly teachers at Marlborough, having come to teaching after a stint in film school and thirteen years as a field engineer and editor for ABC News. She had experienced some of the pressures that awaited these girls outside of school, and she was offended by much of it.

The divorced mother of a Marlborough tenth grader who had already survived the roller-coaster of her early teens, Cope had a mission that had nothing to do with the ability to parse Shakespeare. She wanted to build girls who "spoke in a *person*'s voice, not a woman's voice," she said, girls who did not worry about whether what they said or how they looked was pleasing. Being interesting was a far better goal and a more lasting attribute. Today she had a lesson for them that was not in the text.

"Well, you're *all* beautiful," she said. "Look around the room. Every one of you is beautiful, but look at how different you are. Beautiful? Just a generic reference, I think." A few of the girls blushed, while others succumbed to the giggles. They were quieter after that. It was nice, at twelve or thirteen, to be considered lovely just for being yourself.

Besides, being the object of some boy's adoration was problematic, at least in Romeo and Juliet's time. Cope stopped at the passage where Paris argues for Juliet's hand.

"And what is Paris's argument?" she asked. "'Girls younger than she are happy mothers made.'" Cope glanced up and laughed. "You ready for *that*?"

When Lynn Siegel was in college, she had taken a class in Shakespeare, and she still remembered what her professor said when he handed back the first exam. "He asked, 'Why don't you talk to us?'," she said, "but I just *couldn't.*" She saw a lot of herself in her daughter, Alex. With most of the year gone, Alex's algebra teacher reported that she rarely spoke—but had done so well that she could take honors geometry next year. She could hold her own in a small group in history class, as Myranda Marsh had hoped. French was more difficult. Alex complained to her mother that the other girls spoke up faster, and louder, and drowned her out. The teacher told Lynn and Eric that Alex, who had spent summers in France since she was ten, was the best student in the class, so Lynn suggested to Alex that perhaps the teacher was trying to give the other girls a chance. Alex was not satisfied, even with all A's and a B+ in history for first semester. English was the only class where she felt she made a real contribution. The rest was still a matter of figuring out how to be heard.

Her parents had long since learned to be patient. "It is," said Lynn, "who she is," a direct emotional inheritance from her mother. What mattered to them was that most of the teachers at Marlborough were sensitive to Alex's behavior, which made it easier for her to change. Her math teacher called on her even if her hand was not up. Marsh encouraged her to speak up, and teased her just a bit about always having the right answer. Privately, Marsh was pleased by Alex's frustration; as she had hoped, Alex was no longer content being silent.

In all, Lynn said, "It's been even a better year than I thought it would be." Alex was happy at school. She had a small group of close friends, and she knew plenty of other girls she liked to talk to. "She tells me that no matter what, when she has a free period—very few of her friends have free period with her—she's perfectly happy with whoever's there," said Lynn. "She doesn't have to wait until her close friends are available."

It was a long way from where Alex had been a year ago. She and her parents both remembered how hard it had been for Alex to get ready for school when she was in sixth grade. Every morning, she had spent twenty self-conscious minutes standing inside her closet, wondering what to wear to make the other students think she was cool. It was never a matter of what she liked; she got dressed with an eye to other kids' expectations. Now she woke up every morning and threw on her uniform, eager to get to the bus stop.

And every now and then, there was a glimpse of the girl Alex might become. She had amazed her parents by performing with two friends in the Marlborough student talent show, lip-synching to George Thorogood's blues song, "Bad to the Bone," complete with trashy costumes. It was only a lunchtime show, no parents allowed, but to Lynn it was "a huge breakthrough," not something she could imagine her daughter daring to do at a coed school.

Barbara Wagner was pleased for the seniors who got good news, and proud of the acceptances that she knew would enhance Marlborough's reputation. New student applications for next year were up 40 percent over this year, and the incoming seventh-grade class was the largest in Marlborough's history: ninety-three girls, more than the eighty-five that the admissions office had predicted. As she had hoped, Marlborough was more and more often a girl's first choice, and some of that increased interest came from parents who were impressed by the list of colleges that Marlborough graduates attended.

She was preoccupied, though, with the hard choices some of the girls had to make—particularly Katie Tower, whose dilemma reminded Wagner of a similar dilemma she had faced when she had applied to college. She had applied to the University of Michigan at Ann Arbor, the state's largest and most competitive campus, which had a national reputation and drew a great number of students from out of state—and to Michigan State in East Lansing, a smaller campus that dwelt in the shadow of its better-known sibling. Both schools accepted her, but she got a form letter from Ann Arbor and a personal note from the President of Michigan State. The dean of the school of music there had actively recruited Wagner and had made sure that the president of the university shared, and communicated, his enthusiasm.

She had begun to consider her options from a different point of view: Would she rather be one of more than 30,000 students in Ann Arbor, or attend a less prestigious school where the dean himself seemed to know who she was? For that matter, did she need Ann Arbor to make her feel more important? Or was she sure enough of herself to pick what felt like the right school, instead of the famous one?

She wasn't going to tell Katie or her parents what to do, but she hoped that Katie would have the courage to pick San Diego. The social costs at Berkeley were great; starting in January was like crashing a party that was well underway. The real costs at the University of Chicago were substantial—and in truth, if Katie wanted to pursue science, UC San Diego had a stronger program. Berkeley and the University of Chicago were the famous names, no question, but if Katie's self-confidence had survived the last several weeks, she would realize that she did not need that kind of reinforcement. She was still the intelligent, idiosyncratic kid she had been all along.

For all the talk about curriculum, Wagner believed that the more subtle lessons taught at Marlborough were the ones that made a lasting difference. "It's not just the rigor of the program," she explained. "It's the independence that's fostered. These girls are not overly reliant on faculty spoon-feeding—and that may be partly because of the dialogue that goes on in the classes, but it's more that from seventh grade on we're encouraging independence. The faculty is there to advise."

Toward the end of April, she got a call from Cabel, saying that Katie had finally decided on UCSD. The news was as gratifying, in its way, as the acceptances at MIT had been. Katie clearly had developed what Wagner called "cumulative self-reliance," after years of being encouraged to think for herself. "Katie really thought about what *Katie* wanted," Wagner said. "She was at the center of the program, not looking outside the program— really thinking about what's right for her. Not the brand name." She sought out Katie and told her the story of her own college quandary, a generation before. She wanted Katie to know that she had made an admirable choice.

The site of the 1999 Marlborough School senior prom was the Bel-Air Country Club, and like senior proms across the country, it involved rented limousines, a sit-down dinner, a loud rock band, and a dance floor. What distinguished this prom, though, was the boys—or the relative lack of them. Simple logistics made it hard to find a boyfriend, since there was no way to sit next to a prospect in class, or bump into him in the cafeteria at lunch. If a girl managed to find a boy outside of school, there was little of the usual glory to be gained; no one ever saw them together, at least between the hours of eight and three.

Some parents of prospective Marlborough students worried that romance was artificially absent from the Marlborough curriculum, but most were reassured by the omission. They often confessed that they were frightened by the pace at coed schools, because it seemed far quicker than what they remembered from their own adolescence. Pregnancy was not the threat here, the way it was for the girls in Cindy's biology class at TYWLS; girls at Marlborough were likely to have frank parents and accommodating doctors. The problem, among private-school students, was early sex, rather than unsafe sex, and parents feared that their girls would face decisions they were not mature enough to make. Marlborough was one way to help them apply the brakes. It worked: Even among the seniors, blinding romance was the exception, not the rule.

The girls seemed far more concerned with what the teachers had to say about their dresses. They walked in and struck a pose, waited a beat for the inevitable compliments, and then rushed to stake out a table with their friends. The few girls who had real boyfriends clustered to one side of the dance floor and managed to turn even the fast numbers into something more intimate. The rest of the seniors hung out in little groups, the boys they had brought orbiting the edge of their circle.

Katie Tower's date was a friend from the debate-club circuit, a pleasant enough guy, but hardly a candidate for romance. She was far more excited about the dress she'd found on Macy's sale rack for only sixteen dollars, a column of dark blue satin with an Empire waist. Sommer came with a boy whom she called "the epitome of a friend," having abandoned attempts to turn him into anything more serious. Christina's biggest issue was not finding a date, but figuring out what to do with her insulin pump for the evening, since there was nowhere to hang it on her fitted black dress. She could strap it to the inside of her leg, but this was supposed to be a night of celebration, so for once she decided to leave it at home, along with her eyeglasses.

Katie Briggs and Erica Forneret did not even bother trying to find dates. Katie invoked the grand Marlborough tradition of showing up for dances without a boy, and she announced her intention to dance with other girls who came stag, or by herself, or perhaps with someone else's date. She didn't need to import a boy in a tuxedo to have a good time.

As for Erica, she lacked the diplomacy that seemed to her to be a basic requirement for dating. Her mother had found her a date for a charity ball earlier in the year, and had suggested the names of several potential prom escorts, but Erica was not interested. She was frustrated that it was not easier for her, since the other Internationals had managed to find dates, but they promised her that it made no difference. She knew the boys the other girls were bringing; she knew she could have snared one for herself, had she been willing to try. Instead, she would have to settle for being part of the group. They came to the dance together in a rented limousine, and afterward they planned to go to a club on Sunset Boulevard. The last stop would be Chrissy's house, for breakfast at dawn.

At the last minute, Erica abandoned the dress her mother had found in favor of a pale, clingy silver-green dress with a distinctly 1940s, smart-set look. It was the sort of dress that encouraged the languid pose and the knowing smile, and Erica did her best to live up to it. The next day, some of the Internationals would wonder if her increasingly gay mood was due to nerves, or to something stronger than water in the plastic bottle she carried around with her during the dance. She must have found something to drink somewhere, because by the time the group changed into street clothes and headed to the club, Erica was on her way to being drunk—drunk enough to get wobbly at the club, to get sick at the curb when the girls took her outside for air, to need Chrissy to take her back to the house early and put her to bed.

There was a tiny scandal, of the sort that might come from having been too good for too long. Erica's close friends and their parents worried about how to tell the Fornerets, about what to tell the Fornerets, about whether Erica needed some kind of help, about whether this was an indication of a larger problem. It blew over in days. Rodney Forneret, who had grown up in the easy atmosphere of New Orleans, and Phyllis, who had grown up in a devout Baptist household and did not drink, were of a single mind about their daughter's behavior. Erica had not eaten enough the day of the prom because she was preoccupied with getting ready. Wherever she had gotten the alcohol, which she was not used to in the first place, her body had over-reacted.

As had her friends. After a stressful senior year, Erica's parents felt that she was guilty of nothing more than foolish miscalculation: an empty stomach, some alcohol, and no sense of when to stop. The Fornerets believed that Erica was a Marlborough girl in the best sense; a girl who knew how to find her way back to who she was, even if she briefly lost her way.

23

The Young Women's Leadership
School of East Harlem

May 1999

AFTER A YEAR of diplomacy and exhortation, Cindy Jackson came to work at the end of May drained of everything but the survival instinct. On Friday, May 21, she interviewed for the chemistry teacher's job at the Jacqueline Kennedy Onassis School. The following Monday, she stood at the front of her classroom and studied the faces of the girls in Amy's biology class. They were supposed to be ready to present their special projects on the environment, but Jackson could tell from their vague stares that every girl hoped she would call on someone else first.

They were far more interested in discussing a popular new hairstyle that involved tight braids fitted close against the head in a dizzying number of patterns. Amy tried to get the girls at her table to focus on a little impromptu test preparation, identifying the chambers of the heart, but two of them were too busy studying the hairdo of the girl who held up the plastic heart model.

"That's so cute," cooed one of the girls, oblivious of Amy's efforts. "Oh, your hair is so cute."

The other girl was one of the few who still wore last semester's style, her long hair tucked under a headband. She muttered enviously, "I'm going to do that as soon as I get my relaxer."

Jackson noticed that two girls who were partners had chosen not to sit next to each other—so she walked up to the partner at the front table and asked her to go first.

"We can't do our presentation," came the belligerent response, "because she didn't do her part. *I* did my part. *She* didn't do her part."

"You can still present," said Jackson, who was not in the mood to cut the girls any slack. "But part of a partnership is communication." She walked to the back of the room, where the estranged partner sat, and asked her what had happened. The girl shrugged, shook her head, and drummed a perfectly manicured set of long fingernails, striped black, white, and silver, on the table top.

Jackson strode to the front of the room, barely able to control her anger. The mock Regents exam, a practice test the teachers had cobbled together, was just a week away. The real test was next month. The girls had to get serious.

"Now the truth is," she said, "*this is not a good time of the year to be taking a zero.* There aren't a whole lot of opportunities left to raise your grade. No more definition-of-terms work, which means no more easy grades. You've been on easy street until now."

She picked another team to go first, and reminded them of the stakes. If they defined their assigned terms and presented the material in a self-confident way, with stylish visual aids, they could earn a total of fifty points. This one project was enough to improve a girl's grade for the entire term.

If a team did a sloppy job, their grades would suffer—as would the rest of the class. Any one of twenty-two scientific terms might show up on the Regents exam. Each team depended on the other teams for definitions. Jackson had been banking on group pressure to get even the most reluctant girls to participate. This morning, she was not so sure.

The first two girls, whose job it was to define "parasitism" and "communalism," had taken the opportunity seriously. They had made a small chart that included a general definition of terms, and, to accompany their oral presentation, a huge poster of a deep-sea scene, with blue tissue paper for the water, shiny green paper for the plants, and brightly-colored fish. As they explained how the weather affected the ecosystem, they held up a big orange sun and some gray-green clouds.

When they were finished Jackson asked the other girls to give them a round of applause. "If you're having trouble knowing what you're doing with your presentation," she said, "I'm going to use these girls as an example, because they did such a good job. Wonderful job. You girls go put these posters up in the hall and take some of the old work down."

She turned to the others, eager for another happy surprise.

"Anyone else ready to present?" she asked. The girls got very busy shuffling the papers in front of them.

"Now, look," she said. "These reports were due today and you guys aren't ready. You let it go over the weekend and now here you are. What's going on?"

She did not really want to know. She had heard all the excuses before. Some girls had real responsibilities at home, while others sank to the level of the least-cooperative member of the team. If she caved in and let sympathy run her classroom, the girls would never get to college.

"If your partner's lazy, be prepared to do all twenty-two terms yourself," she said. "That's what happens in the business world. Your group doesn't manage to get a presentation ready, you get fired! You act like this in the business world and you won't have a job very long. You *all* talk about big money. Well, big money doesn't come without sacrifice. So you have nineteen minutes left today, and you have tomorrow, and we have Wednesday to present.

"Do you guys know what I'm saying?" She glared at them. "Get ahead of the game. Now go ahead. Get this done."

Jackson plunked herself down in her chair. The girl at the back of the room silently piled up her binder and textbook and moved to the front table to sit next to her partner. Behind them, Amy woefully considered her visual aids, which were nothing more than definitions written in different colors. This was not a fifty-point presentation. Her partners wondered if they could quickly find some magazine pictures to paste around the definitions, to spruce up the poster a bit.

Jackson watched Amy and wondered what had gone wrong. She had seemed such a promising student at the beginning of the year, but now she barely managed to keep up. She was, as her teacher had already warned her, "on a plunge." She did not do the assigned homework on time, and when she tried to hand it in a month later, Jackson refused to accept it. Amy missed tests and asked to make them up when she felt she was ready. Jackson turned her down there, too, explaining over and over that the point of homework and tests was to get them done during the unit they covered. She had given her a "low C/high D" on her second-semester progress report, but this time there was no compensatory spurt of energy.

Jackson wished she had more time to work with the girls. She had told Chevere early in the year that what she really needed was either a double class period or a classroom period and a lab scheduled together. What she did not need were the special activities that ate into her already-insufficient class time. An off-campus assembly to introduce public school students to the opera was only a good idea if the academic foundation was secure. It was not.

As Jackson waited for the period to end, her mind drifted to the teaching job she had applied for, and to the physical trainer who had encouraged her to get a trainer's license and give up teaching altogether. He had told her that if she worked six days a week, all day, she could clear $2,000 a week.

"Whew," she had replied, marveling at the amount. "That's *too* much money." On the other hand, she had signed up to do a standup comedy routine at the Toyota Comedy Challenge in mid-June. Maybe she would be auditioning for a television show in Los Angeles by the end of the summer.

Amy headed to the library for study hall, where she stood at the center of a noisy knot of girls who were using the computer. When she saw Gary Ryan come in, she broke away and ran over to the table where he was setting up his chess board.

"Those're my friends," she said, a little breathless. "The wild ones."

Gary smiled and set out the chess pieces. He was a self-described "philosopher and theologian" who had gone to Harvard University and now worked for a foundation that taught chess to underprivileged kids. Tito Lopez had started teaching Amy to play when she was in third grade, but she was too good for him now. Amy looked forward to Gary's visits, and she spent study hall with him over a chessboard.

When she made a move that would have led to checkmate, Gary returned her piece, pointed out her mistake, and waited while she figured out the right move. Amy was a good player when she concentrated, and he wanted to encourage her. There was a citywide tournament coming up on Saturday, probably a thousand kids, and he told her it would be great if she could go.

"I *can't*," she said, the resentment rising in her voice. She gave over part of each weekend to studying. "I've got the math Regents."

"I know you can't," said Gary. "I'm just saying it would be great if you could."

Fabrice Fortin came into the library, and Amy looked up.

"Hi, Fabrice," she said.

"Concentrate, Amy," said Gary.

She turned back to the game. After a few more moves, Gary pointed out that she was in a better place than he was. He had decided to resign the game.

"*NO!*" she yowled, loud enough to draw a reprimand from the librarian. "I want to beat you! Get a checkmate!"

Gary smiled, and resigned the game. As Amy collected her books, she bragged that she had become the resident cutup in math class. "You ought to come see me," she said. "I act kind of crazy in there now, because I'm not *into* it anymore. It's the end of the year. I want to be *outta* here."

Gary teased her that soon she would not have enough time for chess. "You've become a real socialite," he said, gently. "The center of your clique."

"That's me," Amy replied, as she sauntered off. "They all revolve around me."

She felt only a tenuous connection to TYWLS. The older she got, the harder it was to live up to her reputation as a smart girl; the gap continued to widen between her grades and the grades her teachers said she was capable of. There were real consequences to her behavior now: From ninth grade on, her grades were part of the official transcript that would someday be part of her college applications. She had always said she would get serious when the time came, but if anything she had become more flagrant in her disregard. None of what Chevere talked about—college, scholarships, a chance to get out of the neighborhood—seemed to matter.

College was not yet real. Graduating from TYWLS might not be real. Amy's parents talked more and more about moving to southern California, maybe when Amy was in tenth grade. That would be the end of TYWLS; in fact, Amy would most likely end up at a coeducational public school. So she did enough to get by and consoled herself with the fading notion of what she *could* do, once she decided to try.

Diana was using her inhaler four times a day instead of her regular two doses; it was the only way she had enough energy to get through the day. She had a huge amount of work to make up from all the days she had been absent, and she had to get caught up in time for the exams. She could always taper the medicine back to the normal dose over the summer. Right now, all she wanted was to feel well enough to catch up.

She walked into English class, deposited a book report and some late work in her teacher's box, and quickly found a place at the front of the carpet, at Sarah Kirkpatrick's feet. Diana had her notebook out and her pen ready; while some of the other girls chatted, she wrote down the vocabulary words that were already written on the board.

Kirkpatrick took her place in front of the girls, and hesitated. The girls waited. She took a shallow, nervous breath and began, "Okay, all of you know from my accent that I'm not from here."

This one time, she might have welcomed an interruption, but no one spoke. "Now, my husband and I have made the decision . . ."

"Oooh," cooed one girl, expecting to hear a pregnancy announcement. "Ta da . . ."

". . . that the best thing for us right now is to go back home."

"That's not good!" yelped another girl, in disbelief.

Kirkpatrick rushed ahead, determined to finish her little speech. "And since I can't commute from New Orleans," she said, with a nervous laugh, "I have to stop teaching here. Now, it's going to be really hard for me, especially with you girls, who I've known for two years, because I love you and I'm going to miss you. And I'll give everyone who wants it my e-mail address, because I want to know what happens."

She sighed. She had been worried for days about how the girls would respond. Some of them, surely, would get angry. Some would reject her for having rejected them, because that was how they would see her decision. She was just another adult who did not really care about them. Kirkpatrick wished that she could convince them otherwise, but she doubted she was going to change minds.

She tried hard not to cry in front of them, and her voice got higher and brighter from the effort. *"I want to know how things turn out for you,"* she said. *"And you haven't seen the last of me. I promise I'll come back."*

No one said a word. Kirkpatrick took a moment to collect herself, and when she spoke again, she sounded like her old self, kind but determined, expecting a little more effort from everyone.

"But until then," she went on, "I just want you to remember that I am in charge. You can't get around me."

One girl looked like she was about to start sobbing, so Kirkpatrick walked over to her to talk about their pending e-mail relationship. What bothered her more were the stoics, the ones who walked out at the bell without saying anything to her. She could read their faces; they were not surprised to be abandoned. She had likely lost them for the rest of the year.

Diana was disappointed by Kirkpatrick's announcement, but not diverted from her task. She made her way upstairs to Fabrice Fortin's math class. It was a slower section than the one she had been in with Maryam; at the semester break, the principal had decided that Diana needed the chance to go back over some of the material she had missed.

Fortin spent the whole period drilling the girls on the sum of the interior angles of a triangle. They worked problems on the board, they worked problems at their desks, and Fortin walked the aisles to see how they were doing. All they wanted to know was whether a particular kind of question was likely to show up on the mock exam. Exasperated, he refused to answer.

"Hey, the point of the mock Regents is to show me what areas we have to work on for the real exam," he protested. "But this doesn't count on your grade, so don't worry in terms of that."

Of the nineteen girls in this class, he was fairly confident that thirteen would pass—including Amy, though he found it increasingly hard to get her to participate in class, and Diana, whose native ability ought to make up for her absences.

The next day, Kirkpatrick found a girl's mother waiting for her outside of room 901, asking for a moment of her time. The English teacher asked one of the secretaries to supervise Amy and Maryam's class, apologized to the girls, and darted back outside—where the irate woman brandished her daughter's recent essay and complained that the grade was "inappropriately low." She had shown her daughter's work to a friend who had a job at an advertising agency and thought it deserved better. She wanted Kirkpatrick to change the grade.

Kirkpatrick was furious. All she cared about were the hardworking students who felt let down because she was leaving, and now someone had taken her out of her classroom, away from the group, to ask a special favor for a single, undeserving student. For once, she allowed herself the luxury of anger.

"Your daughter got a sixty-one on the last assignment," she said, "twenty-eight on the last quiz, she's missed three-fourths of the work, and you're saying, 'She just can't seem to get a break with you'? Come on. The grade was what it was supposed to be."

While she and the woman argued, the girls abandoned their reading lists to study for the math test. Amy was stuck on the logic problems Fortin had reviewed the day before, so Maryam ran through them with her, jabbing the air with her finger to punctuate the pattern of true and false statements. When she was done, Maryam turned to her own work, quietly reading the biology Regents prep book.

A girl at the next table noticed that Maryam seemed to have finished her math prep and moved on to the next subject. "Oh," came the envious stage whisper, "Maryam is *studying* for that test."

Maryam waved her away without looking up. "I'm trying to," she said, "which is hard, given all these distractions."

At that moment Kirkpatrick stormed back into the room, determined to spend what was left of the period on the girls' reading logs. Each girl had to submit a hundred-word synopsis of each of the twenty-five books she had read during the year, as well as longer essays on four books from a single genre, all with proper bibliography listings—even if the punctuation drove some of the girls crazy. She was determined that the girls complete this exercise in responsibility. It would be proof that she had accomplished something.

Several of the girls had failed to read enough books, and now they were struggling to catch up. Kirkpatrick was not in a charitable mood.

"You girls were supposed to keep track of every book you read this year," she reminded them, "and if you didn't, you're going to be scrambling."

One of the girls at Maryam's table had read enough books, but she worried that she would never get the journal entries done on time. Kirkpatrick changed her tone; she supported anyone who made a genuine effort, but not the girls who spent most of their energy looking for a way out.

"Don't worry," she said, her hand on the girl's shoulder. "These don't have to be a great big deal. Just get them done."

Maryam needed no such encouragement. She had long since completed her log and her four essays and was now immersed in a new book. Amy was another story. Kirkpatrick took the chair next to Amy's and showed her her work log for the term. There were two essays still missing.

"I want you to make up the work," she said, sternly. She moved on to the next girl on her list.

Amy clenched her teeth until the little muscle at the side of her mouth began to kick in protest, and for a few minutes she sat there, blank, staring at the wall. Then the bad feeling passed, and she started listening to Maryam and the other two girls at the table, who had gone back to their discussion about the logic problems they expected to find on the mock Regents. Amy despaired of figuring them out, but she frantically took notes as they talked, muttering "true" and "false" to herself as she worked.

One of the other girls listened to her and laughed. " 'True if false'? 'False if true'?" She pointed to her own forehead and raised her voice. "Stupid if smart?"

The fourth girl at the table wailed, "We're going to fail!"

"*I'm* not going to fail," said Maryam.

Back in September, Amy Lopez had looked like she was wearing her big brother's blazer, its lopsided shoulders extending beyond her own, but nine months later she had grown into her uniform. She and two other girls stood in front of their biology classmates with their revised visual aids. They had pasted drawings of animals along the bottom border of their terminology poster and had hastily created two more posters, one with more terms and another with drawings of ocean plants.

Cindy Jackson walked to the back of the room and sat down. "Okay," she said, "as always, we offer our speakers our undivided attention. No playing with your posters or other material on your desk."

At that, Amy made a noise like an old radio transmitter—"beep, beep, beep, beep"—while the girl standing next to her acted the part of a radio announcer at a station devoted to news of the ecosystem. She introduced each new term, and Amy provided the definition. When they got to "competition for ecosystem resources," Amy allowed herself one ad lib:

"Since we're talking about humans in New York City," she said, "that means competition for jobs, transportation, and *romance*." The third girl finished the definitions, and then Amy announced, "That was our news flash. Tune in again at six." Everyone laughed and applauded, and Jackson gave them a roll of tape to mount their posters on the bulletin board in the hall.

She asked them if they wanted to come back to her to see their grade, and they hesitated. Amy looked first, and held up the evaluation form for her partners to see. Forty-seven points out of a possible fifty. They had pulled it off at the last minute.

The next two teams did equally well; even the girl who had refused to sit with her partner had completed a couple of rudimentary posters. It was a long reach for that girl even to complete the assignment, and Jackson was in the habit of rewarding effort as well as outcome. She found herself feeling as optimistic as she had felt blue just days before.

She walked back up the center aisle and faced the girls. The mock math Regents was next period, and she knew the girls were apprehensive. It was time to tempt them with a reminder of where all this hard work might get them. Jackson had a bit of the revival preacher in her; she knew how to get the girls worked up about their future. "Let me talk about some good things we saw today," she said. "You're getting much better at speaking to the group. You keep eye contact, you speak slowly and loud enough, and you're going to be respected, whether you're a public speaker or a businesswoman or talking to a professor in college."

There it was again, the promise that TYWLS was a stepping stone out of the neighborhood, with everything that implied: Money, status, a better view of the horizon. "If you're going to be a presence in your work, with your mate, in your family, you have to be able to speak strongly," she said. "Not loud, but with authority. It's not easy. When I was in seventh grade I was a goofy kid, I didn't have a whole lot up here"—and she knocked her fist on her forehead—"but as I learned to speak, I became more confident."

She praised each girl in turn. Amy's partner, the radio announcer, had "a wonderful presence." Amy spoke "with great authority; you can tell she has support for her ideas." The girl who had at first refused to cooperate with her partner had a great sense of humor.

"You guys are like an engine," said Jackson, winding up her spiel. "We're stoking that engine, you're learning new things, we've got maybe three weeks until the Regents, and *I feel good*. So you feel good, too."

She planted herself in front of them. Everything about Cindy Jackson was emphatic: copper-colored hair, big blue eyes, a puckish grin; when she got going like this she was hard to resist. "Because you know what this means?" she asked.

They waited.

Jackson yelled, "Who's not in the driver's seat anymore?"

"You," the girls called back, in unison.

"And who is?" Jackson asked.

"We are," the girls cried.

Moments later, the girls were crowded around the blackboard in one of the math classrooms watching Paul Winston, the latest addition to the mathematics faculty, do last-minute problems on the board. Winston was TYWLS's surprise secret weapon, a seasoned math teacher from another school who had agreed to spend a scheduled leave at TYWLS. He was supposed to provide after-school tutoring, but need had sucked him in, and now he took over Jenny Long's classes, helped with test prep, and tried to compensate for a year of rotating teachers. People tried not to think about what would happen when Winston's leave at his other school was over. If Fabrice Fortin had been the favorite math teacher all year, now Paul, who had experience as well as good intentions, was the center of attention.

He scrawled a few more equations, ran through them with the girls, erased the board, and told them it was time to begin. They sat two to a table instead of the usual four, with calculators and scratch paper at each place. Two proctors took their places at opposite ends of the room, and the test began. When the air conditioning cut off, the only sound was the sputtering hum of the overhead lights. All the jokes and excuses came down to this: a rehearsal for the real thing, which would be part of their college applications.

By the end of the week, Diana Perez believed she would survive a year of spotty attendance. She knew her grades were good—she hadn't lost the ability to plow through mountains of late assignments—and to her delight, the mock Regents had seemed relatively easy. Summer was always an easier season than winter, in terms of her health, and as the days got longer and brighter, her spirits improved. She had decided not to participate in the intensive summer figure-skating program, but rather to relax a little, do some reading, and spend time with her older sister Linda.

Diana and her mother took to talking about college again, sitting on the couch late at night, Maria's stout arm around her daughter's slender shoulder, speaking low so as not to wake the little girls. Maria loved to listen to Diana's notions about the future. It was like a travelogue. She could sit there in the quiet dark, everyone else asleep, and, if she concentrated hard enough, she could imagine that they had left the apartment behind and gone to some exotic new place Maria had never seen.

They did not know how close Celenia Chevere had come to filing a formal truancy report at the start of the semester in addition to the science teacher's complaint. The principal was obligated to do so if a student's absences were excessive and chronic, but she had agonized about what to do. She knew Diana loved school, and she knew she did her best to show up. Still, Chevere couldn't allow her to think that her actions were without consequence. She had begged Maria to do what she could to get her daughter to school. She continued to beg her, and to tally up the absences, and to wonder how much longer she could pretend not to see the problem.

The names of thirty-three girls, each of whom had earned at least an 89 average, were posted on a framed list outside the TYWLS office. Maryam was one of ten girls with stars next to their names, which meant that they had averages of 94 or above.

By the end of ninth grade, Maryam had designed a routine devoted to progress. She came home every afternoon, did her homework, and only then allowed herself to watch her favorite television shows. She took weekend workshops at New York University as part of a science-and-technology program for high school students, where she had a chance to measure her progress against students from more competitive schools. She had a tutor on Thursday afternoons to work with her on Regents prep.

On Sundays, she went to the Muslim temple near her apartment. Maryam needed something to fortify herself, as her friends talked more and more about boys and parties and the homework they couldn't be bothered to do. She had not made friends in her neighborhood; most of the people she saw carried the threat of a dead-end existence, and she avoided them as though they were contagious. She turned to her family's religion for sustenance and said her prayers five times each day.

Maryam's success at TYWLS had brought her to a place she was not quite prepared to handle. She had become the symbol of what the school could do, and she knew it: One day, she and a friend had defied the uniform code and worn sweaters that were the wrong color, and Maryam had stood by while Chevere confronted the other girl. No one said a word about it to Maryam, as though her grade-point average had bought her special privileges. There was a new rule this semester for girls whose grades had fallen below a C, and every morning, Maryam watched them troop into the principal's office to show her their homework before class began. Maryam would never have to endure such humiliation.

The closest she got to trouble was a score of eighty-three on a recent science report, because she had failed to come up with a decent explanation of her absence on the day of the classroom presentation. Maryam, indignant, decided that her reputation could stand a B for the term. She would not "buy back favors," she said, by doing extra work.

She felt powerful at school, and sometimes she succumbed to heady dreams of the future. She rattled off the list of schools she might like to attend when she graduated, as though she were naming the constellations of the heavens: Harvard, Brown, maybe even Stanford, which was so far away she could hardly imagine what it would be like. Then she remembered how depressed she had been when she left home for a single month at Smith College last summer, and she thought about how sad her mother looked whenever the conversation turned to Maryam's leaving home.

The world was an inviting and scary place, and Maryam tried not to get carried away. "I try not to expect too much," she said, carefully. "I try to think about how much I have." She joked that she might still be at TYWLS when she was forty, passing her own daughter in the hall on the way to class, because she had yet to pass all her Regents exams.

In truth, she felt fairly confident about the tests, but straight A's at TYWLS were not the same thing as straight A's at a private prep school, not even the same as straight A's at a public school in a wealthy neighborhood. Even if she passed all her Regents, she still had to do well on the standardized tests, starting with the PSATs next year. Those were the scores the colleges looked at.

In her three years at TYWLS, Maryam had learned that she wanted a college education, and that she was likely the most attractive candidate the Class of 2002 had to offer. She had learned that her mother's notion of a good education had a distinct geographical boundary around it. Maryam might well get what she wanted, if she was willing to ignore her mother's wishes. It felt like too much choice, and not enough choice, all at once.

The ninth graders were losing their English teacher, and Cindy Jackson had heard that Peter DeWan, Fabrice Fortin, and Shirley Gasich would also not be coming back. If she left, too, they would have new teachers for every academic subject but Japanese next year.

Leaving would have been easy if Chevere had fired her. The decision would have been out of her hands; Jackson could have blamed miscommunication, or a difference in philosophies, and gone on her way. But she had been spared, and for all her frustration she could not quit. She ticked off her problems with the school: too little classroom and lab time, too many interruptions, too much test pressure, too little opportunity to connect with the kids. None of that, finally, was reason enough to walk away.

She had job offers from the two other schools she had looked at, and was not about to turn them down until she had to, in case Chevere had a last-minute surprise for her. Still, it looked like Jackson was safe for another year, responsible for the only continuity her ninth graders would have. She dug in, to make sure they were ready for the real Biology Regents, in June. Maybe she would put off her trip to Los Angeles until next spring.

As the school year drew to a close, Celenia Chevere felt an overwhelming sense of exhaustion. She had cleared out the problem students and the teachers who had disappointed her, but she still was not satisfied. She suspected that she might never be—that the New York City public-school bureaucracy and Ann Tisch disagreed with her on the fundamental philosophy of TYWLS.

Chevere felt that she had been clear from the very start. Her goal was to give girls like Maryam Zohny a chance, "because the Maryams of the world," she said, "in another setting, may very easily fall through the cracks. They get no attention, as long as they don't give anyone problems." She had seen it with her own daughter Serena, who was about to graduate from

Wesleyan University in Connecticut, which was why she had put Serena in a private school.

"I'm the sacrificial lamb to the system," Chevere said bitterly of her own career in the public schools. "I didn't need to give them my daughter as well." She had always seen TYWLS as an opportunity to rewrite history; to create the public school that had not existed when her daughters were children, a school that took care of a bright girl like Maryam.

After three years, she had come to believe that District 4 and the Board of Education saw things differently. The roster of incoming seventh- and eighth-grade students reflected "a different mindset and attitude—it's 'Let's put this kid in there because they're going to fix her.'" When the school started, Chevere had recruited girls whose families understood what she wanted to do and supported her demanding style. Now, Chevere too often found herself arguing with parents who complained that she pushed too hard. She wanted to tell them to go somewhere else, and so open a slot at TYWLS for a girl who was willing to do the work. But the district sent her girls who needed saving, and they expected her to figure out how.

It made Chevere angry. "We're not here to save souls," she said. "In all the years I've worked for the system, I've compromised nothing. So I'm seen as a difficult person to work with sometimes. I will not deviate from the goal."

The effort wore her out. "I still feel pretty gung-ho," she said, but in the next breath admitted that the plans she had made before she came to TYWLS had begun to nag at her, competing for her attention. She had started to work on the children's stories she wanted to write, and had contacted an editor she knew who had offered to collaborate with her. She told herself that she was very good at starting schools, but possibly not the right person to sustain this school. "What I feel," she said, "is that eventually I will leave the school. I know that for a fact." Her younger daughter's college graduation meant that for the first time in her life, Chevere could make decisions based on desire, not necessity. She no longer had to support her two girls. She only had to take care of herself—and doing that would mean leaving TYWLS, unless the conflict she perceived was resolved.

Three years earlier, Chevere had walked into Tisch's dream and made it her own. She was not interested in anyone else's definition of success. "I'm not looking for friendship now," she said, "or for anyone to love me now. I'm not." By June, she no longer spoke of attending graduation ceremonies for the pioneer class, in June of 2002.

Ann Tisch was unaware of Chevere's frustration, because she had always believed that the purpose of TYWLS was to serve all girls who were willing to do the work, whether they got A's for it or C's. Rudy Crew had been right to ask for a replicable school, but he had been talking only about the budget. Tisch defined his request in a broader way. It would be easy to make TYWLS look successful if the school only accepted the most promising students. The real challenge, as Tisch saw it, was to prevail with a mixed group of girls—to send someone like Maryam to a fine college while also guaranteeing that a C student got the diploma she might otherwise have missed. After the pioneer class, Tisch had encouraged Chevere to broaden the range of applicants that TYWLS accepted. If the school served a range of students, then it was a viable model for other school districts. If it took only the best, it was merely a showcase; they wouldn't have proved a thing.

Victory was relative. The effort was what mattered. Chevere might be feeling the strain after three years, but to Tisch it was all part of the process. Next year, she would have a class of eleventh graders—the girls who had come to school a year after the pioneers. If TYWLS was serious about sending them to college, they needed help.

The district did not have spare cash to hire a college counselor, nor had Chevere been successful in trying to find a volunteer. Tisch decided that she had to hire a full-time college counselor, someone who understood how to get this particular group of girls into college—and how to navigate the bewildering financial-aid process with their parents.

College. She could hardly imagine what it would be like when that first batch of acceptance letters came in. That would surely motivate the younger girls.

24

Marlborough School

May 1999

L ES KLEIN DID NOT HAVE children of her own, but she understood something about the bond between a mother and her daughter. When she turned fifty, her mother had sent her a letter reminiscing about their sometimes-difficult relationship. Klein already felt sad about losing some of her favorite seniors—and if that was so, she could barely imagine what their mothers must be feeling. As the senior-class trip to Hawaii approached, she had an inspiration: What if each of the seniors' mothers wrote her daughter a letter? She was one of the chaperones on the trip, and she loved the idea of taking the letters with her to surprise the girls.

Klein wrote a long letter, addressed, "Dear mom of a soon-to-graduate-senior," and laid out her plan.

I would like to invite each of you to write to your daughter. I have not told the girls about this, so it would be a secret until they are distributed to the girls toward the end of our time away in Hawaii. I was thinking that among the things we talk about in my classes and many of the heartfelt moments I have shared with the girls in conversation, many come back to their time with you—the wonderful moments and the not-so-glorious ones too.

She wanted the moms to think about their "feelings about the years behind and the weeks ahead leading to graduation." They could include photographs, or make a list of "poignant memories," or just send a card. "The main thing," she wrote, "is that it would be so incredibly meaningful to *her* that you took the time to reflect on your special bond with her through the past six years (middle/high school) or seventeen/eighteen years of life together."

The plan would not work unless everyone contributed, since Klein could imagine nothing sadder than being the one girl who did not receive a letter. If she got enough complaints about the idea, she would cancel the project, but she urged the moms to deliver something to her mailbox or the main office before May 17.

There were only six girls in Arleen Forsheit's science research tutorial, but she prepared for their final presentation of the year as though it were the academic equivalent of a debutante ball. This was not so much the completion of an assignment as it was the celebration of budding intellects, and that required a festive atmosphere—invited guests, too much food, and an uncharacteristic level of hyperbole from Dr. Forsheit.

She stood at the front of the room, beaming, as parents and faculty members took their seats. When it was time to begin, she introduced Christina Kim.

"Anyone who knows Christina knows she has a powerful intellect for someone her age," said Dr. Forsheit, who appeared to be working hard to control her emotions. "Her scientific writing is the equal of anyone in this room. And she chose what is arguably the most abstract aspect of molecular biology." The others applauded. Christina passed out an outline entitled, "Tyrosine Kinase Receptor Ligand Ephrin-A5 and Axon Sprouting

After Focal Stroke," and explained what she had learned about the regeneration of neural connections after a stroke.

She spoke about axons and growth cones and proteins as though they were terms teenagers tossed around every day. She explained that after ten months of studying induced strokes in laboratory rats, the researcher had yet to see the recovery patterns he had anticipated—so Christina had decided to continue her volunteer work through the summer. She had come to the project with ten years' practical experience with illness, and was herself the beneficiary of ongoing medical research. The terrible swings that had marked her first years as a diabetic were over, in great part, because researchers had figured out a better way to manage the disease. If the tiny insulin pump she wore was not yet a cure, it did enable Christina to lead a semblance of a normal life. She marked time, and defined progress, differently than did many of her peers.

When all the girls had finished their reports, Dr. Forsheit asked them to comment on the class itself; to talk about what they had learned personally from the experience. One of the girls said that she never would have had the nerve to go to an Ivy League college if not for this class. Christina agreed: The tutorial had given the girls a chance to see how their self-confidence held up in the outside world.

"The obstacles were important to overcome," Christina said. "I'd be in the lab with people who were MDs and PhDs, and they'd forget I was only in high school. I'd cram the night before just to *go* to the lab. But then I got the work done. You just have to decide this is what you really want to do."

Robin McCleary, Dr. Forsheit's successor as department chair, wondered if the girls would put together a "Cliff's Notes" version of their presentations for the ninth and tenth graders, but Christina was reluctant.

"I don't want people to think this is the only way to get into college," she said. "It's not. But I've heard even eighth graders talking, and a lot of them think they ought to do this, just for that reason. But it's not for everybody."

Kurt Schleunes was a man who believed in the incremental step, and as the year drew to a close, he was mostly satisfied. He had found fifteen talented ninth graders to take his new accelerated pre-calculus honors section next year, which would prepare them for an AP course in their junior year. He would have to invent a new class to challenge them if they continued with math in their senior year, but he was already talking to Dr. Forsheit about a combined math-and-science research project, something that would have the girls "crunching a lot of numbers" in their work.

He dismissed the recent AAUW report that said that girls could do just as well in a "gender-fair" coeducational classroom. Schleunes did not think that standardized test scores were a useful evaluative tool; at the level of Marlborough or Harvard–Westlake, most students did exceptionally well, with both schools reporting average scores above 650 in both the mathematics and verbal sections of the SAT. What he cared about was whether talented girls studied math in college and at the postgraduate level. Advanced work required a confidence that test scores could not measure, and that, he believed, was where a girls' school made the difference. He was going to build graduates who thought about math when they thought about the future.

The only thing that upset him was the computer-science curriculum for the coming year, which lacked an advanced sequence of programming classes. The woman who had been hired to run the computer center was currently in charge of the curriculum, but she was not a programmer or a formal department chair. Schleunes felt that this sent a damaging message to the girls, as though they had been relegated to the fringes of the technological revolution. In this case, he agreed with the AAUW that "technology has become the new 'boys' club.'" There was a huge difference between people who used computers and people who actually knew how to program them, and he did not want to see girls shut out.

"I see us going down that road of 'Programming's not for girls,' and it makes me *mad*," he told Robin McCleary when they met to discuss how their departments might work better together. "Not too many things make me mad, but this does. You're alive in the twentieth, the twenty-first century, this is the field. Women have traditionally been shut out. It's just awful. We should have a program that leads to an advanced-placement class, and the AP curriculum is such a turnoff. Nobody seems to care, and that's even worse. It's an elective program."

Usually the head of the math department ran the computer curriculum, but Schleunes felt it ought to be a discrete program. Maybe next year. If a lot of girls signed up at the introductory level, he could use that interest as the foundation for a bigger program. The only way to exploit enthusiasm, as Dr. Forsheit had found, was to keep a step ahead of it and design new classes in response to the demand.

McCleary encouraged him to push for advanced programming classes. "You'd be the Pied Piper of this thing," she said. When he hesitated, she offered to back him up. "Okay," she said, "we have a new project, the 'Computer Science I'm Mad As Hell and I'm Not Going to Take It Anymore' project. There. You've got me mad, too."

Sixteen of the graduation dresses that were supposed to come back unhemmed arrived hemmed, which caused a ripple of trouble. If a girl came in for her fitting and found her dress two inches short, she searched the racks for a dress in the same size that was two inches longer. When the intended owner of the longer dress came in, she too looked for another dress. By the middle of alterations week, the two mothers in charge of the project were beside themselves, the seamstress faced the unpleasant task of making replacement dresses if she ran out of swappable garments, and the girls were at a fever pitch.

The prom had been theater. Graduation was tradition. There were stories, from the days of old money and restricted society, of girls whose parents sent to Paris for the proper dress, of long-stemmed roses and an air of exclusivity. The class of 1999 would wear identical, affordable dresses and carry understated bouquets. Still, marching into history required that every half-inch of hemline, every shoulder strap, every dart, every glimpse of a dyed-to-match sandal, be right.

The Marlborough senior class was leaving on Friday, May 17, for four nights in Hawaii. In the remaining weeks before their June 3 graduation, they were expected to show up for classes and take whatever AP tests they had signed up for, and the final exams their teachers might require. Beyond that, they did not have to come to school. As teachers loosened their grip, the seniors suddenly found themselves with a free Friday afternoon or a long, empty morning. School became the place they dropped by to report on the far more interesting things they had done between classes.

They embraced relaxation with the same fervor they had previously reserved for their schoolwork.

Katie Tower clung to a friend as they walked down the hall, elated at her first round of "Hawaii shopping."

"I got a bikini," she crowed. "I am *so* excited." The only real work that stood between her and graduation was a ten-page portfolio for her political-writing class, and it was almost done. At this point she came to school because she was not ready to make a clean break. She lolled around the Living Room and played "Heart and Soul" on the piano, the first time she had played in eight months thanks to the demands of senior year. She hung out with her friends, ignored uniform regulations, and drove the younger members of her carpool home.

The other girls were just as determined to be irresponsible. Erica loudly announced to her English teacher that there was no point in her reading her final paper aloud, because she was handing in the same paper in another class. It was mostly the same girls. Why should they have to listen to it twice? Katie Briggs baked cookies and concentrated on her singing, Sommer took long breaks in Larchmont and wondered about how to wear her hair at graduation. Christina showed up for the English Literature AP exam because she wanted to score a five, the highest possible grade, but even she slacked off on her classes.

Nothing counted anymore. The only reason to show up at all was a vestigial discipline, or the kind of affection that overcame reason.

Katie Tower's last class at Marlborough was Dr. Forsheit's Science and Society, and for once Katie was late and unconcerned. She and her friend Tai breezed in five minutes after the bell, Katie wanting everyone within earshot to know that she had spent two hours at Noah's Bagels with a boy she had met at a party after the prom who had since been promoted to "boyfriend," and that the only reason she had shown up at school at all today was to attend this class. As soon as it was over, she was going shopping.

But first, Tai had to hand in a special project she had roped Katie into helping her with—an eight-page newspaper made up of the girls' articles, book reviews, and editorial cartoons. Tai presented it to Dr. Forsheit, who called for quiet and took her place at the middle of the room.

"Okay," she said. "There's one last thing I want to do here. You all did a great job, but I think we all agree that Tai did a *terrific* job, worked way beyond the call of duty at this, or any other, time." She produced a bag tied with ribbon and handed it across the table to Tai. "So I just wanted to give you this as a way of saying 'thank you.'"

Amid a chorus of "awww"s, Tai reached for the bag and hugged Dr. Forsheit.

"Make a speech, Tai," said one girl.

"Nah," Tai replied. "This is where I just sit down."

Dr. Forsheit insisted that she at least open the bag. Inside was a big plastic drink container from Jamba Juice, a popular fruit-smoothie chain.

"I'm a Jamba Juice *obsessive*," said Tai. She opened the container and found two smoothie coupons inside, and when she held them up, all the other girls applauded.

"And all the rest of you should be very, very proud of yourselves, you did a terrific job," Dr. Forsheit said. "This was just an excellent final project." She would make copies while the seniors were in Hawaii and distribute them when they returned.

That was it. The juniors had a class session on Friday, but by then, the seniors would be on their way to Hawaii. Between hugs and kisses, Dr. Forsheit slipped into mother mode, begging the girls to remember their sunscreen, reminding one with very pale skin to pull her ponytail straight back so that the part in her hair would not burn. After they left, she marveled at how well things sometimes worked.

"It's a moving thing," she said, "when you see girls go beyond the call of duty."

Joan Jacobs Brumberg's views on teenagers and body image might have offended some of the seniors, but a group of ninth graders were already at work on a project about diet and appearance when Dr. Brumberg visited

Marlborough. The younger girls were at a more vulnerable age, too new to their figures to be comfortable with themselves. The idea, explained one of the participants, was "to talk about serious issues in a casual way."

On May 20, they presented their first effort, a series of comic skits about an array of characters: two friends named Heather, who believed it was impossible to be too rich or too thin and ignored their friends' warnings about extreme diets; a girl who confused worries about studying with worries about weight; another who stood on a scale, moaning "Oh, God, I need to lose so much weight" while she planned an exercise regimen; and an athlete who swore that her parents' decision to get a divorce had not depressed her in any way.

When they were done, they offered to answer questions—in character. Immediately the girls in the audience took after the Heathers.

"Don't you think your outlook on beauty, on celebrity, is kind of warped?" asked one girl.

"No," said Heather number one, in an approximation of a Valley Girl's whiny drawl. "Have you looked at *Vogue,* at *YM,* at other magazines? Ever see anybody fat in any of those magazines?"

"No," came the reply. "But are you saying the world is one big *Vogue?*"

"Well—*yes.*"

The girl who played the hardworking, chip-eating student chimed in. "Now, I'm taking five APs, but I'm really not stressed out by it. I just need to do well and go to a great college. Now, some people can't handle it, and I think for them sometimes they develop an eating disorder because it's a way to control at least one aspect of their lives."

The audience was far more curious about the two Heathers; they preferred to think that girls who had eating problems were fools, not candidates for the Ivy League.

"What do you think thin is going to get you?" came a voice from the audience.

"Well, I don't spend that much time on my schoolwork," said Heather Number Two, "so if I want to attract a wealthy husband who's going to support me and take care of me, I better look good enough for him to be attracted to me every morning."

When she had to stop to take a breath, a girl called out, "Why can't you take care of yourself?"

The laughter subsided, and everyone waited for the answer. Heather Number Two smiled, and said, "Because—what would be the point of that?"

The student moderator tried to insert some pertinent statistics. The average American woman was five feet, four inches tall and weighed 140 pounds, she said, while the average model was five-feet seven and weighed only 112. There was no way to keep up with media images, so girls ought to stop their useless dieting. Down that road was a scary fate: While 60 percent of anorexics who sought treatment eventually recovered, 20 percent of those who were not treated would die of the disorder.

The audience wanted to know what exactly qualified as anorexia.

"If you're in the hospital," said the first Heather, "that's anorexia."

"Then what's the *before that*?" came a voice. What was the sign that a girl was headed for real trouble?

"I dunno," said Heather.

Someone in the audience shouted out, "Ally McBeal," referring to the show's extremely thin star, Calista Flockhart. Another girl who liked the actress's bony look immediately hissed, "She's *not* anorexic."

Several teachers had come by to see the presentation. One of them, who had fought anorexia and bulimia, stood at the back of the room with a pained expression on her face. She remembered all the compliments she had received in college when she cut back on her eating and spent more time working out. She remembered eating less and less, until she felt so depressed about herself that she taught herself how to eat too much, how to hide food, and how to mask the smell of having vomited by eating oranges. She had become a master of "making sure nobody saw." She had finally started eating right about two years before, but she still had bad days when she found herself paying far too much attention to the number of calories she had consumed.

Part of her recovery was to offer a sympathetic ear to girls who needed to talk, so she made it her business to know who in this room had problems with food. The senior girls might feel smug and defiant, because they had survived. The younger girls needed the public debate.

———

The seniors' Hawaii trip was the perfect antidote to a year of hard work and anxiety, since the big decisions involved how long to stay in the sun, or whether to have a plate of fresh fruit. The girls lolled, or strolled, or slept. By the time Les Klein called them together to receive their letters, she felt the slightest trepidation. She had decided to ask for the letters because a lot of the seniors had wonderful relationships with their mothers—but some had "less than great" relationships, and Klein did not know how they would react. For that matter, she did not know what the mothers had written. She hoped she had not made a mistake.

She passed the letters out and watched the girls scatter so that they could read in private. Klein, who was determined to be "vigilant" about any negative reactions, wandered around at what she considered "a respectable distance, trying not to interfere," but wanting to be available if any of the girls needed to talk. They seemed not to: It was very, very quiet, save the occasional sniffle or burst of laughter. Almost twenty minutes passed before anything happened—and then, as though someone had flipped a switch, the girls got up and started to move. One contingent sprinted for the public telephone to call home, while others gathered together and read their letters to each other. A couple of girls complained that Ms. Klein had "ruined the 'up' mood," and one disgruntled senior walked far out onto the breakwater to get away from prying questions.

Debbie Briggs had started her letter in a deceptively casual tone. "I can't believe you are practically a High School graduate," she wrote to Katie, "and *I am the one with the writing assignment!*" She griped about having written the letter in her head a half-dozen times, and joked about "brain drafts . . . awash in my own tears," but she abandoned the comedy by the end of the second paragraph.

I'll never forget the way you marched off into preschool, kindergarten, Marlborough, without a glance back. If you didn't have the world by the tail, by God you'd sure look as if you did! Yet in saying that, it seems that I am saying you are good at putting up a false front. There is nothing about you that is superficial or phony. You are one of the most sincere people I know. You just know that whatever lies ahead, you can do it, even if it is one step at a time. I think sometimes you even amaze yourself!

She thanked Katie for sharing her love of singing ("heaven itself!!") and then, having confessed the depths of her affection, she tried to regain her balance. Katie was on her way out of the house, and Debbie had to make it as easy as possible for her to go.

I love you so very much, and the best thing is that I know that you know that. I know that you know how much I will miss you next year, because, in those very RARE moments when you are not having more FUN than you have EVER had, you will also miss me. I am so blessed with the relationship we have had thus far–I can hardly wait to see what the future brings for the two of us. Hopefully, just as many hugs, tears and, most importantly, laughter.

Love, Mom xxoo

Katie loved what her mother had written. She and Debbie had always been close in a way that made Katie feel very safe, and as she read and reread the letter, she could picture her mother "poring over it, and crying too."

She felt happy and sad at once, but not homesick.

Phyllis Louie had a funny habit of dating letters with the day she expected them to be read, not the day on which she wrote them, as though her words were not real until received. It also made the message seem more immediate; these were the things she would say to Sommer if she were sitting right there on the beach with the girls.

"My dearest Sugar-Foot," she began, "I have been walking around for the last few days wondering what I would write to you. There are so many things I want to say to you." She started with memories of her pregnancy, and the "myriad of things" she thought about while she waited for her daughter to be born.

> I have loved you from the moment I knew I was pregnant. When you were born, I knew you were the most beautiful and wonderful child *ever* born. I have admired and loved you *every day*. There are many days when I'm thanking God for you, that I wonder what have I done in my life to have received such a gift—you!

She reminisced about kissing Sommer's feet when she was a baby, which was where the nickname "Sugar-Foot" had come from, and about the time Sommer announced that she did not need to go to school anymore, because she had her first library card and knew how to read. She reminded Sommer of how she had gotten the Civil War and the civil rights movement confused.

"Sommer," she wrote, "you will never know the pride I feel when I would see you dance, act, or recite some poem. Sometimes I would think my heart would jump out of my body." She encouraged Sommer to take advantage of all the opportunities that undoubtedly would come her way, and finished with a quote from Kahlil Gibran: "'Our children are not our children, but gifts from God, to nurture and take care of.'" They both had to get used to the idea that Sommer was leaving—that she was supposed to leave, and they were supposed to be happy about it.

"I will continue to cherish and love you," wrote Phyllis, "and everything about you. I love you infinity!! Your Mom."

Sommer laughed at the business about her baby feet and her library card, and got teary at her mother's declarations of love, but she did not feel the need to call home or share passages with the Internationals, who were grouped around her reading their own letters. For all the petty disputes over who was opening the mail or whether shoulder pads made the wrong statement, Sommer and her mother had made their way to this day together, while her father sang a happy descant of jazz and dance and optimism. Phyllis was the pragmatic one; Sommer's love for her was grounded in respect and gratitude. So she sat still, and thought about everything Phyllis had done for, and with, her, and spoke to no one at all.

Erica Forneret cried easily, like her mother, and as soon as she saw Phyllis's letter, "wrapped in something so bizarre that only she could have found it," the tears started. Phyllis had made a portfolio out of heavy hand-made paper, cream-colored, with little pastel leaves pressed into it, and tied it together with stiff ribbon. Inside, there was a photo collage on the left and a handwritten two-page letter on the right, all of it on paper with a rosebud border.

The photographs were all of Erica as a little girl—dressed in a hula costume, a tutu, a leotard, a veil, and an adult's pink-silk high-heeled pumps; swathed in a fur coat; sitting in the bathtub. The letter was a delirious appreciation of Erica, tempered by just a bit of advice.

> There are so many things in my heart and head that I want to say to you. Most you have already heard—all of your life—how wonderful, talented, and beautiful you are.
>
> But as you go into this newest adventure . . . just remember you are loved and cherished not for how you look or what you do, but by your family for who you are—your honesty, integrity, loyalty to friends, high moral standards, your moodiness, sense of style—be true to yourself in spite of the pressures of those who have chosen another road. You are special—our shining star, and we will miss you very much.

She wrote about how excited she had been to visit Yale with Erica.

> How blessed, how honored, how proud I am of this wondrous, miraculous child who shines so britely under her vintage wicker basket, that her glow was seen and appreciated by a school willing to, no, made the effort to tip the edge of the basket and look be-

yond to discover a multi-talented, passionate, renaissance woman whose gifts will enhance the class of '03.

Since Phyllis always worried about her daughter's tendency to downplay her abilities, she couldn't resist the basket reference. "I only pray," she continued, "that she actively pursues the finest educational opportunity of her life. The wondrous world is yours for the taking—work hard, Erica. Continue your love of learning and love of life."

Her only other request was that her daughter "give back," always, in whatever small ways she could.

Say yes to giving, say yes to learning, say yes to living the extraordinary life of an extraordinary young woman.

Bravo, Erica, my shining star—Shine on, my love, shine on.

Cabel Tower had made a little book for Katie, covered in a dark-red floral fabric and tied with pink ribbon. She had glued photos to every page and written her letter around them in a curly, girlish script:

From the moment you arrived, it was love at first sight! Thank you so much for being born to us! Dad and I loved watching you grow, and as you grew, we did too.

Next to a shot of toddler Katie in the bath, and another of a preschool Katie dressed only in socks and shoes, Cabel went on:

You liked water from the start, and you've always had your own great fashion IQ. I had always thought that the most beautiful sound in the world was the sound of your laughter—until I heard you and Nicholas laughing together. You have always loved music and you have great taste—er, usually. Your loving spirit shines on our family and your friends—old and new.

There was a photo of Katie in her karate outfit, and Cabel had written:

It has been a joy to see your love of nature, your killer instinct! And sometimes you can be a really good sport about things.

You have made me so proud, and genuinely deeply happy. I am so blessed to have you for a daughter—and for completely self-ish reasons: You have made me a better person—more able to love, less hurried, you taught me to listen—even though it seems at times that I don't—you made me look at the world in a different way—you taught me the importance of kindness. Thank you.

Love, Mom.

Katie, who was in tears long before she got to the end of the letter, grabbed one of her friends and ran for the nearby phone. Katie called collect and got her parents in the middle of dinner.

"Are you okay?" demanded Cabel, unnerved by an unexpected long-distance call from a sobbing daughter.

Katie stopped crying long enough to blurt out, "I love you so much," and then it was the next girl's turn.

Some girls, like Katie Tower, got special letters, while some received what Christina considered "the generic, 'Oh I'm so proud I think I'm going to cry'" letters. There were teary readings aloud, accompanied by crashing waves on the beach, the drama of separation and of nature mingled together, and as Christina read her mother's letter she felt her indomitable calm give way.

She refused to surrender the letter to any of the concerned friends and teachers who asked to see it, and refused to say why she cried so violently—but the more they asked, the worse she felt, and later she would estimate that she must have been out of control for easily a half-hour.

She did not know what was more difficult for her—the bitterness and sorrow she felt, as she prepared to leave her mother and their often-contentious relationship behind, or the misguided comfort the others tried to offer. She listened to what she considered to be "all that pseudo-psycho bull-crap—that every mother and daughter had the same issues, and this was a phase, and it all had something vaguely to do with me going away for college," and cried ever harder. She was the elder daughter of a spottily employed painting contractor and his weary wife, a girl who had grown up threatened by serious illness and inflamed by a desire to be the very best. Success meant turning her back on her family, getting as far away as possible and staying there. Her "issues," as she saw them, had nothing to do with the sweet girls who would go to school in California and drive a new car home at vacation time.

So she cried and swatted away the sympathizers. The girl who awed her classmates with her literary analyses was, for the moment, incapable of explaining herself in real life.

25

GRADUATION DAY at Marlborough School was always too hot. The only place large enough to accommodate the crowd was the parking lot behind the library, which was transformed each year into an outdoor auditorium. The seniors sat on risers that faced east, which meant sun beating on bare shoulders, but the parents and teachers had the worst of it, sitting in the dead-on glare of the setting sun.

This year the weather forgot itself. Two nights before graduation, rain soaked the artificial turf that had just been rolled out to cover the parking lot. The next day, as the girls assembled for their final rehearsal, Barbara Wagner studied the threatening sky and consulted with a few parents and teachers. She had been up much of the night wondering whether to hope for the best or find another venue, and today she had contacted the nearby church that served as the bad-weather site. If she was going to rent a party tent and canopy instead, at indefensible expense, she had to make up her mind in the next few hours.

As if on cue, the last scrap of blue sky slid behind a cloud just as the girls climbed onto the risers to begin their rehearsal. The nine employees of Classic Party Rents unloaded big potted plants, but no one felt optimistic enough to take out the stacks of folding chairs.

When Katie Briggs heard the rumor about a possible relocation, she became terribly upset—and surprised at how much the news bothered her.

"I had no idea it meant so much to me for graduation to be at school," she said. "But it did."

She huddled close with her friends, all of them moping around in ragged jeans and tired sweatshirts. They hid their mounting disappointment behind unnecessary sunglasses. What was supposed to be a day of brilliant promise was shaping up to be a soggy disaster.

Wagner stepped up in front of the group. "Okay," she said. "How many of you will receive your diplomas tomorrow if you're chewing gum?" She looked at that sea of woeful faces, weighed the financial and emotional cost of moving the graduation ceremony off-campus, and made a snap decision. She smiled and raised her voice. "I have just decided to tent this whole area for tomorrow," she announced, to a suddenly animated audience. "My worst nightmare is that it'll be eighty degrees and sunny tomorrow and we'll regret it, but we have to live with it. Now, please. Do stop talking."

The girls were revived. "What *color*?" yelled someone in the back.

"White," Wagner said, laughing. "And now Ms. Jones and Ms. Klein, the consummate liner-uppers, will line you up upstairs and you'll pro-*cess* down as you'll pro-*cess* down tomorrow." The girl standing next to Sommer jumped up on Sommer's back, and Sommer carried her, piggy-back, over to the stairway.

The seniors climbed up to the second floor and formed two rows by ascending height. One girl looked at the classmate who stood facing her, and called out, "Do we come down in pairs?"

"No," said Susanna Jones, the departing Upper School director, "because every member of your family wants to see just you."

At that, the accompanist began to play a goofy version of "Pomp and

Circumstance," embellished with improvised flourishes and trills. Klein took up her position at the gate where the girls entered and either hurried them along or held them back, to even out the space between them. The line still did not look right. Several sets of friends of disparate heights had bought their shoes together—heels for a short girl, flats for her pal—so that they could stand next to each other on graduation day. In their sneakers, they punctuated the otherwise-smooth line with dips and exclamation points.

"Okay," said Wagner, once all the girls were in place. "You're standing. You're smiling. They'll applaud. But if they don't, I'll say, 'Please join me in welcoming the class of ninety-nine.' Then they'll applaud. When that is finished, you'll sit down."

One girl doubted that her ability to reason would survive tomorrow's ceremony. "You'll only say that if they don't applaud?" she asked.

"Don't worry," said Wagner, with a weary smile. "I've been through a few of these. I will not let you down. Then I'll introduce half the world, thank some other people, talk about the tea dance, introduce the four legacy graduates. Then I introduce the commencement speaker, yada, yada, yada. Then the Chamber Singers will sing." She waited, but the singers did not respond to the cue.

"If they *don't* move toward the aisle, they won't sing," she continued. The Chamber Singers rose like sleepwalkers. "If they move this slow, they won't sing. The ceremony will be over." Dutifully, they sped up. Wagner ran through the list of student speakers until she got to the final cue, for the valedictorian's address.

"Now I introduce Christina—'Please join me in welcoming Christina Kim.'" Wagner waited a beat, so that they could all imagine that Christina was talking. "Now her speech is over. Now we award the diplomas."

Most of the seniors arrived at school on graduation day looking as though someone had cut a head out of one magazine and a body out of another and pasted them together. From the neck up, they were hothouse beauties. From the neck down, in their ragged jeans and necessarily button-down-the-front shirts, they were neighborhood kids on a day off from school.

After six years of deferred vanity, appearance suddenly seemed to be the only thing the girls cared about. The hairstyles were extravagant and romantic, the kind that could not possibly be created in the frenzied confusion of the dance studio, which had been transformed into a dressing room. Sommer had spent seven hours the day before having her shoulder-length hair braided into dozens of tiny braids, anchored behind one ear with a spray of rosebuds. Erica wore a crown of fresh flowers that trailed a long ribbon bow. Katie Tower's pageboy had geometric precision, Katie Briggs's baby-fine platinum bob was newly trimmed and held together with hairspray, and Christina had managed to terrorize her long bangs, which had retreated from her forehead in meek obedience.

"Don't touch my hair," yelled Katie Briggs, as friends approached her. "You might get *stuck!*"

The dance studio resembled nothing so much as a communal fitting room during a big sale. The graduation dresses hung in labeled bags on garment racks in the dance studio, and each girl had a folding chair upon which she could set her purse, her street clothes, her beauty supplies, and an extra pair of pantyhose. Several of them put on their dresses right away, but others hesitated, not quite ready to complete the transformation that marked their departure from Marlborough. They darted around with disposable cameras, hugged Ms. Klein, or consulted on a friend's eye shadow. A dozen mothers lined the back wall of the studio or paced the hallway outside, ready with tissues or advice, not wanting to push but hoping to be asked.

Once dressed, Katie Tower fled the small studio and headed for Caswell Hall, which was empty save for a girl whose mother and sister were applying her makeup. Katie and two of her friends whirled across the wooden floor, their skirts fanning out as they spun.

Katie Briggs slipped in, a troubled look on her face, and waited for them to stop. She needed someone to watch her walk. Her dress was doing something funny, and she wanted the others to tell her what the problem was. Katie started off across the room, straining against the hem, and someone yelled at her to stop before she tore the dress. The solution was simple: Katie had to take shorter steps than she was used to. Tradition was a little narrow-minded about how an independent young woman ought to behave.

Katie Tower decided against any more twirling. She slipped back into the studio to see how the rest of the girls were doing.

"It's so unreal," she confided to one of her friends. "I don't feel like it's happening." She caught sight of herself in the mirror and edged closer, to make sure she still approved of her appearance.

"Does this look okay?" she asked, nudging her pageboy into place.

"Sure," said the other girl, who sported a similarly unadorned bob. With a mix of resignation and envy, she surveyed the array of twists and braids and cascades of long hair. "But it doesn't matter. We can't do anything else."

Nearby, Erica stood still while her mother adjusted the ribbon in her hair. "I'm tired already," muttered Erica. "I just want to get it over with and go home."

Cabel Tower was one of the mothers leaning against the back wall of the dance studio just in case their daughters needed them. Cabel had worn a white dress and carried a bouquet at her Connecticut College graduation, but what she remembered most about it was what she did not do, which was to take her mother's advice about the future. Her mother, possessed of some private romantic notion about Cabel's life, had asked her to consider going to a bilingual French-English secretarial school in Manhattan, so that someday she might marry a French businessman. Cabel quit after three days to take a speedwriting course, since she believed it would buy her a more interesting future.

She marveled at how different it was for Katie and her friends. Their teachers might agonize about how best to prepare these girls for the constraints of the real world, but Cabel was not worried. "These girls have no encumbrances," she believed. "There's nothing they can't do."

She glanced at her watch. Jon had arrived home from an all-night job at seven o'clock this morning and had gone right to sleep. He had set the alarm clock, but she wanted to make sure he was up and out of the house.

She darted outside to call him on her cell phone, hoping that he wouldn't answer.

One by one, the teachers ducked into the faculty restroom to change into their graduation outfits. By the time Les Klein emerged, trying to subdue a floral scarf that refused to do her bidding, the girls had filed onto the lawn for their class photograph. Klein stood near the photographer's tripod and watched the seniors take their places, the shortest girls arrayed sidesaddle on a white cloth on the lawn, the next row seated on folding chairs, with three more rows of girls standing behind them.

For ten minutes they posed for choreographed posterity:

"Lean to the center."

"Lean forward."

"Don't lean back. You'll have a double chin."

Then they headed back to the dance studio to check the damage that an errant breeze or emotion had done. There was a buffet table set out for the girls, and as they walked by, Katie Tower, looking dazed, grabbed a little sandwich on a French roll and ate it leaning forward, away from the full skirt of her dress. One hovering mother warned her nervous daughter away from a piece of chocolate, while another girl decided to forego the lemonade her parched throat yearned for. She eyed the cup suspiciously.

"I can just see it spilling," she said, and headed inside.

Another girl, having temporarily misplaced her autonomy, wailed, "Mommy, what'd you do with my flowers?"

Klein followed them into the dance studio and watched as they lined up in front of the mirror again. Earlier in the afternoon, she had invited Katie Briggs and Katie Tower to get together over the summer; Klein had a year-end ritual of buying books for a handful of favorite students, and she prided herself on the perceptive match of title and recipient. This year, she hadn't had time to go shopping, but she wanted the girls to know that she hadn't forgotten.

Now that they were in their dresses, Klein held back, wistful. There was no more time for hugs. What had felt supportive just an hour ago would threaten the image they were trying so hard to create. She was surprised at how timid she felt. They seemed far out of reach.

"It makes me feel a little sad," said Klein, "but you know what? You can't stop the river. They're in another place today. Within themselves. They have moved on. I feel like I want to move forward, but . . ." She took a half-step, and stopped.

Cabel Tower stood nearby, and one of the other moms gave her a long, mute hug. The woman sighed, and blinked to keep from crying. "I know," said Cabel. "I have a whole package of Kleenex." With their arms around each other, they turned to watch their daughters. Some parents had already begun to file into the tent to find their seats, but Cabel lingered until the girls were almost ready to line up for the processional.

Timothy Bruneau, the choral director, had gathered the Chamber Singers together for a warm-up session in the music studio next door—the seniors, like Katie Briggs, in their gowns, and the juniors in dresses.

"I just want to say, you're going to be feeling a bit more emotionally charged today," he said. "But don't sing any bigger. Don't do this"—and he sang with a sob in his throat—"and don't sing anything more than you can control."

At 2:30, the singers took their place to the left of the stage for a quick final rehearsal with the house band, which included Kurt Schleunes on drums, another math teacher on bass, and one of the science teachers on guitar. The first song was "Set Me As a Seal," a contemporary piece whose words came from the Song of Solomon. The second was a gospel rendition of the pop song "Stand By Me," and when the girls got to the chorus, Bruneau addressed the gowned seniors in the front row.

"*C'mon,*" he exhorted them, snapping his fingers. His voice was full of the emotion he had warned them to avoid. "*Last time.*"

The tent protected the audience from the rain that never came, but there was no way to stave off the dank cold. At 3:30, the eighty-three shivering members of the 1999 graduating class took their places along the second-floor hallway, while 770 guests waited in the transformed parking lot. There were flowers everywhere: garlands wound around the staircase, huge sprays on either side of the platform where the girls would receive their diplomas, vases alongside the speakers' platform, and smaller arrangements across the front of the stage. Three official photographers and three video cameramen waited to record the event.

A bagpipe player began to play, the seniors allowed themselves one tremulous, collective yelp, and the processional began. Barbara Wagner came down the stairs first, followed by members of the board and faculty, and the girls cheered as favorite teachers passed—Arleen Forsheit, the departing Susanna Jones, and Les Klein, who stopped at the gate to monitor the girls' pace. Christina Kim, the class valedictorian, came first, followed by the rest of the class. Katie Tower entered giggling, pausing for an instant as she passed her parents so that Jon could take a photograph. Erica Forneret floated in, her head held high, as though she already had her eye on the next phase of her life. Katie Briggs was quiet, eyes down, trying hard to concentrate on every detail of what was happening. Sommer Louie strode down the aisle, victorious.

Barbara Wagner took her place in front of the girls. Every year when this moment came, she imagined that she knew what it was like to be a parent of one of these girls. She felt so proud of them. She knew their dreams; she knew what their parents wanted for them.

It was, she said, "a magical moment. It's never looked so good, and it will never look this good again." For days, she had been yelling at the seniors about when to stand up and when to sit down, and here they were, she thought, "looking like angels." Marlborough graduation was a humbling experience, even for the wise guys in the class.

She took a long moment to look at them, with their plain white dresses and their bouquets. Lisl had rebelled and put on a cardigan sweater over her dress, but the other girls braved the cold for the sake of tradition. Wagner was glad that she had not caved in to pressure for caps and gowns instead of long dresses, even though she understood the argument that long dresses were a vestige of another era, while caps and gowns defied gender. The photograph of this year's student-body president would be hung on the wall in the Living Room alongside portraits that dated back to 1926, every one of them of a girl in a long white dress.

"A Marlborough graduation doesn't look like everyone else's," she thought.

The crowd applauded without provocation, but Wagner wanted to be sure that the girls got their first cue right, so she turned to the microphone.

"Now, will you join me in congratulating this wonderful, wonderful class," she said. The audience cooperated with more applause, and the girls sat down. Wagner welcomed everyone, and introduced four legacy seniors, two of whom were the third generation of Marlborough graduates in their families.

The commencement speaker was the writer Joan Didion, journalist, novelist, screenwriter, and herself the mother of a girls' school graduate. If anyone onstage or in the audience had hoped for a sentimental send-off, ripe with praise for what the girls had accomplished, they were quickly disappointed. Didion intended to "nag," she said, as she had when she spoke at her daughter's graduation from the University of California at Berkeley. "And what I want to nag you about—another surprise—is working hard."

She read from letters that F. Scott Fitzgerald had written to his only child, a daughter, Scottie, after she had broken a rule at boarding school and been asked to leave. Fitzgerald's wife, Zelda, had had a nervous breakdown and been hospitalized years before, and he saw a lesson there for Scottie. "'She realized too late that work was dignity,' Fitzgerald wrote about Zelda in his letter to his daughter, "'and tried to atone for it by working herself, but it was too late. She never knew how to use her energy . . . and one of my chief desires in life was to keep you from being that kind of person.'"

Didion believed that the next few years were crucial for Marlborough's seniors, as they had been for Scottie Fitzgerald, and for her own daughter, "because these are the years that female children of the middle class either take hold of their lives—or don't." She warned her audience that everyone sent "more complicated, more mixed, more nebulous" messages to their daughters than they did to their sons, even parents who were enlightened enough to have sent their girls to a single-sex school.

"We say we want them to be happy," she said, "which is certainly true, but it is just as certainly an inadequate prescription for living. . . . We assign them instinctively a passive role in their own fate." This preoccupation with happiness ignored "the possibility that comfort and security at twenty, or even thirty, often lead to boredom and dissatisfaction at forty and fifty." What was the point of a Marlborough education if a girl retreated into a referential life, as someone's wife and someone's mother?

Didion finished with a story of her own, about a missed Christmas in 1969. She was supposed to be in Los Angeles with her family. Instead, she was in a deserted office building in New York City, trying to finish an article for *Life* magazine. She called home to speak with her husband and young daughter, and after she hung up, she began to cry.

It had taken her twenty years to figure out why. It was not because she had missed the holidays with her family. It was because of the story coming over the Associated Press wire about Altamont, the 1969 rock concert near San Francisco where four people died and thirty more were injured—an event, Didion recalled, that "many people saw as the end of an era."

"I should have been at Altamont," said Didion deliberately, as though she were not yet done chastising herself. "But I was sending myself too many conflicting signals to realize it."

This was the lesson for today's graduates: The world would do its best to confuse and distract them, and they had to resist, as they had for the last six years.

"I think my wish for all of you today is that metaphorically you get to Altamont when Altamont is happening," said Didion. "That you make a decision to live in the largest world possible, not to protect yourselves from it, but to live in it; to try to get the point. To accept the risks and insecurities of trying to perform better than you can. To live recklessly, to take chances, to pick up your work and stick to it, take pride in it."

Her own daughter had gone to Central America after she graduated from college, and had called her mother once she got past the soldiers with submachine guns at the airport. She said that she was scared and excited, and described her mood as crying and laughing all at once.

"What I wish for, for all of you, four years from now, is to be crying and laughing all at once," said Didion. "Thank you."

After the Chamber Singers performed their first number, Barbara Wagner stepped to the podium to deliver her remarks. Like Didion, she knew that the girls were about to enter a world where opportunity was sometimes hard to find and often harder to embrace. She wanted them to remember how fortunate they were just to have the chance to be confused. Wagner read from a letter written by a Marlborough alumna who had graduated in the late 1800s: "'Whether we graduated from school or not made very little difference,'" she read, "'because we did not have careers before us. . . . Some of us undoubtedly dreamed of careers, and distant horizons, but for the greater number of us this turned out to be a matter of wishful thinking.'"

Wagner asked the girls to do something with the chance they had earned for themselves. "The class of 1999 has had the most impressive array of college acceptances we have *ever* seen at Marlborough," she said. "Next year, unlike 1899, each of you will enter a college or university of your choice. You will also have career opportunities that we have not yet envisioned today.

"I offer my most enthusiastic congratulations," she said. "I might even cry again." At that her voice choked and she fanned her hand in front of her face, as though trying to beat back tears. She smiled at the audience. "I've been crying all week, you see."

When she had collected herself, she introduced Christina Kim, who as valedictorian was one of the day's three student speakers. Christina began with a disclaimer. "Who am I kidding, anyway?" she asked. "I am a seventeen-year-old almost–Marlborough graduate who has spent not all but much of the past six years simply making sure my homework was done on time. . . . The one thing I'm really sure of is that a fraction of a point doesn't give me any kind of authority to tell you about life."

She went on, in an uncharacteristically soft voice, to list some of the things other people had said about the meaning of life: that it was an overlong drama, a moderately good play, a box of chocolates—or a video game, "since no matter how good you get, you're always zapped in the end."

"Life is just one damn thing after another," she said, finally allowing herself a sly smile. "Life is the same damn thing, over and over."

What she really thought was that life was a process, "a rough draft, I guess, and this just happens to be one of those snapshot moments, where looking back in a couple of years you'll be able to summon this vague image of people dressed all in white. But the end result doesn't seem to mean half as much as how we got here."

"It's all about the struggle, I guess," she said. "Yes, Señora Loles, *hay que luchar.*" Christina glanced at the rows of girls seated to her right. "I guess there's not much more to do than to go out there and be all that you can be," she said, with a smirk for having expropriated the Army's advertising slogan. "You know you'll be fine. And just remember: the next time you find yourself on a sunny beach in Hawaii, the higher the SPF, the better."

With a shrug, she sat down.

The first faculty prize, the Florence Elise Mead prize for music, went to the graduate "who by her example has enriched her peers, her school, and her community by reason of her skills and discipline in music," said Wagner. It went to Katie Briggs, who made her way to the podium amidst shrieks from her classmates and applause from the crowd.

Wagner announced a half-dozen other academic awards before she got to one of the most important awards of the afternoon—the Faculty Prize, which went to the student who "best caught the ideals and spirit of Marlborough." This year there was a tie—and one of the winners was Katie Briggs.

Her mother, Debbie, had barely recovered her composure after the announcement of the music award, and now she burst into tears all over again and covered her face with her hands. Jeff Briggs held out his arms, as though somehow he could embrace his daughter from his seat half-way back in the crowd, and began to applaud, shaking his head in wonderment.

There were more speeches, and then the slow parade of graduates as each girl came to center stage to receive a diploma from the president of the board of trustees and a hug from Barbara Wagner. To end the program, the Chamber Singers sang "Stand By Me," which prevented Debbie Briggs from regaining her self-control for another five minutes. Cabel Tower sang along, while onstage her Katie started to cry. When the song was over, Katie Briggs turned her back to the audience and applauded the other girls in the group.

The weather cut a ragged edge around the tea dance. What should have been a languid afternoon of sitting at tables on the front lawn, eating little sandwiches and trading good wishes, was instead a frenetic display of adrenaline and nerves. A graduate who stopped moving long enough to eat soon had goose bumps down her arms, so most of them flitted from table to table or found refuge in a circle of warmly dressed well-wishers. The photographers set up along the walkway near the back lawn to take family photos as well as any impromptu groupings the girls came up with, which further disrupted the afternoon. Sommer and Erica and the other Internationals all had to have group photographs, and they ran from one ensemble to another just in time to pose and smile. Other girls yelled to their friends as they passed, and for a while the front lawn was left to teachers, distant relatives, and bored younger siblings.

The band set up in the front courtyard, with its small temporary dance floor, and when the music began, the girls grabbed their fathers for the first dance, a crowded number that was over before they had much of a chance to absorb what was happening. From that point on, it was chilly chaos; a few dancers, a few girls visiting with the guests, and the magnetic pull of what came next, which drew many of the girls back to the dressing room before their parents were ready to give them up.

Graduation night was an extravagant, orchestrated celebration designed to reward the girls without once giving them the chance to lose their heads. The parents had hired a bus to take the girls, and whatever dates they had managed to find, on a recreational tour of the city, from supper to bowling to a ride on the new subway to dancing and dessert. They would pick them up at one of the girls' homes after breakfast.

The seniors filed toward the bus looking much different than they had only hours before. The promise of all those girls in plain white dresses, clutching their bouquets, had been replaced by an almost mocking joy: an all-night party and no consequences; not a single paper due, no looming exams, freedom from everything that had defined their lives for six years. They fairly pranced onto the bus, the boys in their wake, and more than one parent commented that the girls seemed larger than the boys, even though it was not always true.

The last bit of Marlborough discipline involved checking in as each girl or boy got on the bus, to make sure that everyone who was supposed to be there, was. Katie Tower waited impatiently in line, telling anyone who cared to listen that the leather skirt she was wearing had been a gift from her father to her mother twenty years ago. She darted over to say goodbye to her parents, did a quick pirouette to show off the skirt, and hopped onto the bus with the boy she had met after the prom. Senior year was over, and with it all the anxiety and confusion of figuring out what to do next. Life, at this very moment, had nothing to do with academics, and it was perfect.

The buses pulled away at six, though a blanket of clouds as sleek as a seal's coat made it seem much later. Most of the parents had already left, cloaked in a protective sense of purpose: they had other children to feed and put to bed, or a restaurant reservation with visiting relatives. They had things to do; there was no reason to linger. The catering staff dismantled the party, and the breeze, without girls in big skirts to get in its way, took aim at the stragglers, who hugged themselves to stay warm.

A small knot of people, Cabel and Jon among them, stood on the front lawn, disoriented by the weather and the knowledge that there was no longer any reason for them to remain. They consulted the evening's itinerary one last time and drifted slowly toward the street, amid shouts of "See you at breakfast," "Get a good night's sleep," and "They're going to have a great time." Jon, whose exhaustion was starting to catch up with him, hurried Katie's brother toward his car.

Cabel hesitated. She took out her car keys and looked down the street. Katie was gone. It was time to go home.

26

The Young Women's Leadership
School of East Harlem
October 2001

CHRIS FARMER WAS one of those earnest young men who
made even the most idealistic goal seem feasible. If Ann Tisch
wanted to send every single TYWLS graduate to a four-year college, all he needed was an office, a strategy, and nights and weekends to
handle the paperwork that might overwhelm the girls' parents. Tisch hired
him as TYWLS's full-time college counselor in the summer of 1999, but
his job title barely began to describe his responsibilities. Farmer was the
girls' guide to a world they had been dreaming about since they came to
TYWLS.

He had to move faster than he would have liked. By now, the oldest
students at TYWLS were starting eleventh grade, which to Farmer was a
year too late to start making college plans, and the pioneers were in tenth
grade, a time when they ought to start thinking about where they wanted
to apply. His plan to help them catch up required a lot of public relations
work. Farmer had spent six years in the admissions office of a small New

England college, so first he called former colleagues at schools around the country to sell them on TYWLS. Then he had to turn around and sell the girls on college.

Farmer winced every time he heard a girl talk about what she would study *if* she went to college. He, too, had been an "if," he said, the first in his family to attend college, his parents eager to send him but with no idea of how to make it happen. He wanted to change the way the girls thought about the future—to make sure they debated what to study *when* they went to college.

To do that, Farmer said, "I have to get the vocabulary and the rhythm going." He piled his desk with college brochures and hung triangular flags from various schools along the walls of his tiny office. He encouraged the girls to drop by whenever they had free time, and like Cindy Jackson in her reproductive biology class, he answered any questions they had: What is a sorority? What does the bathroom look like in a coed residential hall? What is the deadline for financial aid?

He tried to get them to think of college in concrete terms, and this only confirmed how little they understood about the choices that faced them. When he asked the girls whether a multicultural campus was important to them, most said that it mattered but was not a critical consideration.

So he asked, "What percentage of students of color would make you feel comfortable?"

The consensus, among girls who did not have a single white classmate, was that 80 percent students of color would be an acceptable ratio. They were stunned to learn that a more realistic figure, aside from historically black colleges, was about 18 percent.

Farmer found their naïveté "charming and a little bit scary," and admitted that he was extremely concerned about how the girls would do once they left TYWLS and its controlled, supportive atmosphere. "It's going to be culture shock," he said. "You can't prepare enough. A girl wants to get her hair done and no one in town knows how to do kinky hair—that's going to be a shock for her no matter how much you talk about it in advance."

In the fall of 2000, the first senior class began the application process, and suddenly Farmer had even more to do. He ran his own SAT-prep class after school. He insisted that everyone take the SATs twice, once at the end of eleventh grade and once during senior year, as well as the SAT 2 achievement tests. He met with the seniors' parents. He made sure that the English teachers wrung the very best college essays out of the girls.

There might not be a law in New York that required girls to apply to college, but Farmer behaved as though there were, and did not mind if the girls misunderstood. No one escaped. By November, his life had become a bureaucratic pinball game as he shot from phone call to conference to impromptu counseling session. On a typical morning, he got a call from a mother who was stumped by a financial-aid question about her checking-account balance. Should she list today's balance, which included a welfare check she had just deposited and might make a college think she had enough to pay for her daughter's education? Or should she pay her bills first and list the remaining balance, which would be close to zero—and might make it seem that her daughter needed more money than a college felt like spending?

She wanted to tell the truth, but she had worked herself into a state trying to decide which truth was the right one. Farmer wearily rubbed his forehead, took a long breath, and asked her to bring in all her financial records. He would fill out the financial-aid forms for her. It was faster than tutoring all the families in how to work their way through the maze.

His diligence paid off. Every graduate in the class of 2001 went to a four-year college except one girl who chose to enlist in the military. Graduation was an emotional, exhilarating day—but Celenia Chevere did not attend. She had announced her resignation a year earlier, at the end of the pioneers' tenth-grade year, with a letter stuffed into staff members' mailboxes on one of the last days of school. She did not tell the girls, and by the time word got out, school was over for the summer. Many of her students never got to say goodbye, which made for resentment and some hurt feelings, but Chevere had never been one for the emotional farewell.

She preferred a quiet departure and a clean start. Chevere left TYWLS to start another new school in a downtown Manhattan district, an ambitious K–12 project called New Explorations Into Science, Technology, and Mathematics. It was a daunting effort for a woman who had flirted more than once with retirement, but Chevere had learned something in her four years at TYWLS: She was better at invention than she was at the sustained effort.

Her successor disagreed with many of Chevere's basic tenets, particularly the one about the relationship between the girls' home life and their future. She embraced the things that Chevere had encouraged the girls to discard—the jewelry, the hairstyles, the makeup—because Chevere's brand of assimilation sounded to her suspiciously like selling out. The girls were not to be ashamed of the way they looked, but to venture into the world proud of their differences.

It made for a confusing year, and by the end of it, many of the pioneers yearned for Chevere's brand of discipline. When they returned for senior year, they were relieved to find another new principal, Kathleen Ponze, who prized organization and dedication to task. TYWLS was again the kind of place they wanted to be, especially now that they were preparing for college. Maryam expressed the prevailing sentiment: The girls had come to appreciate Celenia's strict expectations, but they no longer felt that she held their fate in her hands. Back in seventh grade, Chevere had been an almost mystical symbol of promise. By twelfth grade, they understood that they would have to create the future for themselves.

Amy Lopez breezed into senior year with the same blithe abandon that had characterized her previous five years. Since ninth grade, she had locked in her reputation as a girl who was smarter than her record showed, and although she was embarrassed by some of her grades, she no longer made any pretense of reform.

"It's *such* a relief to be a senior," she said. "I've been waiting for this since third grade." To clear the way for the experience, she had spent the summer in what she called a "huge college rush," buying books and reading brochures, and right before school began, she had called more than a

dozen schools to request applications. For once, Amy did not procrasti-
nate: She got all the early work out of the way so that she could enjoy senior year without distraction.

By late October, she was nearing the end of what she called her "little
break," and getting ready to polish her application essay and fill out all the
forms. Her list of colleges reflected her family's yearning to leave East
Harlem: a half-dozen schools in California, three in Arizona, and only
three in New York. She had her heart set on Cal State Hayward, where several of her church friends went to school, or the University of San Diego, a
small private college with a debate team. Her mother Sandra's part-time
progress toward a bachelor's degree had forced Sandra and Tito to delay
their departure for another year or two, but Amy could get out, and they
urged her to do so.

She made only one concession to the process, which was to take test
preparation seriously. Amy had "winged it," she admitted, on her junior
year SATs, and came away with a combined score of 1020–just above the
national average of 1000. It was not a number that made a competitive girl
like Amy happy. This year she signed up for Chris Farmer's after-school
SAT-prep class, read the prep book, and even attended a Saturday program
outside school. She took the achievement tests on the first testing date, in
October, to buy extra weeks of preparation time before the more important
SATs. As November 3 approached, she did her best to prepare herself psy-
chologically for the event.

"Now that I know what I want," she told herself, "I'm going to go in
there and get it. I want something a little higher. At least an 1130."

Her mother insisted that Amy was "more on task now" than she had
been when she started at TYWLS. She surely had done better than she
would have at a big public school, where acting up was the norm and not
the foolish exception. Amy still talked to her parents about becoming a
doctor someday; perhaps she would find her rhythm once she got out of
the city and landed at a small campus where the best thing she could be was
smart.

For somewhere, underneath her seeming indifference, was a girl who
desperately wanted to do better. In one of the drafts of her college essay, she

wrote about how her mother "helped mold me. . . . From my schoolwork to my spiritual life she is always offering a word of advice and aiding me in my studies. When I fail to do what is right, my mother is there to help me get back on my feet." If some school would just give her the second chance her mother was willing to give her, she knew she could improve.

Maryam Zohny never wavered. For six years straight, she pulled in all A's, and began her senior year the putative valedictorian of the class of 2002. She signed up for AP sections of biology and Spanish, made plans for an expanded after-school journalism program, and started a theater group, underwritten in part by Ann Tisch's foundation, for seniors who wanted to see Broadway shows. The only disappointment in her academic life was what she called a "horrible" experience with the SAT test in May of her junior year, where she scored no better than the other girls. There was no room in her plan for a problem, not this late in the game.

"I don't let those tests get to me because I don't think they reflect your intelligence," she said, defiantly. "If you have to pay to do well on a test—if you have to be *trained* to take it—then I don't personally think it reflects your intelligence. Minority women have the worst case, and I fall into that category."

She refused to worry. She preferred to believe what everyone had told the girls from the very start: that colleges looking for a diverse student body would be eager to recruit them, even if their scores weren't equal to those of other candidates. She was the best student TYWLS had to offer, so she compiled an impressive list of colleges she would like to attend: Columbia's school of engineering, Brown, MIT, Cooper Union, New York University, Barnard, Princeton, and Tufts.

Over the summer, she had spent seven weeks in a special program at Brown, but it did nothing to allay her mother's concern about Maryam leaving the city, and Maryam felt homesick the whole time. Staying in the city might be the best choice, after all. Maryam decided to apply to the engineering school at Columbia, early decision, even though she preferred Brown.

"Brown is still my first choice because it's my favorite school," she said, "but because family is important to me and my mom wants me to be here,

I'm happy to stay. I want to be close to my family." At Columbia, she could have the experience of living on campus without breaking her mother's heart.

When it came time to write her essay, Maryam went to Chris Farmer for help. In the wake of her SAT test, Maryam was determined to show the admissions officers that she was someone special—that she had overcome great obstacles to do as well as she did. She decided, finally, to tell the story of her father's death, and the lie at the center of it, and her strength in the face of it. She wrote, and then she and Chris talked, and then she rewrote, over and over, until she had it right.

Maryam told of the day when the ambulance came to take her father away, as it had several times before—and what her mother and grandmother told her, days later, when she asked why her father had not come home. Maryam was not yet three when her father died. Her mother had decided that she deserved a little more life before she found out about sorrow.

"They told me he was in Egypt," she wrote, "receiving treatment from the best cardiologists. . . . Although their explanation did not satisfy my curiosity, it kept me quiet because I wanted him to come home."

For three years, Maryam was on her best behavior, believing somehow that her father's recovery would come more quickly if his youngest child was obedient. When her kindergarten class made Father's Day cards, Maryam wrote, "I aimed to make the best card and write the sweetest letter to make my father recover sooner." She proudly showed it to her teacher, expecting a lollipop and words of praise in return. Instead, the woman took her aside and gently told her that her father was dead. Surely Maryam knew that. It was not a good idea to pretend like this.

"I tore my card to pieces and secluded myself from everyone," Maryam wrote. She could not talk to her family, because they had kept the truth from her. She would not talk to her teacher, who had broken her heart. Throughout her years at TYWLS she had kept quiet about what had happened, taking refuge, as she always had, in good behavior. She would honor her father's memory with her achievements: she would have the best grade-point average and the most appearances on the honor roll; she would be the girl the other students whispered about in awe, one of those whom Ann Tisch knew by name. She never confessed the kind of suffering that might lead to a teacher's compassion or, worse, to pity.

But now she could write about it. Maryam had finally learned what her ninth-grade history teacher, Peter DeWan, had been unable to teach her: to take a chance. She believed that it might never have happened had she gone to another school. "I started out shy at TYWLS," said Maryam, "and if I'd been at a coed school I would have stayed that way. I would always have wanted to be in the background, never speak up. Going to this school, it built me up. Gender doesn't matter. If I want to do something I'll just do it, and I don't care."

TYWLS teachers spoke with a particular urgency to the best students, but in the summer before tenth grade the real world began to whisper in Diana Perez's other ear. Her older stepsister Linda showed up one day with her bags and a police escort and told Maria and James that her boyfriend had beat her up. This was not the first time, Linda said, but it would be the last. She wanted to move back in with her folks.

Diana was thrilled to have Linda around, but soon the persistent phone calls began, and then the boyfriend started hanging around. Diana was out with Linda one day when he showed up, and the two girls ran home together. When he called, begging to speak to Linda, Maria refused. She and James got a screening service that required a caller to identify his phone number so that they could ignore the boy's calls.

It went on for months, and along the way, Maria said, Diana developed "this fear, of not being able to do anything." TYWLS told her that she could do whatever she set her mind to, but life said it was impossible.

In October, the boy got Maria on the phone and asked for Linda. When she refused to put her stepdaughter on, he said that he had been talking to Linda for weeks. Who did Maria think had taken her to that amusement park?

It turned out that Linda had started to see him again without telling anyone in her family. She had lied and said she was at the amusement park with some of her girlfriends. When Diana found out, she fell apart. Maria still remembered Diana screaming at Linda, over and over again, "How could you do this? We did everything to try to help you, to save you!"

"She went in her room that night, and that was it," said Maria. "Because Diana always had this idea that she's a young woman, but she can do whatever she wants. No one else can make her do something. To see this? It just devastated her."

Diana sank into depression. She had trouble sleeping, woke up tired, cried at the slightest provocation, and found no respite at school. She complained to Maria that there was no point in even going to school, "because I feel the same way there." Some days it was too hard to get out of bed in the morning, and Maria, who had to get the other girls out the door and get to work herself, let Diana stay behind. As the weeks passed, Diana gave up her after-school activities and dropped out of the Figure Skaters of Harlem program.

Celenia Chevere could not continue to ignore Diana's increased absences, so tenth grade became a nightmare dialogue with representatives of the city's truant-control and child-welfare offices. Every morning, Maria begged Diana to get up and go to school, as the truant officer encouraged her to do, but after a while, Maria began to doubt her own pep talk. There were three buses between the projects and TYWLS. What if Diana felt a wave of hopelessness along the way?

"Frankly, I would rather have her at home where I can watch her," she said. "She says she's going to school, but what about the one day she decides not to go? Teen suicide is a big problem—and once she leaves the house I don't know where she is."

But the truant officer didn't want to hear why Diana was home; all that mattered was that she was not in school. Her report triggered a round of visits from a child-welfare worker: Was there food in the refrigerator? Could she see the girls' bedrooms? The worker told Maria that Diana was using her depression as an excuse to skip school, which was more than Maria could bear.

"I said, 'If you were talking about any other girl, I'd say yes, but not Diana. She really *likes* to be there. She says to me, 'I miss being with the girls,' and she misses all the activities.'" Maria had run out of ideas. She was only trying to protect Diana until she felt better, and yet people treated her as though she were harboring a budding delinquent. All the while, the clock was ticking: If Diana did not start going to school more often, she might have to repeat tenth grade.

It was school, finally, that saved her. In the spring, TYWLS built Diana a safety net, and a half-dozen people held it in place: Celenia Chevere, the school's guidance counselor, a volunteer social worker, and the psychiatrist she referred Diana to, a member of the school's office staff, and Maria.

The social worker and guidance counselor sent Diana to a psychiatrist who put her on a low-dose antidepressant, and after a month, she was able to get up and go to school for a week straight. When she arrived, she checked in at the office, where a woman who had worked at TYWLS from the beginning spent a few minutes chatting with her before she went off to class. Diana was never to feel alone.

One of the teachers invited her to join a new running club, thinking that the exertion might help with her asthma. For the first time since Linda had shown up at the door, Diana was tempted to try something new.

"But mom," she said, "I don't think I can run from here to the corner."

"Well, even if you come in last," Maria replied, "it could be a start to get back into things."

Diana joined the running club. She shoveled assignments until she was almost caught up—and if her grades were not what they had been in the past, she managed at least to pass her midterm exams. Her chemistry teacher loudly singled her out.

"Look at this," she said, waving Diana's test. "She did better than most of you who were here all the time."

Diana's friendship with Maryam did not survive tenth grade, because they no longer marched in tandem from one class to another. Diana had to pick up a chemistry credit in summer school to begin eleventh grade with her class, and was assigned to easier sections of some of her classes, so she watched Maryam's progress from a distance. She didn't mind. Diana began, slowly, to regard tenth grade as an aberration. She got her pace back, and as she settled into a routine, she allowed herself to think, again, about the future.

Everyone at TYWLS had been so kind to her. A year later, as she began her senior year, she still marveled at it. "People stood up for me," she said. "They knew me on a different level than they would have if there had been boys here. If I missed things, the other girls would get my assignments, check out books for me."

As a senior, she quickly got caught up in the rush of applications and interviews, and part of what sustained her was the knowledge that she mattered to her classmates and teachers. "They remembered me," she said, as though she had been on a long journey. "That's what's different about this place." She moved Chris Farmer to tears with an early, overlong draft of her college essay in which she wrote of her depression, but the intensity of the experience unnerved her, and she refused to show successive drafts to anyone else.

Maria watched Diana's return with a weary satisfaction, her faith in TYWLS made even stronger by the events of the past two years. Education was Maria's religion, and if anyone doubted its restorative powers, they had only to look at what had happened to Diana and Linda. Circumstance had slowly loosened Linda's grip on a bright future: She got pregnant, moved back in with her boyfriend, and had to drop out of the college classes she took at night. She had abandoned the one part of her life that held promise. It was exactly what Maria had worked all her life to spare her daughters.

"She can't get from Point A to Point B," Maria complained. Linda was on her way to becoming just another young woman who made a couple of foolish mistakes and would likely pay for them for the rest of her life.

"I would have hoped at this stage of the game for her to be at another level," Maria said. "To me, education is everything. Ignorance is the worst. It keeps us down. Keeps us from doing what we can do."

She might have lost Diana, too, had it not been for TYWLS. Now they were back in step, Diana taking two AP classes and working in an after-school tutoring program, and Maria on the graduation committee. They had started to talk about college again. If it was not quite so grand a scenario this time around—no talk of England, or of California—it was sweeter for the fact that they could talk about it at all.

Diana told her parents that she looked forward to leaving home. She felt ready for it.

In the name of escape, Maria and James encouraged her. "The farther the better," they said.

Epilogue

May 2002

FULL RIDE.

For the girls at TYWLS, financial aid was as much a part of the college dream as was acceptance at a favorite school. Maryam Zohny had done everything she could to get into Columbia University, and now she waited, atop a valedictorian's straight-A record, to see if the university would come up with enough money to make it possible. Amy Lopez still yearned to go to school in California—but even if she got in, even with financial aid, there was the unspoken question of how her family would pay for visits home. Diana Perez's uneven attendance and academic performance put her in an even more precarious position. A college financial-aid officer might not consider her to be a wise investment.

For six years, the girls had been tutored in the causal link between effort and reward, so a mix of momentum and faith got them through the application process. They applied to schools with an attitude of happy abandon, one that stood in stark contrast to the Marlborough seniors' more knowing anxiety: Maryam to Columbia's liberal arts program, early decision; Amy to a slew of schools, despite a chronic case of senioritis that compromised her already wobbly record; Diana to Skidmore College, her first choice, and to a handful of others. Chris Farmer looked out for the whole class—watching deadlines, reading esssays, filling out financial forms—but he set himself a specific goal for Diana: He was going to place her at a four-year college outside of New York City. She had to get out of there.

When Columbia deferred Maryam's early application, the mood changed. Like Christina Kim at Marlborough, Maryam was the best student TYWLS had to offer, and the scenario for her future had not included any kind of bad news. Chris Farmer called the admissions office and was assured that Maryam would get a spot when the rest of the class was filled in the spring, but the deferral made some of the other girls reevaluate their odds. What had seemed reasonable before now felt extravagant. In truth, the world could be unkind to high school seniors with good records, even to girls whose accomplishments were so dramatic when compared to those of their peers in the public school system. The TYWLS seniors began to scale back their hopes.

Amy shied away from the highly competitive schools like Columbia, and she received acceptance letters from eight of twelve schools. She could have attended any of three Cal State schools, but by the time the letters came, she had arrived at a surprising conclusion: She did not want to go away, after all. Although Chris Farmer had assumed that Amy would go to Cal State's Fresno or Hayward campus, she backed off and chose Manhattan's PACE University instead.

"Just in case college doesn't go the way I planned," she said, "I can be home and not in foreign territory." The Lopez family still talked about moving west, but Amy would deal with that when she had to. For now, she wanted to be with her family. Simply going to college felt like change enough.

Maryam was home for spring break the day her news came. She was up early, and when she checked her e-mail, she found an acceptance from Columbia's liberal-arts program. Maryam had a full ride; the only contribution she had to make was to participate in the university's work-study program.

She ran into her mother's bedroom to tell her the news, and then she began to call her friends. As always, she was circumspect about her emotions, remembering what early rejection had felt like, not wanting to seem a braggart to girls who had been turned down by a favorite school—but she had to tell them, and she was gratified at how happy they were for her. That was the lasting legacy of TYWLS: what Maryam called the "mushy stuff," the friendships that outlasted good luck and bad.

Diana was almost lucky. Skidmore College and Bard College both put her on their wait lists, but there would be no final word until May 1, when contracts were due. An admissions officer told Chris Farmer that Diana was first in line at Skidmore, but that was little solace, with almost a month to wait. Farmer watched, warily, as Diana began to miss school, the way she had in tenth grade. He could see that she was having a hard time, and he feared another bout of depression. "The wait list is torture," he said. "She's kind of a fatalist in general—the glass is half empty—and this plays right into that. She's feeling unwanted. The girls this happens to, it hurts their pride."

Her mother, Maria, came in the day before the contract deadline to tell the college counselor that they were putting Diana back on her antidepression medication. They had tried pills to help her sleep, but right now she needed more than that. Farmer called Skidmore that afternoon, and heard what he had spent a month hoping he would not hear: The admissions officer did not anticipate accepting anyone from the waiting list. There was better news at Bard, where Diana's acceptance was "a pretty sure thing," but he had to call both schools back late the next day, once the deadline for responses had passed officially.

So he held his breath for twenty-four hours, and then he called back. Bard College, which cost about $34,000 per year, offered Diana Perez a place in its freshman class for about $2,000 per year, in the form of a loan. Grant and scholarship money covered the rest. Skidmore College kept her on the wait list, but as far as Farmer was concerned, she was going to Bard. Diana was safely placed; he had to prepare for a week of "negotiating, begging, pleading," for a handful of other girls who were still on wait lists, and for girls who had only been accepted by community colleges. Some four-year schools were about to find out that they did not have enough students in their freshman classes, and when they did, Farmer intended to be there to press for "girls with real potential."

The one person who wasn't going anywhere was Cindy Jackson, the science teacher. Or rather, Cindy Jackson, the Program Chairperson, the Science Department Chair, the liaison for student teachers, the member of the school leadership committee, the public-speaking teacher, and, along with an art teacher, the most senior faculty member at TYWLS. Cindy was the only core academic teacher to have made it through six years with the Class of 2002, and she had no doubt that she would stick around. She continued acting, and, in April, she appeared in a three-night run of an off-Broadway play called "Stop Kiss." Still, TYWLS took up more and more of her time; she was an educator who acted on the side.

As for Celenia Chevere, her retirement was delayed again by yet another irresistible start-up. In September 2001, she opened a new K–12 public school in downtown Manhattan called New Explorations into Science, Technology and Math. Eleven girls followed her from TYWLS, so the school's first tenth-grade class was all girls.

The Marlborough girls from the Class of 1999 enjoyed such a lush array of opportunities that a few of them looked back and decided they could have handled more of life, sooner, than Marlborough had allowed. Only Christina Kim stayed on campus for her junior year at MIT; Katie Briggs, Katie Tower, and Sommer Louie studied in Italy, and Erica Forneret went to Yale's Mellon Centre, in London.

Christina continued at the driven pace she had set for herself in high school. Having declared a major in neuroscience, she added a second major, in linguistics. It was all part of a long-range plan eventually to conduct research in some area of overlap between cognition and linguistics. Three years out of Marlborough, her appetite for knowledge—and for a weighty challenge—was undiminished.

If anything, she was more impatient than ever. The farther she got from Marlborough, the less certain she was of its relevance. "There are plenty of girls here at MIT who are very sharp and very smart because they actually are smart," she said, "that is, *not* because they were coddled and over-encouraged and positively-reinforced into *thinking* they were smart just because they were girls. In the end, you have to earn what you get."

She distanced herself from her alma mater, as she had set herself apart from her family toward the end of her senior year at Marlborough. Christina was always trying to wrestle her way out of the past, which was by definition constraining, and into the endless, promising future. She was prepared to admit that there had been good things about her Marlborough experience, but unwilling to take the time to enumerate them.

"I think I've moved on," she said.

Katie Briggs had shed her skin—what she called her "cautious Katie" persona—in stages. She had found a boyfriend during her freshman year, and then, despite her commitment to him and to science, she had taken an entire year to study in Italy. She took courses that had nothing to do with teaching biology, which was what she thought she might want to do. It was a slightly delayed, and unusually productive, teenage rebellion. In classic fashion, it involved rejecting the past.

"I really feel that I was ready to be out of that environment a lot sooner than I was 'let out,'" she said of Marlborough. "Not so much because I missed boys, but because I felt suffocated. . . . I was pigeonholed into a role." But when she was done complaining, she admitted that she would let her daughter go to a girls' school, someday, if that was what she chose. Perhaps Marlborough had helped make Katie the kind of person who was not afraid to be frank.

"In the end, I think Marlborough put me on the road to being how I am today," she said, "but a lot of it was already there in my heart."

The other girls, in the mist of their own junior-year adventures, were willing, even eager, to credit Marlborough for preparing them for the larger world. Sommer Louie was the most devout, certain that Marlborough had given her "a lot of my confidence and positive self-image as a female." Specifically, she felt confident enough to change her focus from medicine to law, with a double major in sociology and Policy Studies, and to find a boyfriend and then leave him behind while she spent four months in Perugia. Girls who went to coeducational schools did the same things, she knew, but she found that she prized her "very different" experience.

"I have absolutely no regrets," she said.

Nor did Erica Forneret, whose life had become a rather hyperbolic experience. She had spent the first half of her junior year living with five other girls in a beautiful flat in the center of London. She traveled to Venice ("the most gorgeous little city on this big earth"), Florence, Naples, and Rome. She flew to Scotland. ("The Scottish breakfast complete with beans and haggis is now my favorite thing.") She saw Barcelona and Amsterdam and came back to classes in modern British theater, Portuguese, and Skyscraper Architecture of Jazz Age New York.

Everywhere she looked, she found reason to be astonished. She had declared a double major in History of Art and Political Science, and hoped to go to law school after graduation, but it was hard to imagine her confined by a single course of study. Erica was far too busy looking around.

Marlborough's contribution to the action was, to Erica, both simple and profound. "It made me extremely self-sufficient," she said. "I always assumed—but I didn't know for sure until I lived really on my own, across an ocean—that I was completely capable. Competent in all things. I think that's amazing."

The girls had taken theory for a test-drive to see if it translated into practice, and had come home satisfied. They found themselves able to cope on their own, and, more important, willing to tolerate ambiguity. They were not afraid of a little constructive bewilderment. Katie Tower left for a semester in Italy having decided on a double major in molecular biology and history, and came home with no more idea of what she would do with that major than she had had when she left. She intended to go to graduate school in biology; beyond that, she would wait and see.

She came out of Marlborough with a certain fearlessness—"I am not afraid to stand up for myself or for someone else, because I was always encouraged to speak out and make my opinion known," was how she put it. The Marlborough admissions director spoke approvingly of incoming sixth-graders who seemed willing to take risks, because that kind of girl seemed to flourish in an all-girls environment. Many graduates emerged with their enthusiasm for taking a chance intact; six years of structure and support had made it safe to be brave. Six years of challenge had taught them to take credit for their own accomplishments.

Alexandra Siegel was in tenth grade now, where grades counted, and she had begun to imagine a future that would have seemed ambitious even for a more outgoing girl. A straight-A student, she talked about Oxford University in London one minute and Stanford University the next. Or she might choose an Ivy League school with a strong writing program, like Yale or Princeton or Dartmouth. It was too early to make a list, but not too early to think about where she might be happy—and that was in an elite school, the sort of place where a girl who excelled at everything might want to go.

Alex would never be the first one to shout out an answer, but she was no longer the silent, circumspect girl she had been in Myranda Marsh's history class. "She's still quietish," said her mother, Lynn, "but she's secure in her way. She has matured so much. She's comfortable in what she knows."

Myranda Marsh did not get to witness Alex's transition. She had left Marlborough at the end of the 1995–2000 school year, and was in charge of curriculum development at a new charter school for poor minority students. But she had gotten Alex started.

The Siegels credited Marlborough with everything good: their daughter's newfound self-confidence; her willingness to extend herself in every class, regardless of subject; the fact that she talked about heading to London for college. She might be restrained, but she was brave, now, too, and her parents were convinced that where she went to school was the determining factor.

"Marlborough has been instrumental in all of this," said Lynn. "If there were boys, it would change who these girls are."

"And even if Alex didn't change," said Alex's father, Eric, "some girls would. And that would change how the girls related to each other."

Let the researchers continue the debate about whether single-sex schools made a difference, and for whom, and how much. The Siegels looked at

Alex, and at her gregarious younger sister, who had just entered seventh grade, and were satisfied that they had made the right choice for both girls.

Barbara Wagner presided over it all with a growing sense of purpose. If she strove for diversity in the student body, she worked toward consensus, among the faculty, about what mattered: an ever-expanding advanced curriculum in math and science, an increasingly competitive athletic program, and a commitment to a rigorous academic approach that survived the occasional skeptical parent. There was plenty of fun on the side, from the winter carnival to the annual pajama day, but from the day a girl set foot on campus, the message was clear, and spoken by the faculty in chorus: This was where a girl came if she was prepared to work hard and wanted to excel.

In 2002, Marlborough could not take a single girl from its wait list, because ninety-eight girls had chosen to attend, far more than the usual response of seventy-five to eighty-five girls. Ten years earlier, girls would have been less likely to choose Marlborough. Now, they were less likely to turn it down.

The questions that had plagued educators and researchers for decades remained unanswered: Was subtracting boys the defining reason for girls' improved performance and self-image, or was it the small classroom, the passionate teacher, the supportive staff? If anything, new studies only complicated the issue. Research on boys showed that they might be better off in a coeducational classroom, and this posed a tangled problem for educators who wanted to do what was best for everyone. The brain research that JoAnn Deak had cited to Marlborough math teachers was truly a work in progress: Anyone, on either side of the debate, could find data to support his position.

David Sadker, who, with his late wife, Myra, had begun the debate on gender in the classroom, dismissed much of the research for asking the wrong questions. Numbers were not to be trusted; the statistics about women outnumbering men in college sounded impressive, for example, but women dominated two-year schools, not the Ivy League, and there were more of them in social work than in math and computer technology.

Sadker preferred to listen to "stories that resonate," he said, and they told him that the coeducational classroom still did not offer girls an equal education.

More and more parents agreed with him. They put their faith in smaller, more intimate samples; they listened to friends with older daughters, not to often-contradictory studies, and they decided to take a chance on what might work. For private-school students, it was a matter of finding the right school, but public-school students needed to have options created for them. Politicians arrived at their own consensus: The No Child Left Behind Act of 2001 included a bipartisan amendment sponsored by Senators Kay Bailey Hutchison (R–Texas) and Hillary Clinton (D–New York), which called for single-sex schools and programs as one of twenty-seven "Innovative Assistance Programs." In the spring of 2002, the Department of Education announced its intention to loosen Title IX guidelines to allow for single-sex public education.

Six years earlier, Maria Perez had wondered why her daughter, Diana, should be denied what the rich girls had, and in reply she had gotten complaints about gender discrimination and paeans to equal access. Now, there was a new response, fashioned by an unlikely alliance of conservatives and liberals desperate for a way to reform the nation's schools. The public school system had offered its birthright, of late, to entrepreneurs and to religious schools, but TYWLS represented an alternative that worked within the system, based on the successful reforms begun over twenty-five years earlier in District Four. Another public girls' school had opened in Chicago, and the new legislation guaranteed that there would be more such efforts, for girls and for boys.

Critics worried that the law would nudge children back into limiting stereotypes—or that it was meant to serve as a gentle introduction to vouchers, and erode the public schools even further. Supporters, including an optimistic Ann Tisch, envisioned a network of schools like TYWLS that better served their students and strengthened the school system at the same time.

Pocket reform—one ambitious school at a time—was working, where larger ideas did not. Single-sex schools got results, while cries for a general overhaul went begging, and finally, people got tired of waiting. Until the unlikely day that research retired the notion, parents and policy makers were ready to take the chance that some girls would profit from school without boys—and that all girls ought to have the chance.

Why should Diana Perez miss what the rich girls had? No reason at all.

Selected Bibliography

American Association of University Women. *How Schools Shortchange Girls*. Marlowe & Company, 1995.

_____. *Separated by Sex: A Critical Look at Single-Sex Education for Girls*. American Association of University Women Educational Foundation, 1998.

Brown, Lyn Mikel and Carol Gilligan. *Meeting at the Crossroads: Women's Psychology and Girls' Development*. Harvard University Press, 1992.

Brumberg, Joan Jacobs. *The Body Project: An Intimate History of American Girls*. Random House, 1997.

Deak, JoAnn. *How Girls Thrive*. National Association of Independent Schools, 1998.

_____. *Girls Will Be Girls: A Parent's Guide to Cultivating Confident and Courageous Daughters.* Hyperion, 2002.

Fennema, Elizabeth and Gilah Leder, editors. *Mathematics and Gender.* Teachers College Press, 1990.

Fliegel, Seymour, with James MacGuire. *Miracle in East Harlem: The Fight for Choice in Public Education.* Times Books, 1993.

Gilligan, Carole, Nona Lyons and Trudy Hanmer, editors. *Making Connections: The Relational Worlds of Adolescent Girls at Emma Willard School.* Harvard University Press, 1990.

The National Coalition of Girls' Schools. *Math & Science for Girls: A Symposium.* The National Coalition of Girls' Schools, 1992.

Orenstein, Peggy. *Schoolgirls: Young Women, Self-Esteem, and the Confidence Gap.* Doubleday, 1994.

Pipher, Mary. *Reviving Ophelia: Saving the Selves of Adolescent Girls.* G. P. Putnam's Sons, 1994.

Sadker, David and Mary. *Failing at Fairness: How America's Schools Cheat Girls.* Charles Scribner & Sons, 1994.

Acknowledgments

A book like this only happens if people say yes, so I want to thank Barbara Wagner, head of school at Marlborough School, and Celenia Chevere, the first principal at The Young Women's Leadership School of East Harlem, for letting me spend a year at their schools. Ann Rubenstein Tisch helped with access and filled me in on everything that happened before TYWLS opened its doors.

A group of families at each school allowed me to accompany their daughters to class, to come home with them, and to talk to their teachers and advisors. It was a particular pleasure to watch these girls grow up, and for that I thank Katie, Debbie, and Jeff Briggs; Erica, Martine, Phyllis, and Rodney Forneret; Christina, Youngsook, and Young Cheol Kim; Alexandra, Lynn, and Eric Siegel; Katie, Cabel, and Jon Tower; Diana, Maria, and James Perez; Amy, Sandra, and Robinson Lopez; and Maryam and Afaf Zohny.

At Marlborough, teachers Arleen Forsheit, Leslie Klein, Myranda

Marsh, and Kurt Schleunes realized early on that I intended to camp out in their classrooms, and they spent time they did not have talking with me about what went on there. I also want to thank Timothy Bruneau, Susan Cope, Jeff Gadette, Jeff Girion, Laura Hotchkiss, Susanna Jones, Susan Lewandowski, Genevieve Morgan, Julie Napoleon, Sandra O'Connor, Deborah Parker, Della Schleunes, Jim Skrumbis, Katie Ward, Monica Ward and Jeanette Woo-Chitjian for their contributions. Wanda Horton, Nancy Long, Laura Morrison, and Michelle Svihovec helped with scheduling and documentation.

AT TYWLS, Cindy Jackson shared her passion for teaching and provided valuable continuity between visits. Peter DeWan, Fabrice Fortin, Shirley Gasich, Suzanne Kerho, Sarah Kirkpatrick, Jenny Long, Nina Ostrov, and Holly Simon went out of their way to be helpful to me.

Educators and researchers shared their perspectives on education, equality and gender discrimination: I thank JoAnn Deak, Seymour Fliegel, David Sadker, and Susan McGee Bailey at the Wellesley Center for Women. Joan Jacobs Brumberg provided an enlightening look at teenage girls' changing self-image.

I thank Laurie Brown for helping with introductions at Marlborough— and Chiari Coletti and Karen Finney of The New York City Board of Education for helping with the permissions process at TYWLS. As always, Jacci Cenacveira provided comprehensive research materials, and Sue Clamage and Freddie Odlum efficiently transcribed taped conversations. Clare Muldaur made sure—with humor and efficiency—that daily life ran smoothly.

At Riverhead Books, Julie Grau was enthusiastic and involved from the start, and Erin Bush Moore offered a level of attention that could make a writer feel spoiled.

I am extremely grateful to my agent, Lynn Nesbit, for her professionalism and genuine support. Tina Bennett and Richard Morris provided valuable help, as did CAA's Brian Siberell.

William Whitworth read *All Girls* in manuscript; I was the fortunate beneficiary of his insights and generous encouragement.

Harry Shearer read the manuscript as well, the culmination of our three years of arguing about single-sex education; I thank him for forcing me to defend everything I think.

I thank Carolyn See for sustenance, on the plate and off.

My friends offer distractions when I want them and support when I don't; for that I thank Ginger Curwen, Vicky and Hummie Mann, Judith Owen, Kathy Rich, Marcie Rothman, and Patty Williams. I was glad to have Lori and Roy Rifkin, Phyllis Amaral, and JoAnn Consolo to talk to as our daughters applied to middle school.

Sarah Dietz is the reason I wrote this book, and I thank her for being exactly who she is. Larry Dietz supports my work in ways that a line of acknowledgment can barely express. I love them both, and am grateful every day that we are together.

Karen Stabiner
Santa Monica, California
January 2002

KAREN STABINER is the author of the national bestseller and *New York Times* Notable Book *To Dance with the Devil: The New War on Breast Cancer,* and the national bestseller *Inventing Desire,* an acclaimed portrait of the advertising industry. Her work has appeared in *Vogue, Redbook, Ladies' Home Journal, The New York Times Magazine, Los Angeles Times Magazine,* and *The New Yorker.* Stabiner lives in Santa Monica, California, with her husband and their daughter.